COLLECTIBLE CERAMICS

An Encyclopedia of Pottery and Porcelain for the American Collector

by
MARCIA RAY

CROWN PUBLISHERS, INC., NEW YORK

Library of Congress Catalog Card Number: 73-92104

Prepared and Produced by Everybodys Press, Inc.
Printed in the United States of America

This Edition Prepared for Distribution by
CROWN PUBLISHERS, INC.

Introduction

China is not a mere fancy, it is a complete education.

"A Well Known Collector,"
in *Pottery and Porcelain Review,* May 1896.

More books have been written about pottery and porcelain than any other facet of antiques collecting. Most of them have been concerned with wares of the 18th and 19th centuries; many are intensive studies of one particular factory. Continued research constantly brings new information which adds to or corrects earlier published data. When "new" antiques come into popularity, books are written about them.

This very quantity of published material makes for confusion. The casual collector with one or two pieces to identify, the housewife who wants to talk intelligently about her grandmother's dishes, the dealer who wants to check on something unusual, quail at thumbing through a library for scattered information.

In this compilation—actually it is an encyclopedia—collector, housewife, and dealer find their answers easily. Here, information assembled from various sources have been checked against earlier and later versions, and presented in brief to give the most accurate data currently available. Covered here are 18th century wares, most often found in museums; wares of the early and late 19th century, generously available in antique shops; some of the early 20th century wares now coming on the antique market; and a few present day wares which are being collected for the future.

Books are suggested in the text for further study, selected because they seem presently to offer the latest, most accurate coverage, and should be readily located in most Public Libraries.

The photographs used, excepting those of museum pieces and a few from private collections, purposely do not show unusual examples. Rather they illustrate the kind of items to be seen today in antiques shops and shows; it will not be difficult to find similar or even better examples.

ACKNOWLEDGEMENTS . . .

Special appreciation goes to *Spinning Wheel* for permission to use copyrighted photographs which have appeared in that magazine, to the Frank Moffits of Kingsport, Tenn., the Webb McCurleys of Taneytown, Md., and to Ruth's Antiques of Funkstown, Md., who supplied many items for photographing. Thanks also to the private collectors who graciously furnished photographs: Mr. Paul Evans, Mill Valley, Calif.; Mr. Paul Fitzpatrick, Lancaster, Pa.; and the late Mrs. Nancy Fitzpatrick; Mrs. Louise Henzke, Fort Worth, Texas; Mr. & Mrs. Carroll Hopf, Mt. Joy, Pa.; Mrs. Linda Hopkins, Glen Burnie, Md.; Mrs. C. Albert Kuper, Baltimore, Md.; Mrs. Henry J. Langsenkamp, Jr., Ft. Lauderdale, Fla.; Mrs. Lowell W. Olson, Atlanta, Ga.; Mrs. Lawrence A. Prentice, Stuart, Fla.; Mr. A. Christian Revi, Hanover, Pa.; Mr. & Mrs. Richard Robey, Hanover, Pa.; and to the various museums, present day manufacturers, and those private collectors whose photographs are credited in the text.

First of all and quite simply . . .

Pottery in its broadest sense is anything made of clay, shaped, and baked—from a common flowerpot to a Dresden teacup. The basic ingredients, the manner of mixing them, and the degree of temperatures at which they are fired make the difference. In general use, though, pottery denotes the coarser ware—the earthenware and stoneware; the finer is porcelain.

Paste is the body material. *Hard Paste* is a true porcelain as it originated long ago in China—a mixture of kaolin and china stone, fired at very high temperature. It can be eggshell thin or thick enough for furniture, i.e., a Chinese garden seat or a Meissen desk. It is translucent; you can see the shadow of your hand through it. It is tough, doesn't scratch, is cold to the touch, and "rings like a bell." The first hard paste porcelain in Europe to successfully copy the Chinese ware was developed at the Meissen factory in Germany about 1710.

Soft Paste is what eighteenth century English potters (and some French ones, too) came up with in their efforts to produce Chinese porcelain from materials at hand. Soft paste porcelain is fragile, scratches, is warmer to the touch than hard paste. It is porous, and the color in the decoration sinks in deeper, giving it a soft effect. It is usually opaque. Soft paste in England dates from the 1740s.

Bone China, a mixture of bone ash, kaolin, and feldspar which English potters discovered about 1800, is a sort of in-between hard and soft paste. It was the English answer to the Chinese and Continental hard paste; practically all English porcelain is soft paste or bone china.

Stoneware is produced from "natural" clay, that is a single clay to which no other clays are added. It is fired only once, but at such intense heat that it comes out vitrified, very hard, and non-porous. It can get along without a glaze, but usually salt is thrown in the kiln to give it a glossy finish and an impervious coating.

Earthenware is a softer pottery than stoneware. It is fired at a low temperature, at least twice, and because it is porous, it requires a glaze to seal the pores. Most inexpensive tablewares today are of earthenware.

Glaze is an applied mixture of silicates and water that makes china shiny and seals the porous earthenware so it is usable for domestic purposes; common flowerpots don't need it. The usual procedure is to dip the pottery, once-baked and called "biscuit" into the liquid glaze, which is rather thin and slightly grainy, then fire it again.

China covers the world of crockery. It is a handy, overworked, all-encompassing word.

ALBARELLO

An albarello is a waisted cylindrical drug jar—a type found in twelfth century Persian and Mesopotamian wares, and in today's museums. The name itself has an ancient Oriental connotation. It is Italian, of course, adapted either from the Italian word meaning "little tree," referring to its resemblance to a section of bamboo in which Orientals shipped their drugs, or an Italian corruption of the Persian *el barani*, meaning a vase for drugs. (*See* Drug Jars.)

The example pictured is of French faience, ca. 1585.

ALBION WARE
See *Bennett Pottery*

ALLEN CROCKERY CO.
See *Illinois Potters*

ALPHABET PLATES

The engaging ABC plates today's grandmothers so often collect for their grandchildren—and keep for themselves—were in pleasant demand from the 1820s to the 1860s, though they were still being made much, much later. The earliest were of creamware with the alphabet embossed around the rim, and a picture with elevating verse or motto, hand-printed and hand-colored, in the center. Leeds made many of these, as did other early potteries. Then followed the ironstones, with cheap transfer prints, crudely colored with splashes of red, blue, green, yellow, and orange. The borders taught the alphabet; the verses, how to behave, often carrying moral instruction far beyond primary age.

Davenport and Wm. Adams & Company broke the "Be Good" monotony with sets picturing wild animals—elephants, tigers, zebras, and such. Another variation was a center letter, illustrated and exampled, as "B is for ball," used with a daisy-embossed border. As ABC plates departed more and more from precepts, there appeared Robinson Crusoe sets, Mother Goose sets, and an Everyday Life series where Victorian children were pictured at their normal pursuits. Some were obligingly printed for the hard-of-hearing with deaf and dumb alphabet borders. ABC mugs were made, too, but they are harder to find now than the plates.

The alphabet plate pictured is hand-printed and brightly hand-colored, featuring "Harry baiting his line, for to fish he doth incline," ca. 1840-1845.

AMERICAN ART CHINA WORKS

See *American Belleek*

AMERICAN BELLEEK

Belleek porcelain is thin and light of body and of a singular translucence. The ware—and the name—originated in Ireland in the mid-1850s. In the 1880s and 1890s, several factories in the United States were making Belleek, many of which imported Irish workmen to advise them.

Around Trenton were the old Jersey City Pottery; Ott & Brewer, known as the Etruria Pottery (John and William Bromley came over from the Belleek factory in Ireland to work there); the American Art China Works (Rittenhouse, Evans & Co.); the Columbian Art Pottery; and the still continuing Lenox China, which developed from the Ceramic Art Company. In East Liverpool, Ohio, Knowles, Taylor and Knowles made a quantity of Belleek in the 1880s; and in Baltimore, Maryland, Bennett produced it in a limited amount about 1886. Richard Carter Barret, of the Bennington Museum, reports in recent researches that the factories at Bennington were the first in this country to produce Belleek.

All these companies made decorated tableware; some added novelties; most of them furnished blanks for amateur decorators.

American Belleek is heavier and less translucent than the Irish and cannot be mistaken for it. (*See:* Irish Belleek; Lenox; Lotus ware; Bennett Pottery.)

The Belleek tête-a-tête service pictured was made by Bennett in Baltimore, ca. 1886. The set included a second cup, not shown in the photograph.

AMERICAN ENCAUSTIC TILING COMPANY

This Zanesville, Ohio, company was one of the first producers of floor and wall tile in the United States, and at varying times in its long life, from 1875 to 1936, was listed as the largest tile producer in the world. Its decorative tiles with relief figures were very handsome, winning gold medals at Paris in 1900 and at the Pan-American Exposition in 1901. Especially fine work was done in the early 1890s when Herman Mueller was the director, and chemist Karl Langenbeck was working with him. Besides tiles, the company made many novelties—plaques with Greek or other figures in relief, candlesticks, vases, and for today's lucky bottle collectors, a wondrous wine bottle in the shape of a monk with removable head. Most of their pieces, large or small, are marked "A.E.T.Co" on the back to make identification easy for us. (*See* Mosaic Tile Company.)

AMERICAN MARINE PATTERN
See *Ashworth*

AMERICAN POTTERY CO.
See *Apostle Jugs*

AMERICAN VIEWS
(Also called Staffordshire Blue or Historical Blue)

The making of chinaware got off to a slow start in America. There were more important things to do in settling a new country than to bother with a "luxury" product. By the beginning of the nineteenth century, when everyday Americans were ready and financially able to discard their pewter and wooden dishes for china, the potteries in Staffordshire were well established and geared to produce inexpensive ware for export.

American housewives of the early 1800s liked best the Staffordshire ware, transfer-printed in deep cobalt blue; it was doubly alluring when it was decorated with an American scene. Enterprising English potters arranged with artists travelling in America to sketch the sights for their blue ware. Hardly a section of the settled country was overlooked. Scenic views of the Catskills, the White Mountains, Sandusky, Ohio, and Louisville, public buildings of all sorts, from the "Penitentiary in Allegheny, near Pittsburgh, Pa." to the "Octagon Church, Boston," appeared on plates and teapots, platters and tureens.

Leading Staffordshire potters like Adams, Clews, Meigh, Ridgway, Stevenson, and Wood, and hundreds of obscure ones, made American Views. Sometimes they back-stamped their pieces; more often they did not, but the distinctive designs each potter used for his borders were almost as good as a signature. Views were occasionally pirated, the borders seldom were. (The same potters made English Views for home consumption, in the same deep blue, and with their same borders.)

From 1820 to 1830, a rich clear cobalt was the color used most. It was an easy color for potters to work with—it fired well under high temperatures, and it economically covered any defects in the china.

After 1830, the shade of blue lightened; other colors came to the fore—pink, red, black, green. By 1850, potters were using quite pale shades, colors in combination, and had abandoned American views for those of the romantic East.

But American scenes never lost complete favor, nor did the rich blue color. The Bennett Pottery in Baltimore produced a "Pickett's Charge, Gettysburg" platter in dark blue after the Civil War. Numerous designs were made by English potters at the time of the 1876 Centennial Exposition in Philadelphia; and there was a great flurry of blue American View souvenir plates by Wedgwood, Minton, and others, in the early 1900s. The later ones, of course, are most easily found today.

For further reading: *Anglo-American China, Part 1*, by Sam Laidacker; *Historic Staffordshire*, by Ellouise Baker Larsen; *The Book of Old China*, by J. Hudson Moore; *Staffordshire Blue*, by W. L. Little (1969). (*See* Historical Blue Ware, Late.)

The illustration is one of John & William Ridgway's "Beauties of America" series, a 6¼ inch plate portraying the "Atheneum Boston," (1814-1830).

APOSTLE JUGS

Gothic Revival at its mid-Victorian best well describes the fine stoneware Apostle jugs, molded in relief design as crowded and elaborate as the carvings on a mid-Victorian sideboard. Around these rather heavy white or putty colored octagonal pitchers is a frieze of eight arched niches in each of which stands a robed apostle; the other four are less commodiously accommodated. One is on the handle, one inside and one outside the lip, and the twelfth just below the lip.

Charles Meigh of Hanley made many of these. John Ridgway of Shelton and Samuel Alcock of Burslem also found this style satisfying to public taste. Other English potters made them, too. Most of them put their marks on the jugs, and some added the diamond registry mark. In America, the American Pottery Company in Jersey City, N.J., around 1840, was also making stoneware Apostle jugs.

The same type body was used for other pitchers with similarly molded designs, often of Gothic inspiration. Meigh used classic figures on some of his; Ridgway made one called the Tournament pitcher; Alcock, particularly, liked to set white figures against a colored ground; the American Pottery made some with hunting scenes.

ARABIA PORCELAIN FACTORY

Though the Arabia Porcelain Factory, just outside Helsinki, in Finland, currently turns out in the neighborhood of 250,000 finished pieces a day, including household wares of feldspathic porcelain, earthenware dishes, objets d'art, and hand-painted giftware, less than twenty per cent of it crosses the ocean to the United States. Their hand-painted children's mugs and cereal sets are special favorites here; mothers have been known to cry when a piece was broken.

The pottery was founded in 1874 for the manufacture of porcelain decorated in Islamic style, but never quite made the grade until, in 1916, it was taken into a cooperative "Swedish modern" movement then sweeping Scandinavia. It has prospered mightily since. Some excellent artists are now at work there, and present-day wares, even utilitarian ones, are worthy of interest.

ARCADIAN CHINA
See *Gossware*

ARC-EN-CEIL

Zanesville Art Pottery in Color, by Louise and Evan Purviance and Norris F. Schneider, lists this company under "Smaller Zanesville Potteries," as: "A. Radford and Company 1903 . . . became Arc-en-Ceil 1903-1905, under the management of John Lessell . . . operated as The Brighton Pottery 1905-1907." Here were made the usual art-type pitchers, vases, dresser bottles, and small decorative items, though its frequently used gold lustre glaze was distinctive. The mark was "Arc-en-Ceil" in a circle, usually ink stamped. You will run across a piece now and then even though the company was not in production long. Alfred Radford helped construct the plant, and for a short time worked there, perfecting a special type of decorated jasperware. This, however, was not marked, either with his name or Arc-en-Ceil. (*See* Radford Jasper.)

AREQUIPA POTTERY

The Arequipa Pottery operated only seven years, from 1911 to 1918—a therapeutic attempt to make the tuberculosis sanitorium at Fairfax, California, self-supporting and to bring in to the two dozen or so young woman patients a little money to help pay for their treatments. The girls did the decorating and lighter tasks; older boys from a San Francisco orphanage were brought up to the sanitorium to do the heavy work. As far as the pottery itself and the enthusiastic response of the patients were concerned, the venture was a success, though little financial gain accrued to the sanitorium.

Robert Blasberg, writing in *Western Collector* (October 1968) describes the ware, "if not always of museum caliber, nonetheless a good example of what we may call bungalow pottery—sturdy, honest ware with straightforward decoration. The glaze treatments are well done and the use of local motifs particularly interesting."

The originator and first director of the project was Frederick H. Rhead, who, from 1902 to 1908, had been art director at the Roseville Pottery in Zanesville, Ohio. The second director Albert L. Solon, son of Marc Louis Solon, was an accomplished potter who learned his craft in England. He was followed by F. H. Wilde, who had established other successful potteries in California. Rising costs and general conditions at the time of World War I put an end to the project. (*See:* Roseville; Solon, Marc Louis.)

Various impressed marks were used on Arequipa pottery. All save one—an AP monogram—included the name "Arequipa" and "California." Since this pottery was sold through various outlets in Chicago, New York, and Boston, as well as San Francisco, you do not have to go to California to find a piece. Incidentally, Arequipa means a "place of peace."

The illustration shows a vase in soft mat green, with relief ivy decoration around the top.

ASHWORTH

George L. Ashworth & Bro., as such, came into the potting picture in 1862, when George Ashworth purchased from Francis Morley the pottery which Morley had purchased from Charles Mason in 1848. Ashworth had been in partnership with Morley in that venture from 1858 to 1862, and took over when Morley retired. Ashworths continued to use the molds, patterns, and processes developed by Mason, just as Morley had done. The company is still making   modern version of Mason's Ironstone in tablewares today. (*See* Mason's Patent Ironstone.)

The Ashworths also originated many patterns of their own. Their transfer-printed ironstones in bistre brown and sepia were very popular in this country in the 1870s and 1880s, and the company exported heavily.

The plate illustrated is the *American Marine* pattern, originated by Morley and continued by Ashworth for many years, in fact, into the twentieth century. (Pieces after 1891 will bear the word "England" in addition to the Ashworth mark.) This particular plate is in brown, but it was also printed in a pale blue. For the length of time this pattern remained in production, it is surprising not more of it is seen in shops today.

AUGUSTUS REX

A regally intertwined AR mark on some beautifully decorated porcelain may send you into an awed "Augustus Rex" whisper. This was the monogram of the Elector of Saxony who set Johann Bottger on his way to inventing hard paste porcelain, the first in Europe, and who founded the Meissen factory. Look carefully. Probably no other mark has been so copied. For many years the Dresden firm of Wolfson used it openly until they were finally made to desist by a lengthy lawsuit. Wolfson's wares may be old, but they are not Dresden. Be aware, too, that the true AR mark was never used on teaware. (*See:* Meissen, Dresden.)

AVALON WARE
See: *Clifton Ware; Chesapeake Pottery*

AVON POTTERY

For a short year and a half—1886-87—Karl Langenbeck, who had been associated with the Rookwood Pottery in Cincinnati, Ohio, and who was one of America's foremost ceramic chemists, operated his own Avon Pottery in Cincinnati. He concentrated on ornamental pieces, favoring the graceful classical forms then so popular. You'll find his applied handles in the form of elephant's or ram's heads, maybe in mat glaze, maybe in a glaze similar to some used at Rookwood. All his pieces are marked Avon, and there aren't many of them to be found.

In 1891 Langenbeck was in Zanesville, Ohio, as head chemist for J. B. Owens, soon moving to the American Encaustic Tiling Company. In 1894, he helped organize the Mosaic Tile Co., also of Zanesville. His accomplishments as a chemist, and his influential *Chemistry of Pottery,* published in 1895, so overshadowed his Avon pottery venture that it is often overlooked in his list of credits.

JOHN AYNSLEY & SONS, LTD.

Because we associate the Aynsley name so firmly with present day bone china, we tend to forget this same company has been making fine bone china for over 200 years, leaving a trail of early tea and dessert ware pieces for today's collectors.

The John Aynsley who established the pottery in 1775, started his career as a director of the Fenton Park Colliery Company, but he became so enamoured of the porcelain objets d'art then so new and highly favored that he switched from coal mining to potting. He set up his factory in Longton—it was known as Lane End until about 1848—and the present company, managed by his descendants, is still there.

At first he specialized in beer and cider mugs, decorating them in color from his own engravings of sporting, political, and humorous events. One mug, made about 1790, now in the Victoria and Albert Museum, depicts a prize fight which took place January 9, 1788, at Odiham in Hampshire between Richard Humphreys, the Bath Butcher, and Mendosa, the famous pugilist who invented the straight uppercut.

As tea drinking became more and more fashionable in England, Aynsley turned to tea and dessert services, and by the turn of the nineteenth century he was making them of bone china, still the present company's specialty. Aynsley marks varied slightly with the years, and a study of them in any good marks book, along with proper attention to the style of the piece and its decoration, will indicate the period in which the occasional early pieces you may find were made. Some of them were quite splendid in painting and execution.

Pictured is a pierced basket dessert plate, patterned in gold with raised turquoise filling, hand-painted center, early 19th century.

BANDED CREAM WARE
See *Mocha Ware*

BARROWFIELD POTTERY
See *Glasgow Potteries*

BARTLETT, MRS. ANNIE LATHAM
See *Southern Highland Potteries*

BASALT
See *Egyptian Black*

B

BAWO & DOTTER

Bawo & Dotter was first of all an importing firm, established in New York City in 1864 by Francis H. Bawo, a native of Germany, and Charles T. Dotter of Brooklyn. Among the china manufacturers for whom they acted as American agents were such well-known English firms as W. T. Copeland and W. H. Goss, and the German maker of bisque doll heads and dinnerware, Simon & Halbig.

Soon the business began to expand in directions of its own. In 1872, Bawo and Dotter acquired a decorating shop in Limoges, France, the Elite Works, and in 1883, another decorating works at Fischern bei Carlsbad, Bohemia. China marked "Elite/Limoges" and "Carlsbad/shield/China/Austria" came from their decorating shops. In 1896, they began to make their own whiteware in Limoges, but apparently they always bought the Carlsbad china they decorated.

Mr. Dotter retired in 1888, and C. F. W. Bawo, presumably Francis Bawo's son, joined the firm. The style of the company remained the same. That year, Bawo and Dotter established a glass factory and decorating works at Steinschoenau, Bohemia, to manufacture engraved, decorated table glass and fancy articles.

By the mid-1890s, they had opened stores in Paris, London, Berlin, Hamburg, and Brussels as outlets for their own products. Their main offices were in Dresden, Germany, and in Barclay Street, New York. Importing was still part of their business until at least 1900. What with so many irons in the fire, the firm could—and did—use its name on a variety of articles, as manufacturer, as decorator, and as importer, to the confusion of today's collectors who fail to find Bawo and Dotter listed among chinamakers.

BEARDMORE, FRANK & CO.
See *Sutherland Art Ware*

BEAVER FALLS ART TILE COMPANY

At this factory in Beaver Falls, Pa., organized in 1886, some most attractive tiles were turned out, mainly designed for solid wall decorations "for libraries, dining rooms, and bathrooms." Excellent designers worked here, and the plain enamel, embossed, and intaglio tiles they made have begun to interest collectors. (*See* Tiles.)

BELL, JOHN & MATHEW PRESTON
See *Glasgow Potteries*

BELL POTTERY

Foremost among the Shenandoah Valley potters of the nineteenth century were the Bells, beginning with Peter, Jr., who is credited with originating the process of glaze and color that marks Shenandoah pottery as a whole. He worked in Hagerstown, Md., and Wincester, Va. (1800-1845). His son John Bell worked in Waynesboro, Pa., (1826-1881), to be followed by his sons, John W. Bell (1881-1895) and Upton Bell (1895-1898).

Peter's other sons, Samuel and Solomon, had a pottery in Strasburg, Va. (1834-1882). This was carried on by Samuel's sons—Solomon was a bachelor—Samuel, Richard Franklin, and Charles (1882-1908).

Distinctive Bell marks appear on all kinds of useful articles—household crocks of brown pottery, blue decorated stoneware, glazed turk's-head molds, bureau supports, mixing bowls, soap dishes, chamber pots, grinding pestles, pie plates, shaving mugs, banks, cuspidors, colanders, picture frames, and whatever else they could think of that people might want.

The characteristic glazes they used were bright and clear—brown, yellow, red, chocolate, green, white, gray, and blue, alone or in all sorts of combinations.

The second-generation brothers, John in Waynesboro and Samuel in Strasburg, kept close in touch, sharing examples of coloring matter and clay and also the results of their experiments. Most of the Bell wares have a certain similarity, only the marks are different.

For further reading: *The Shenandoah Pottery,* by A. H. Rice and John Baer Stoudt (1929).

John Bell impressed his name on the bottom of the tan and brown "feather glaze" mug pictured. This is a hearty size, being 4 inches tall, and 3½ inches in diameter. (From the McCurley Collection, Taneytown, Maryland.)

BELLARMINES

As early as 1520, the Germans in Cologne were making a coarse stoneware jug with a portrait of a bearded man on its neck. They called it a Bartman jug, meaning "bearded man." Then, in the early 1600s, Cardinal Bellarmine came to the Low Countries to oppose the progress of Reformed Religion. He was heartily hated, and because of the fancied resemblance of his unpopular features to the ugly man on the Bartman jug—both did have the same square "cathedral-cut" beard—people began calling the jugs "Bellarmines." In England, about this same time, the jugs were called Gray-beards, and appeared in all sizes, qualities, and degrees of ugliness. The shape continued to be made for years, but the faces are of the very, very past.

Not long ago, when a river in Surrey, England, was being widened, a workman found the Bellarmine pictured, buried deep in mud. The inscription, in Flemish translates to "Drink and Eat. Forget not God." It dates about 1560.

BELLEEK

See: *American Belleek; Irish Belleek.*

BENNETT, ARNOLD (1867-1931)

The only reason Arnold Bennett gets mentioned here is because he set so many of his novels in the English pottery district. To learn, most vividly, what life was like in early Staffordshire, look for his *Anna of the Five Towns* (1902), *Tales of the Five Towns* (1905), *Grim Smile of the Five Towns* (1907), *Clayhanger* (1910), and *Hilda Lessways* (1911). You may appreciate your old Staffordshire teapot all the more, knowing that ten-year-old boys got up at four to tend fires and worked through till dark at night "learning the trade." Bennett was born in Hanley and knew the background well.

BENNETT POTTERY

The first industrial pottery south of the Mason-Dixon line was established in Baltimore, Md., in 1846, by Edwin Bennett, a native of Shropshire, England. He was already an experienced potter when he came to this country in 1841. Here he worked for a short time at his brother James's pottery in East Liverpool, Ohio, then traveled about a bit to potteries west and south. He ended up in Philadelphia, Pa., at the Gillinder glassworks where he stayed until he was ready to start his own business in 1846.

His pottery operated from that date until 1936, under three generations of the family, and under various firm names—E. & W. Bennett (1848-1856); Edwin Bennett Pottery (1856-1890); Edwin Bennett Pottery Co., Inc. (1890-1936). Edwin Bennett died, at ninety, in 1908.

Over the years, Bennett made almost everything in the pottery line, from cheap yellow-glazed kitchenware to an elaborate porcelain on the order of Irish Belleek. They made caneware; Rockingham (*see* **Rebecca at the Well**); blue ware (*see* **American Views**); whiteware, after 1869; porcelain, after 1890 when a decorating department was added; Parian (*see* **Parian**) and Albionware.

The last named was produced in limited quantity in 1896-1897. It was a decorative ware, vases and such, with figures built up in colored slip by the artist and covered by a clear glaze. The Albion ware vase pictured was done by artist Kate Dewitt Berg, then employed at the Bennett Pottery.

The clays used in most of the Bennett products were locally

16

mined in the Markey Creek area. Production was at its peak during the Civil War when more than 100 men and boys were employed, turning out some 3,000 pieces a week.

Baltimoreans have always regarded Bennett pottery highly, the lesser as well as the finer pieces. Souvenir pitchers, given to ladies attending the Shakespeare Commemorative production at Ford's Theatre, Baltimore, in 1892, seem to have been consistently treasured; they show up frequently in the Baltimore area, though more often in home collections than in shops.

BENNINGTON

Bennington is the name of a town in Vermont where various potteries were located. It is not the name of a specific company, nor is it the correct name for the mottled brown and yellow glazed pitchers and pie plates and other household objects, including cuspidors and bedpans, which were made there. That handsome utilitarian ware has a name of its own—Rockingham. It was first made at an earthenworks in Swinton, England, and was named for the Marquis of Rockingham on whose property the factory stood. Edward Butler is said to have been the originator.

In the last century, practically every potter in this country and England made Rockingham ware, but because that made at Bennington potteries was so outstanding as to shape and glaze, status-seeking collectors liked to think all their pieces were made there. Soon everyone was calling the ware "Bennington" or "Bennington-type." It is a usage hard to overcome—and one which tends to make us forget that many other wares were made in Bennington. Yet Parian was produced there in great quantities, equal to anyone's best, and their porcelain, though never made in profusion, was excellent. (*See* American Belleek.)

There were two potteries at Bennington. The older, The Norton Pottery, established by John and William Norton in 1793, made gray stoneware until 1894. Christopher Fenton, who married the founding John Norton's granddaughter, directed the other, which began independent operation as the The Fenton Pottery about 1847. Over the years there were various partnerships and designations for both potteries. The history of each, the marks they used, and the wares they made are covered fully in Richard Carter Barret's *Bennington Pottery and Porcelain,* a book you should find in your public library.

Of all made-in-Bennington ceramics, the deer, lion, and poodle pairs, made in the 1840s and 1850s, are the most sought and perhaps the most expensive. Several variations of flint enamel lions were produced—with molded mane or coleslaw mane, with tongue up or tongue down, with a base or without, and in combinations of such variations. The standing poodle with basket in mouth, pictured, was the only individual dog designed at the Bennington potteries. He appeared in Rockingham with a mustache, sometimes with a topknot, sometimes with both. According to Mr. Barret, sitting poodles in Rockingham were made at East Liverpool, Ohio, and though sometimes attributed to Bennington, were never made there. (*See* Rockingham.)

BING & GRONDAHL

This Danish porcelain manufactory in Copenhagen was started in 1853 by Frederick Wilhelm Grondahl, an artist with an idea—he had previously been a sculptor at the Royal Copenhagen works—and H. J. Bing, a stationer who had money to invest. The company still operates under the styling Bing & Grondahl though Grondahl died soon after the enterprise began. Only Bings are in the firm now.

Like Royal Copenhagen, Bing & Grondahl makes dinnerwares and figures as well as Christmas plates. Like the older factory, too, the characteristic glazes they have developed, their blues and whites, and their fine porcelain bodies seem magical in perfection.

Among early twentieth-century ceramic artists of the world, B & G's Carl Petersen, Kai Nielsen, Jean Gauguin (son of the famous French painter), and Margretha Hyldahl rank high. First editions of their works are on display at the firm's museum in Copenhagen. Any of their figures are choice collector's items today—art museums already have many of them. It does not, in truth, take long for excellence in porcelain to reach the collector's shelf, and current pieces are good buys for present enjoyment and future gain. B & G's figures of children and animals are particularly appealing. (*See* Christmas Plates.)

"BIRD & FLY"

See *Prestopans*

BISQUE

The word comes from the term "biscuit," and is applied to unglazed earthenware or porcelain which has been fired once. Medallions, busts, and small groups of sculpture are found in this ware. Chaffers describes it as "like a new clay tobacco pipe without the least gloss on it." In the late nineteenth century French and German factories turned out much of this ware for export in varying degrees of workmanship, the fine pieces showing great delicacy in modeling and color. Few of these bisque figurines are marked. One of the few companies who did put their stamps on their bisque wares was Gebruder Heubach of Lichte, Germany. They also used the same rising sun mark on their bisque doll heads. (*See:* Piano Babies; Heubach.)

The bisque figurines illustrated are large ones, unmarked, of the 1880-1890 period, very colorful, and exquisitely molded.

BLANC DE CHINE

Enough to say this is the name applied by collectors to plain white Chinese porcelains of all periods. Those of the Ming period are considered the finest. The example pictured is a writer's cup of the Chi'en Lung period (eighteenth century). The figure of one of the immortals is intrinsic with the cup; the stand is carved teakwood.

BLUE-DASH CHARGERS

You'll find more of these early English Delftware chargers in museums than in your grandmother's cupboard. They are very large dishes or platters for carrying meat—a boar's head, perhaps, or a roasted peacock. Old Delftware is a coarse earthenware, with an opaque tin glaze, and often pitted. The decoration is free style, and "blue dash" refers to the border of slanting blue lines on most of them. The center designs, crudely and quickly executed, show blue and white kings and queens, seascapes, landscapes, and lively would-be Chinese floral patterns, or polychromed designs of tulips and flowers which proclaim them sure ancestors of the later "gaudy" wares so beloved by the Pennsylvania Dutch. (*See:* Delft; Lambeth Delft)

Illustrated is a 12½-inch Lambeth Delft coronation plate, decorated in blue, yellow, and manganese, with blue-dash edge, showing Charles II in coronation robes within Westminster Abbey. It is inscribed and dated, "C 2 R 1661." This is part of the Burnap Collection in the Nelson Gallery, Atkins Museum, in Kansas City, Missouri—one of the most outstanding sources for study of seventeenth century English wares in this country.

BLUE ONION PATTERN

This familiar pattern, found on dinner and teaware and on all kinds of kitchen tools from egg whips to meat pounders started off humbly enough about 1730. It was intended for kitchen

utensils, but in no time at all it moved up in the world to the dining table. Johann Haroldt of the Meissen factory in Germany introduced it at a time underglaze blue was just being developed. He "borrowed" the design from an earlier Oriental pattern, incorporating the Tree of Life, the pomegranate, the chrysanthemum, and a stylized peach. Haroldt's peach was promptly mistaken for an onion.

Almost at once, other European factories began to copy it. A few went so far as to make their copies exact, even to the Meissen crossed swords mark. Fortunately for collectors, most of them, like Villeroy & Boch and Royal Copenhagen, were proud to reproduce it, with minor variations, under their own backstamps.

The pattern is still used today on both very good and very cheap china. Pieces made at the Meissen factory carry the crossed swords mark in the design as well as on the backstamp.

BOEHM BIRDS

Though Boehm Birds are still being made and are broadly distributed, they are of a class and quality which warrants their inclusion here as "antiques of tomorrow." Skillfully and painstakingly crafted, with a degree of detail unusual in today's commercial products, the birds and their backgrounds have been faithfully rendered in bisque. As works of art, they are already found, in sets or as individual pieces, in museums around the country. Fortunately they are not yet so expensive but that almost anyone who really wants one or two, or even a whole collection can afford them. (Of course, you may have to skimp on butter for the next few years, but why not?)

Back in the 1950s, Edward Marshall Boehm, a ceramic sculptor deeply interest in ornithology, began to manufacture small ceramic figures, animals, bowls, vases, and the like under the name Ozzo Ceramics. The company has since become Edward Marshall Boehm, Inc., specializing in the production of the handsome bisque Boehm bird scenes. There is an excellent chapter about Boehm in *A History of American Art and Porcelain* by Marion D. Schwartz and Richard Wolfe (1967).

BONE DISHES
See *Wedding Present China*

BO'NESS POTTERIES

Of all the potteries in Scotland, those at Bo'ness on the River Forth seem to show the most originality, life, and color in their products. The principal manufactory there, the Bo'ness Pottery, established in 1784 by Dr. John Roebuck, changed hands many times before it closed. The various owners, in order of possession, were: McCowen, Alexander Cummings, James C. Cummings, Shaw & Sons, Jameson & Co., Redding Coal Co., John Marshall (1854-1899). Charles W. McNay operated the Bridgeness Pottery there. Only the last two are mentioned in Godden's *Encyclopaedia of British Pottery and Porcelain Marks*.

Under Jameson production, Staffordshire-type blue printed ware was the specialty; most of it was made for export to the United States. It was usually marked with the pattern name—the Bosphorus pattern was one of their most successful—and sometimes the firm name, too.

The West Lothian Pottery Co., also at Bo'ness, did a brisk business in a type of colored ware decorated under glaze with quick sure brush strokes; it was backmarked with an impressed star only. The handsome horses, pictured, were made at the West Lothian Pottery. Also produced here were many flatback spaniels and other "Staffordshire" dogs, thinly potted and hollow, with a small round vent hole in the base. (*See:* Scottish Pottery; Carpet Bowls; Cottage Ornaments.)

BOOTH'S
BOOTH'S "WORCESTER"

Booth has been a familiar name in The Potteries since the mid-1700s and before. Enoch Booth, of Tunstall, who excelled in salt glaze, has left us a scratch-blue decorated mug, signed with his name and date—1742. It's now in the Fitzwilliam Museum in Cambridge, England. Various Booths went on and on, though not always in continuity. Godden devotes three full pages to Booth marks in his *British Pottery and Porcelain Marks*.

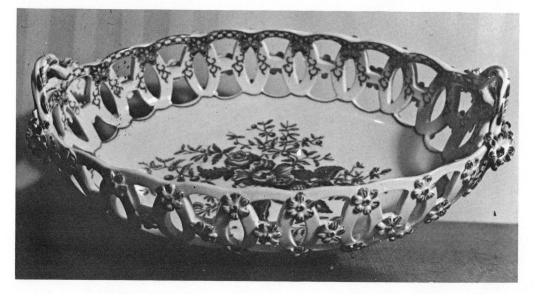

The Booths which interest Americans most, the ones who made the later wares we find so readily today, began with Thomas Booth & Co. (1868-1872), became Thomas Booth & Son (1872-1876), then Thomas G. Booth (1876-1883), then T. G. and F. Booth (1883-1891); then Booth's Ltd. (1891-1948).

In 1948, if you care to follow its later fortunes, the firm joined with Colclaugh China Ltd. to form Booth & Colclaugh, Ltd., which in 1954 joined with seven other potters to form the present-day Ridgway Potteries, Ltd. Each company has its own factory and sometimes gets to put its individual name on the backstamp along with "Ridgway's Potteries."

Back now to Booth's as it was. The company always made earthenwares, including in its early days an Ironstone they called "Parisian Granite." As for later Booth's, their proud innovation was Silicon China, a hard white opaque earthenware, not porcelain at all. On their dinner services, vases, and such in this ware, rich blue was a dominant color, and many of the early English patterns were revived. One of them, Lowestoft Deer, was used on a dinner set in the early 1920s, a sort of Chinese Willow pattern design with a spotted fawn in the center. It delighted housewives then, and "late" antiquers now.

Along in the early 1900s, Booth's made some copies of early Worcester porcelain types. Since they used their Silicon China as the body, the pieces could never be mistaken for originals. But so good was the potting and decoration, they might have given the experts a bit of puzzlement in attribution had they not marked each piece with a cypher combining the Worcester crescent and "B" for Booth.

The illustrations show one of these Booth's "Worcester" pieces, and the cypher. The twisted handles are finished with underglaze blue, and there is a blue transfer border inside the edge. The center engraved floral transfer, in classic style, is also in underglaze blue.

BOTTLES

Though we think of bottles as being of glass, collectors should not overlook the many varieties in china and pottery. Amusing figurals, made over the years, are to be found in all shapes and sizes, in all types of pottery, intriguingly colored. There are, for instance, shoes and legs, hands and fists, cockatoos and clowns, pretzels and present-day Jim Beams. You may find nineteenth-century snuff bottles, Meissen-type porcelain ladies purveying Florida water, twentieth-century miniature cats and dogs.

There are earthenware bottles that once contained beverages like Ginger Beer, gin, or lager; earthenware ink bottles, too. In 1895, the Keystone Pottery Co. of Rochester, Pennsylvania, was advertising, along with glazed stoneware for packaging preserves, a "large stock of Ink, Beer, and Porter Bottles."

As for the Jim Beam Collectors Editions, recent entrants in the collecting field, these bottles, well designed and colorful, were the happy thought of its distiller to promote Jim Beam bourbon. Special editions usually come out at the Christmas Holidays or to commemorate some special event. After 1968, we are told, only six to eight specials have been issued each year—and never re-issued, as has occasionally been done in the past. Each edition is limited, with only so many allotted each state—even California was allowed only 2000 cases (24,000 bottles) of the Cable Car bottle. Best to place your order for new editions early—from your liquor store; they may be cheaper full than they will be empty three months hence! Some reproductions have been reported.

BOW

Bow is a name to know and honor for it is probably the earliest of English porcelain factories. In 1748, Defoe wrote in his *Tour of Great Britain:* "The first village we come to is Bow where a large manufactory of Porcelain is lately set up. They have already made large quantities of cups, saucers, etc., which by some skillful persons are said to be little inferior to those which were brought from China."

Bow porcelain was, of course, soft paste. For the most part, its early useful wares, the "cups, saucers, etc.," were decorated in blue under glaze, copying the Chinese. Enamelled pieces, which included many figures, were at first sparsely decorated, but became more elaborate as time went on. The factory closed in 1776.

The place to find Bow porcelain is in museums—the Schreiber Collection in the Victoria and Albert Museum in London is perhaps the most complete in the world. One of the pieces at the Victoria and Albert is the Bow porcelain inkwell pictured. It is 4 inches in diameter, and inscribed "Made at New Canton, 1751," New Canton being the name Bow manufacturers used at this period.

E. BRAIN & COMPANY
See *Forley China*

BRAMELD & COMPANY
See *Rockingham*

BRISTOL POTTERIES

Bristol porcelain is museum fare, but it's good to know a bit about it even from an untouchable distance. Benjamin Lund and William Miller began to make a soft paste porcelain at Bristol about 1749. In 1752, they sold the concern and its surplus stock to the Worcester Porcelain Works, who moved it away. As you can imagine, authenticated Lund-Miller examples are few and far between, and their attractive shapes and forms are all mixed up with early Worcester.

About 1770, William Cockworthy set up a hard paste porcelain manufactory in Bristol. Three years later, he sold his patent rights to Richard Champion, and retired. Champion carried on the works as the Bristol China Manufactory, turning out simply decorated tea things, figures, unglazed porcelain plaques or armorial bearings and the like. Trouble with patent rights and the expense involved in straightening it out proved too much for his finances. He discontinued the works in 1781 and, in 1782, sold the remaining stock of china from his London warehouse.

Earthenwares were also made at Bristol, long before and long after the porcelain ventures—Delft types, stonewares and creamwares, with a great number of potters engaged in the action. For intensive study: *Old Bristol Potteries,* by W. J. Pountney (1920).

Pictured is a Bristol Delft plate, of earthenware with tin glazed back, 8⅝ inches in diameter. It is decorated in blue and red with flowers and leaves, and inscribed, "I B A 1724." Included in the fabulous Burnap Collection, this plate is on view at the Nelson Gallery, Atkins Museum, Kansas City, Missouri.

BROOKCROFT POTTERY

One of several art potteries established by women during the Depression of the 1930s which became extremely successful over the years was the Brookcroft Pottery at Plymouth Meeting, Pennsylvania. Mrs. Naaman Keyser was the founder and guiding spirit, concentrating on reproductions of the slip and sgraffito wares as they were made in early Pennsylvania. The pottery still continues, now owned and operated by Mrs. Keyser's daughter, Mrs. June Adams. It is still making slip and sgraffito wares, adapting them to present-day usage; they are extremely popular as meaningful souvenirs of the Pennsylvania Dutch country.

Brookcroft pottery is marked with an impressed tree with a capital K beside it.

BROWN POTTERY
See *Southern Highland Potteries*

BROWNIES

The Brownies, a combination of good fairies and gnomes created by artist Palmer Cox, burst on the young folks' world

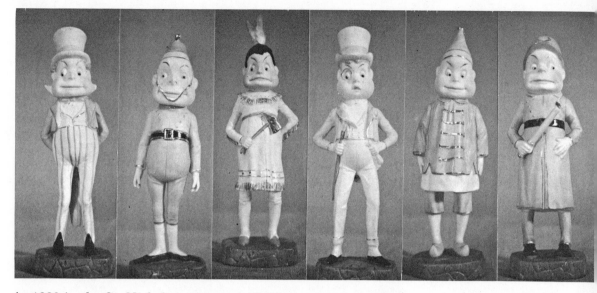

in 1883 in the *St. Nicholas* magazine. Children were enthralled with their antics, and these mischievous little fellows enjoyed a great and long-lasting vogue. Not only did they appear in book form, but they popped up on all sorts of items to intrigue the young—as paper dolls, as printed rag dolls, on souvenir spoons and mugs, as figurines.

According to the *Glass and Pottery World* (March 1895), Miss Mabel C. Dibble, a teacher of china painting in Chicago, and herself a talented artist—she exhibited a case of decorated china in the Woman's Building at the Chicago World's Fair and won a medal—was the one to introduce the Brownies in china painting, "a happy thought that has been often copied." From that, it would seem that amateur hand-painted pieces with Brownie decoration can be put on the "to-look-for" list of Brownie collectibles.

The bisque Brownies illustrated are undoubtedly German though they are unmarked. Expertly decorated with gold and bright pastels, they are about eight inches tall counting the gold-flecked platforms on which they stand. This set, which is exceptionally fine, consists of Uncle Sam, Bellhop, Indian, The Dude, Chinaman, and London Bobby. It is part of the Margaret W. Strong Collection, Rochester, New York.

BUENO RETIRO
See *Capo-di-Monte*

BUFFALO POTTERY

Should you find a piece of semi-vitreous china or pottery backstamped "Buffalo Pottery," sometimes with a buffalo pictured, sometimes without—several different backstamps were used—you may be assured it was made in Buffalo, N.Y., sometime between 1901 and 1920, and most likely before 1914. Occasionally the date is incorporated in the mark. The company is still in business; it turned to hotel ware and after 1920 made nothing else.

This company had a roundabout beginning. In 1875, John D. Larkin and his brother-in-law, Elbert Hubbard, later of literary fame, were partners in the Larkin Soap Mfg. Co., in Buffalo. Larkin made the soap and Hubbard dreamed up ways to sell it. His direct sales and premiums idea proved so successful they decided it would be cheaper to make their premiums than buy them.

They established the Buffalo Pottery in 1901-02 for this purpose, though they also sold their china through regular trade outlets. Besides their popular Blue Willow, they made at least a dozen other dinner sets with such names as Queen, Princess, Maple Leaf, and Tea Rose. Their blue ware was especially well done, and they used it for a Dr. Syntax series and various commemorative and historical pieces.

In 1908 they came out with Deldare, a striking art pottery, rich olive green in color, decorated with English scenes—The Fallowfield Hunt was very popular. Other art wares followed—Abino, Lunaware, Ivory, and Cafe au Lait. None of the art-wares seem ever to have been used as premiums.

Deldare, by far the best known of Buffalo's art wares, is currently enjoying great favor among collectors. Little 6-inch plates, high-priced at $7.50 five years ago, bring more than six times that today. For a comprehensive study of Buffalo Pottery, with many pictures to look at, turn to *The Book of Buffalo Pottery,* by Seymour and Violet Altman (1969).

BURGESS & GODDARD

See *Ironstone*

BURLEY & WINTERS

See *Western Potters*

BUTTER PATS

Butter pats were distinctly *comme il faut* in the 1880s and 1890s and were included as a matter of course in all proper dinner sets from the daintiest Haviland to the heaviest white Ironstone. These small dishes, sometimes round, sometimes square, for holding individual pats of butter, were seldom more than 2½ inches across. Because of their size, they were forever being lost or broken or used as doll dishes, and in the 1900s, they were to a great extent replaced by the larger bread-and-butter plate.

For today's collectors who look for small inexpensive items that are colorful, of good quality, and of growing oldtime interest, butter pats offer spice and variety. Seldom found in sets any more, they can be purchased individually. They show up in Delft, in Dresden china, hand painted with portraits or fruit centers, with Leeds-type feather edge, in flower-shaped majolica, in Moss Rose pattern, and in Rose Medallion, indeed, in almost every pattern and type of china and pottery imaginable.

For displaying such small pieces, shelves made to accommodate their size, or shadow boxes similarly shelved, work into distinctive wall decorations.

The butter pat pictured, is from a Touraine pattern flown blue dinner set, made by the Stanley Pottery Company, England. The design was registered in 1898.

BUTTONS

The mania for porcelain which swept England and the Continent toward the end of the eighteenth century extended even to buttons. Hand-painted porcelain button sets came into high favor; they were new and exotic, and the brocaded silk cases they came in bespoke the importance in which their fashionable owners held them. These pictorial buttons came in sets, usually six large and six small, though whatever the number each button in the

set bore a different picture. In France, amorous couples, cupids, and cherubims were favorite subjects. All the finer French china manufactories produced them; so did the Royal Copenhagen factory in Denmark, and the Dresden factories in Germany.

In England, Josiah Wedgwood, a great producer of buttons in his early days, noted in his catalog of 1787: "The cameos are employed for buttons which have lately been worn by the nobility of different parts of Europe."

The fad was not long lasting; the style in gentlemen's clothes changed with the new century, and the French were too busy with their Revolution to indulge in fripperies.

It was not until the turn of the twentieth century that porcelain buttons came again into high fashion—this time for ladies' shirtwaists and light dresses. About 1905, Minton was making bone china buttons in hand-painted floral designs in "fairly large quantities." So was Coalport, and so was Wedgwood. Wedgwood was still making bone china buttons in 1925. In 1951, that company put out a "limited edition," especially for collectors, reproducing some of their finest designs and earliest successes.

The china buttons and stud sets of the 1900s, like those pictured, were made in many European factories; some of them marked their wares, others did not. Some were factory-painted, others were sold in the white to be painted in decorating shops or at home by amateur china painters.

There were, too, some pottery buttons made about this time. Ruskin's, a hand pottery established in 1898, continued into the 1920s to produce pottery buttons as thin as porcelain, glazed back and front. Another hand pottery, producing Royal Barnum Ware—they marked their buttons CHB Barnum—made a heavy earthenware button richly glazed in red, blue, green, or brown, sometimes mottled. Their button years were from 1920 to 1940.

From Japan came Satsuma buttons, which sold in great quantities some sixty years ago. Their classic decorations included enameled dragons, butterflies, peacocks, scenes of Mt. Fuji, and Japanese people in colorful dress. The best Satsuma buttons are those where the glaze is finely crackled and the decoration, hand-drawn and colored, is most artistic. Reproductions within the last ten years have come on the market—mainly for button collectors—and new occidental designs added.

THE BYBEE POTTERY
See *Southern Highland Potteries*

BRITISH REGISTRY MARKS

The diamond-shaped registry marks often found on British-made products were in use from 1842 through 1883. There were two slightly different versions, the first used from 1842 to 1868; the second, from 1868 through 1883. The difference in design lay chiefly in the placement of the symbols within the diamond.

Study of the drawings and the tables below will help you determine to the day when a British piece was registered. It cannot be older, though it may be later, for some patterns had a long span of popularity and were made for years.

If the piece you seek to identify has the registry mark

but no maker's name, the Patent Office of Great Britain, London, England, will provide it if you send an accurate drawing of the mark, plus 50 cents with your request.

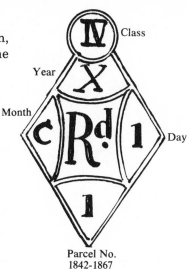

Class
Year
Month
Day

Parcel No.
1842-1867

Month of Manufacture Table
1842-1883

A — December	I — July
B — October	K — July (and December 1860)
C (or 0) — January	K—November
D — September	M — June
E — May	R—August (and Sept. 1-19, 1857)
G — February	W—March
H — April	

Year of Manufacture Table

First Registry Mark
(1842-1867)
Year Letter at the top

A—1845	G—1863	M—1859	S—1849	Y—1853
B—1858	H—1843	N—1864	T—1867	Z—1860
C—1844	I—1846	O—1862	U—1848	
D—1852	J—1854	P—1851	V—1850	
E—1855	K—1857	Q—1866	W—1865	
F—1847	L—1856	R—1861	X—1842	

Second Registry Mark
(1868 through 1883)
Year Letter at Right

A—1871	F—1873	K—1883	U—1874
C—1870	H—1869	L—1882	V—1876
D or W—1878	I—1872	P—1877	X—1868
E—1881	J—1880	S—1875	Y—1879

Note: In 1878, an error crept into the official sanctum and the letter W was used as a year mark from March 1 to 6. The error was caught and the mark changed to the correct D. *Since there was no W designation during the term of use of the second registry mark, either D or W can be designated as the year 1878.*

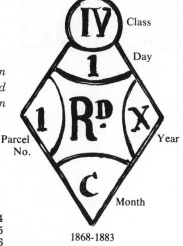

Class
Day
Parcel No.
Year
Month
1868-1883

Design Registration numbers on wares from 1884 to 1910
(These took the place of the triangular marks)

Rd. No. 1 ....registered January 1884
Rd. No. 19,754 ....registered January 1885
Rd. No. 40,480 ....registered January 1886

Rd. No. 64,520	registered January 1887
Rd. No. 90,483	registered January 1888
Rd. No. 116,648	registered January 1889
Rd. No. 141,273	registered January 1890
Rd. No. 163,767	registered January 1891
Rd. No. 185,713	registered January 1892
Rd. No. 205,240	registered January 1893
Rd. No. 224,720	registered January 1894
Rd. No. 246,975	registered January 1895
Rd. No. 268,392	registered January 1896
Rd. No. 291,241	registered January 1897
Rd. No. 311,658	registered January 1898
Rd. No. 331,707	registered January 1899
Rd. No. 351,202	registered January 1900
Rd. No. 368,154	registered January 1901
Rd. No. 385,500	registered January 1902
Rd. No. 402,500	registered January 1903
Rd. No. 420,000	registered January 1904
Rd. No. 447,000	registered January 1905
Rd. No. 471,000	registered January 1906
Rd. No. 494,000	registered January 1907
Rd. No. 519,500	registered January 1908
Rd. No. 550,000	registered January 1909

After 1902, the figures are approximate

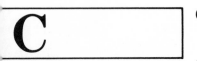

CADOGAN TEAPOTS

You may never see one of these curious pots in a lifetime; then, again, you might run into half a dozen at tomorrow's antiques show. They're nice to know about, just in case. This one-piece peach-shaped puzzle pot has no lid, and the hole in the bottom has no stopper. It's filled through the bottom where a tube from the opening goes up inside and spills the liquid over into the cheeks of the pot. Originally a Chinese wine pot, the form turned up in eighteenth century England as a teapot. Quantities were made, in all sizes, in the mottled brown glazed Rockingham ware. It is said to have taken its name from an early Lady Cadogan who liked to keep her tea guests guessing.

The example pictured is a Chinese wine pot, of the *Ch'ien Lung* period, ca. 1775. The teapots look just like it!

CALENDAR PLATES

If you like your collectibles neatly dated, calendar plates are for you. There's no mistaking the age of these advertising give-aways since the decoration includes calendar pages for the year in which they were distributed with Compliments of the Season. No one seems to know when or where these novelties originated but, from 1906 to 1921, whistle-stop butchers and bakers and candlestick makers from Maine to Arkansas gave them away by the hundreds.

Since the information we have about them comes from studying collections and discussing with dealers the plates which have passed through their hands, this must be a report rather than definitive data. There's general agreement that it is impossible to complete a run from the earliest known (1899) to the present, though die-hards keep hoping.

The 1899 plates are very scarce—a Pennsylvania dealer, in 1968, priced his at $50. These seem to have been a trial run, not too successful, for no others show up till 1906. From then to 1921, they blossomed in abundance. By the 1920s, the premium craze had subsided and calendar plates along with it. One dealer found some 1928 plates in Canada, made in England for a Canadian merchant, and one collector reported a 1929 American-made plate, but none for the intervening years from 1921. About 1951 calendar plates without advertising began to appear in gift shops; a run from that date to the present is not impossible.

In general the 1906-1921 plates are semi-vitreous china, variously decorated with flowers, landscapes, puppy dogs, pretty ladies, and other sentimental subjects along with the calendar leaves. The merchant's name and message were stamped in gold on the face.

Judging from the backstamps on calendar plates, most of them were made in East Liverpool, Ohio. D. E. McNicol, with agents in Boston, Chicago, New York City, Philadelphia, and New Orleans, seems to have been the most prolific producer. Dresden, Sterling, A. Harker, and Knowles, Taylor and Knowles were other East Liverpool potteries to backstamp their plates. Some, marked "Limoges," were made by the Ohio Pottery Co., of East Palestine, Ohio.

Sentimentalists who look for single plates to mark a birth year or for those distributed by stores in their home towns keep the stock low in antiques shops.

The calendar plate pictured was made by Knowles, Taylor and Knowles for Ott Bros., Taneytown, Maryland (incorrectly spelled "Otto" on the plate), showing calendar pages for both 1911 and 1912.

CALENDAR TILES

Jones, McDuffee & Stratton, Boston ceramic dealers and importers of fine chinawares, sponsored the making of the first Wedgwood Historic U. S. calendar tiles. The firm was amazed at the enthusiastic acceptance of these small desk pieces and continued their annual issuance for thirty years, from 1881 through 1910.

With few exceptions, the scenes, transfer-printed on the tiles, were of historic interest to the Boston area where most of the tiles were distributed. They were small, about 3½ by 4¾

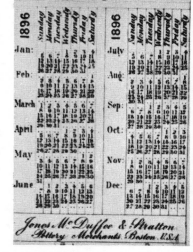

inches, ¼ inch thick, suitable for a lady's as well as a man's desk. Brown was a popular color though, through the years, blue, red, or puce appeared. The calendar occupied one side, the scene the other. All are signed Wedgwood or after 1891, Wedgwood, England.

Can you stand a list of subjects used? It sounds like a Boston Baedeker! 1881—Washington's Headquarters, Cambridge. 1882—Washington Statue, Public Gardens. 1883—Ribbon Badge. 1884—blank. 1885—Map of Boston 1722. 1886—Portland Vase. 1887—SS *Britannia* and SS *Etruria*. 1888—Josiah Wedgwood's Portrait. 1889—Faneuil Hall. 1890—Old State House. 1891—Adams Lean-to Houses, Quincy. 1892—Mount Vernon. 1893—Independence Hall, Philadelphia. 1894—Boston Public Library. 1895—State House, Boston. 1896—Trinity Church, Boston. 1897—Old Federal Street Theatre. 1898—King's Chapel. 1899—Washington Elm. 1900—John Hancock House. 1901—Bunker Hill Monument. 1902—Old North Church. 1903—Elmwood, Home of James Russell Lowell. 1904—United States Frigate *Constitution* in Chase. 1905—The Stephenson and Twentieth Century Locomotives. 1906—Jones, McDuffee & Stratton Co. Store, Franklin Street. 1907—Harvard Stadium. 1908—Harvard Medical School. 1909—Boston Art Museum. 1910—*Mayflower* approaching Land.

CAMBRIAN POTTERY
See *Swansea*

CAMBRIDGE ART POTTERY

This small art pottery in Cambridge, Ohio, was one of the many that sprang up in the Ohio Valley in the late 1890s and early 1900s, taking advantage of the native clays and natural gas, flourishing for a few years, then fading into oblivion. The few examples of its work which occasionally turn up engage—and often confound—today's collectors.

The Cambridge Art Pottery, working from 1895 to about 1910, turned out ornamental wares, vases, and table pieces, marking all its ware meticulously. This pottery's most distinguished product was its "Terrhea," which closely resembled Louwelsa, Utopian, and Rookwood's brown glazed ware. Don't turn down a piece just because it isn't one of the better known; keep it, if only for comparison.

CAMPBELLFIELD
See *Glasgow Potteries*

Luneville rooster pattern plate, 8½ inches diameter. Chalkware pigeon, 10½ inches high; Spatterware plate, morning glory design, 8½ inches in diameter. All early 19th century.

Nodder, Dresden, ca. 1830; 6 inches high. Rose Medallion teapot and cup from a "travelling" basket, ca. 1840; 6 inches high. Cadogan, Chinese wine pot, ca. 1775, 6 inches high.

Wemyss breakfast set, ca. 1880; cream pitcher is 2¾ inches high.

Parian corn pitcher, with 1843 British Registry mark; 8½ inches high. Crown Derby ewer, swan top, ca. 1850; 11 inches high

Teapot, Staffordshire transfer-printed ware, 4 quart size, ca. 1880, 12 inches high. Late Spatter (Late Sponge) mixing bowl, more often found in blue and white, ca. 1890; 11 inches diameter.

CANTA AND BOEHME

See *Victorian Trinket Boxes*

CANTON CHINA

Canton china in the Blue Willow pattern is dear to historical hearts as a relic of the China Trade and gallant clipper ship days. Sea captains in the eighteenth and early nineteenth centuries brought back quantities of it from the port of Canton, often using it for ballast. In England, the same ware is known as Nankin, presumably because theirs came from the port of Nanking rather than Canton.

The pattern itself depicts an old Chinese legend, and the Oriental blues have historical as well as mythological significance. The style and shape of the dishes, though, conformed to the needs of the West.

CAPO-DI-MONTE

This famous Italian manufactory near Naples was established about 1740 by Charles III, King of Naples. He and his queen, Amelia of Saxony, were genuinely interested in porcelain, proud of the manufactory they sponsored and the pieces made there. When he left Naples to become King of Spain in 1759, he took with him his finest workmen, models, and clay. At a country house near Madrid, called El Bueno Retiro, he had a factory set up. Here was made soft paste porcelain quite similar to that of Capo-di-Monte. As long as Charles reigned, this porcelain, which he called Bueno Retiro, was made only for royal use or for gifts to other sovereigns.

But back to Capo-di-Monte. The factory stood idle until 1771. Then King Ferdinand of Naples set it going again, and soon moved it to Naples. In 1821, the factory closed; later the molds and such went to the Ginori factory at Doccia.

At Capo-di-Monte, only soft paste porcelain was made; most of it was unmarked. At Naples, both soft paste and hard paste porcelains were produced, and a variety of marks were used, the most familiar to us being the crown over "N." In common with other potteries of the day, decorations tended to the Oriental in conscious imitation of Chinese porcelains. Mythological subjects were also favored in decoration, executed in either high or low relief, tinted in colors on a white ground. Flower swag borders were characteristic. It is this type of high relief decoration we commonly call Capo-di-Monte today, hoping almost against hope to find some day a genuine and early piece.

The Marchese Carlo Ginori had commenced the manufacture of porcelain at the Villa Doccia near Florence in the 1730s, a factory which is continued to this day. After the Capo-di-Monte molds were acquired in 1834, copies from them seem to have been Doccia's chief product, though Italian majolica also was in production. The Capo-di-Monte reproductions are not equal to the originals, and vary greatly in quality. Some, of course, are quite old now; and many are of fine workmanship. Often pieces are marked with the familiar N under a crown, which has proved an easy mark for other imitators to copy, too.

CARLSBAD CHINA
See *Bawo & Dotter*

CARLTON CHINA
See *Gossware*

CARPET BOWLS

Now that collectors and importing dealers are rustling the back counties of the British Isles for the presently popular "everyday" items, once thought too ordinary to be interesting, carpet bowls are no longer a rarity over here. These solid china balls, about three inches in diameter, are decorated in a variety of simple sponged and checked patterns in lively underglaze colors.

Though you may hear them called Staffordshire, they are actually of Scottish origin, and a great many were made in the potteries at Bo'ness on the River Forth in Scotland. This outdoor game, played on a carpet of grass, called for six pairs and a "Jack," a plain white ball. It was so popular in the border counties in the late nineteenth century that bowling clubs were formed to regulate the pastime.

The illustration shows some of the popular patterns in which carpet bowls were made; these are all from Scotland.

CAUGHLEY

See *Salopian*

CELADON

Celadon was one of China's earliest decorative wares, having been made from the Sung dynasty (950-1279). The body is thick and heavy, and some of it is decorated under glaze with florals or figures in relief. The color is a peculiar soft green, designed to resemble precious jade, sometimes pale and watery, sometimes darker and slightly brownish. Over the centuries the word celadon has come to be used for the color itself, whether it refers to ceramics or to living-room walls.

CENTENNIAL SOUVENIRS

Centennial souvenirs of any description, local or national, are a fascination to collectors and historians alike. As this present decade holds a second Centennial for the United States of America, the hunt is on for mementos from our first one in 1876. In that year, souvenirs appeared in great profusion, many of them at the Centennial Exposition in Philadelphia and almost as many in stores across the country for stay-at-homes. Dated articles in pressed glass, made for the occasion, are still readily found. Souvenirs in porcelain or pottery are less easily come by, but perhaps the more interesting on that account.

The pitcher shown here was made by Wedgwood. It has a light red earthenware body with a buff colored glaze, transfer-printed on both sides. One side shows the State House in Philadelphia in 1776; the other, one of the Exposition buildings in 1876. The names of the thirteen original States are embossed on a ribbon around the throat of the pitcher. Today Wedgwood catalogs list it a rarity; most fine one-occasion productions are.

Sometimes little-known events, immortalized in china, will

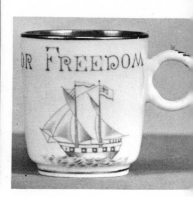

send you scurrying to old history books. A cup and saucer com-
memorating "The First Blow of the Revolution" pictures on one
side the snoopy British coast guard schooner, *Gaspee*; on the
other, the date, May 10, 1772, when staunch men of Providence,
Rhode Island, boarded and burned it.

Souvenirs of local Centennials are also of historical collecting interest. A plate issued in 1957 for the Centennial of Emporia,
Kansas, is pictured in this book under *Spode*.

CERAMIC ART POTTERY
See *Lenox China*

CHALKWARE

Less than a hundred years ago, peddlers were calling at
farmhouse doors with trays of cheap "chalkware pretties" to sell.
Today collectors of primitives look long to find good examples,
for chalkware is "in" again.

Actually these figures are not chalk but plaster of Paris.
Though they are generally attributed to the Pennsylvania Dutch,
the first ones in this country were imported from England. News-
papers of the early 1760s in New York, Boston, and Philadelphia
advertised them as "images." Later they were brought in from
Italy, France, and Germany, though, by that time, they were
being made locally. In fact, Henry Christian Geyer of Boston,
a stonecutter, was making and advertising plaster of Paris
images—Kings, Queens, parrots, sheep, dogs, etc. as early as 1768.
Many others followed Geyer's example. These images were easy
enough to manufacture and they sold well, staying popular, particularly in the Pennsylvania Dutch country, right up into the
1890s.

The early plaster figures were usually cast in two-part
molds, the two parts being cemented, leaving the center hollow;

they were sized and painted with oils. Later ones were much more garish, haphazardly decorated with water colors, without sizing. Cats with their wild grins seem particularly to have enjoyed this slapdash paint work. Pure red, green, black, yellow, and brown were the colors most frequently used.

Many of the figures appear to have been molded directly from Staffordshire ornaments, particularly the dogs, cats, and deer. There are birds to be found, sheep and goats, squirrels carrying nuts, often with slots to show they are banks, elaborate fruit arrangements, rare angels, and even rarer houses. Practically all the old plasterware pieces found today date from 1850-1890, not earlier.

Chalkware is far from inexpensive nowadays and counterfeits are around, though easily detected. Plasterware doesn't age overnight and counterfeiters have never quite been able to master faded colors and the aged surface texture to which the colors have been applied.

CHANTILLY

This important French factory was making soft paste porcelain in 1725, using Oriental patterns and designs. The factory flourished under several very able directors right up to the French Revolution when it was closed. Its distinguishing mark, a hunting horn, was copied at Worcester, and extensively forged in the nineteenth century.

The factory was briefly revived in 1803 by a M. Pigory who added a "P" to the hunting horn mark. These later wares were hard paste porcelain, and not quite up to the earlier standards in either workmanship or decoration.

CHELSEA KERAMIC WORKS
See *Dedham Pottery*

CHELSEA PORCELAIN

The Chelsea Porcelain Works was established in London in 1745, but its days of fame and flourish occurred while Nicholas Sprimont owned it from 1750 to 1769. His soft paste wares were decorated in the Oriental style or in the manner of Dresden and Sevres; his figures, often in arbors of flowers and foliage, had, by 1760, reached a peak of extravagant gilding and costuming; his rich claret color was never produced elsewhere, and his dark blue was the best in England. No wonder Chelsea is the most highly priced and highly prized of all eighteenth century English porcelains—and the most imitated, too. (Beware of European reproductions, both early and late.)

In 1769, when Sprimont was ready to retire, he sold his factory to James Cox who, a year later, sold it to William Duesbury, proprietor of the Derby factory. For almost two decades, Duesbury continued the works, (the Chelsea-Derby period), mainly as a London decorating establishment. Then he dismantled it and moved what materials and molds he wanted to the Derby works in Derby. (*See* Derby.)

Much has been written about Chelsea procelain. For an enthusiastic short account, we suggest Litchfield's *Pottery and Porcelain;* for intensive study, *Chelsea Porcelain, The Triangle and Raised Anchor Wares* (1948); *Chelsea Porcelain, the Red Anchor Wares* (1951); *Chelsea Porcelain, The Gold Anchor Period* (1952); and *English Porcelain Figures of the 18th Century* (1961), all by F. S. Mackenna.

The Chelsea teapot, pictured, depicts a man holding a parrot. It is soft paste porcelain, ca. 1745, and is now in the Colonial Williamsburg Collection.

CHESAPEAKE POTTERY

The Chesapeake Pottery in Baltimore, Maryland, commenced operations under the management of Henry and Isaac Brougham and John Tunstall in 1880. Two years later it was taken over by the D. F. Haynes Co., also of Baltimore, and the name Haynes was thereafter associated with it until its discontinuance in 1914.

The skill and artistry of David Francis Haynes were remarkable, and he achieved distinction for the beauty and originality of his designs as well as the variety of his excellent bodies and glazes. He was always experimenting—and successfully so—particularly with native clays.

His Clifton and Avalon wares, introduced in 1882, were highly regarded; his Parian, first produced in 1885, was of the finest; and Severn ware, with its fine body of a subtly grayish-olive tint, was perhaps his most original and refined of all. In 1886, his semi-porcelain dinner set in Arundel pattern appeared; other dinnerware followed. Everything Haynes had a potting hand in was high standard.

Other potters, in this country and abroad, copied his designs. Grimwade Bros. of Stoke-on-Trent, for one, copied his "Montessan" toilet set; a western U. S. potter, for another, copied his "Torquay" toilet set. Grimwade was enjoined not to market his set in the United States; the western potter was forbidden by court order to do so. Imitation was not flattery Haynes appreciated.

After some enthusiastic expansion, the company found itself in financial difficulties and, in 1887, it was put up for sale. Edwin Bennett (*see* Bennett Pottery) came to the rescue, but in a few years, he sold his interest to his son, E. Huston Bennett, and David F. Haynes. The company then became Messrs. Haynes, Bennett & Co. When Huston Bennett retired in 1895, David Haynes's son, Frank R., purchased his interest. From then on the firm was styled D. F. Haynes & Son. All these dates and changes of name will prove less dull should you find a marked piece and seek to date it!

The pottery was continued by Frank R. Haynes after his father died in 1908. Porcelain clock cases were the chief product of these later years, along with cracker jars, ferneries, cuspidors, and larger pieces like jardinieres, tall flower stands, even floor lamps. (*See* Clifton Ware.)

CHESSMEN

The game of chess originated in Persia, untold centuries ago. Mohammedan conquerers brought it with their armies across Africa and into Spain. It spread like wildfire over Christian Europe. From the twelfth to the eighteenth centuries, it was the Royal game, favored by royalty and nobility; Richard Coeur de Lion and Queen Elizabeth I were among its devotees. Later it moved to taverns and country inns and everyone who could master it played it. Shakespeare had Miranda in *The Tempest* playing at chess with Ferdinand; Benjamin Franklin, George Washington, and other Revolutionary bigwigs were adept at the game.

Chess is played on a checkered board with thirty-two pieces—sixteen to a player, consisting of two rooks or castles, two knights, two bishops, eight pawns, and a King and Queen.

Chess sets, being used in all countries, in all ages, and by all conditions of men, were made of a wide variety of materials. They were fashioned in solid silver, chased gold, and cast iron. They were carved of jade, of wood, and of ivory. An elaborate French set was of carved coral, bisque, and lapis lazuli. They were made of porcelain, some at Meissen. Wedgwood, in 1785, offered sets designed by Flaxman, in white jasper on bases of blue and green; Mrs. Siddons, the actress, and her brother, John Kemble, served as models for the King and Queen. A century or more later, the Martin Brothers (*see* Martin Ware) were potting their individual stoneware versions.

None of these, or other china chess sets in between, are for faint-hearted auction bidders or bargain seekers with skimpy purses. While the elaborate porcelain sets are for collectors of wealth and distinction, individual pieces show up now and then to delight the less affluent. Even these, when they can be found, are in the luxury class. (If you must have a chessman or two for your curio cabinet, try to be happy with carved ivory examples—you'll more likely find them.)

The chess Queen pictured is of jasper, by Wedgwood, modeled and signed by experimental modeler, Harry Barnard, in 1920.

CHESTNUT BASKETS

In eighteenth century England, chestnuts were served at table, an elegant dessert when skinned, peeled, then roasted or boiled. They were served, piping hot, wrapped in a damask napkin, in elaborately pierced silver bowls. By mid-century, these silver bowls were being imitated in perforated porcelain, and through the Wall period at Worcester (about 1752-1792), nothing was lovelier or more practical than their perforated chestnut baskets, complete with stand and cover, in which the dessert could be served without a cloth. By 1790, Leeds Pottery was adding pierced creamware chestnut baskets to their dessert sets, in their own distinctive patterns. The Worcester, Dr. Wall period, chestnut basket was sketched by Edith Lovell Andrews of St. Ives, Cornwall.

CHINA TRADE PORCELAIN
See *Oriental Export Porcelain*

CHINESE EXPORT PORCELAIN
See *Oriental Export Porcelain*

CHRISTMAS PLATES

The best known of Christmas plates are the pure blue and white porcelain editions put out by two Danish factories. Bing & Grondahl has been issuing them each year since 1895; the Royal Copenhagen Porcelain Manufactory, since 1908.

In both factories the design for the year is chosen by competition among their artists and employees. The motif is always Danish, rooted in folklore or history, or portraying Danish Christmas customs or familiar landmarks. Workmanship is of the finest. On Christmas Eve the mold is broken, never to be reproduced. Hence the current plates immediately become collector's items. The plates by both factories are seven inches across, and have holes for hanging. The Royal Copenhagen plates now have a border design, the same each year; the coupe-shaped B & G plates do not.

Some of the back issues are extremely rare and consequently expensive, but full sets can still be amassed, one by one, at a price. If you feel no urge for a backward collection, you can start with the current year and build forward as the plates come out. You'll find yourself with a goodly collection in no time, especially if you collect from both factories. Christmases come and go very fast!

A list of titles of all the Danish plates published and their current values can usually be obtained wherever these plates are sold. Most fine china shops carry them, and many gift shops.

The history of the plates, the artists who designed them and the motifs they used is told in the *Story of Bing & Grondahl Christmas Plates,* and *The Story of Royal Copenhagen Christmas Plates,* both by Pat Owen. (*See:* Bing & Grondahl; Royal Copenhagen.)

The Rosenthal Christmas plates were first issued in 1908. These are of fine Bavarian china, with Christmas scenes decorated in color on white. Muted blues, greens, browns, and yellows are the usual hues. "Weihnachten" and the year are embodied in the border design; the title of the scene and the artist's name are shown on the reverse of the plate. These are slightly larger than the Danish plates, being 8½ inches across.

Unlike the Danish plates, the Rosenthal Christmas plates are not made in limited editions; the number produced each year depends on the firm's estimate of anticipated sales. Rosenthal's New York City office will advise you of retail dealers in your locality. It is possible to collect back issues of these, too, should you wish to make a complete run. (*See* Rosenthal China.)

Late comers, but still very collectible, are the Christmas plates made in this country by the Frankoma Pottery, Sapulpa, Oklahoma. Designed by Mr. John Frank, these have been made in limited editions since 1965, and the mold is broken Christmas Eve.

The title of their first plate was "Good Will Towards Men"; of the 1966 plate, "Joy to the World"; of the 1967 plate (illustrated), "Gifts for the Christ Child"; and of the 1968 plate, "Flight into Egypt." These plates are slightly larger than the European Christmas plates. A reddish brown clay with a whitish glaze and low relief designs make them distinctive and extremely attractive. Being pottery, they are much less expensive new than the European plates, which are of porcelain. Back issues, though, will cost as much if not more. (*See* Frankoma Pottery.)

Rare finds are the Christmas plates the Buffalo Pottery made from 1950 through 1962 (1961 excepted). These were not for commercial sale but were given to customers and employees. (*See* Buffalo Pottery.)

For an example of Norway's 1970 contribution to Christmas plate collectibles, *see* Porsgrund. Swedish Christmas plates, made at Rorstrand from 1904 to 1926, were resumed again in 1968. (*See* Rorstrand.)

41

CINCINNATI ART POTTERY

This Ohio pottery, 1879 to 1891, used as its mark a turtle, alone or with "Kezonta," the Indian word for turtle, and "Cincinnati." You'll find it on pieces of faience with underglaze decoration, usually in dark blue embellished in gold with arabesque designs, sometimes in red on its studio-decorated pieces. Quite a bit of undecorated ware—simple bowls, plates and vases—was sold to home china painters; on these, only "Kezonta" appeared in the mark.

CLIFTON WARE

In 1882, the Chesapeake Pottery Company in Baltimore, Maryland, brought out a variation of majolica, backstamped "Clifton." The body was of an ivory tint, and the glaze was exceptionally rich and soft. The principal Clifton motifs, in raised design, finely detailed and painted in natural colors, were blackberries, strawberries, grapes, geraniums, and ivy. For "Avalon," a similar majolica which followed shortly after, sprays of flowers were used for decoration. In a contemporary report, these majolica products of the Chesapeake Pottery "were pronounced by judges equal to the famous Wedgwood of that grade." This was considered highest praise. (*See* Chesapeake Pottery.)

The Clifton pieces shown are from the collection of the late Mrs. Nancy Fitzpatrick of Lancaster, Pennsylvania, whose excellent article on Chesapeake Pottery appeared in *Spinning Wheel* magazine for September 1957.

CLOCK CASES

Sears, Roebuck & Co., of Chicago, Illinois, was established as a mail order house in 1893. The merchandise they presented so bounteously in their wonderful wish books was never the extreme of fashion, but it was what most people knew about and were aching to buy.

The porcelain clocks offered by this concern in their 1897 catalog were not new on the market; they had by then reached a point of mass production and popular price. Yet read what their chatty 1897 pages have to say, for this is the type of porcelain clock case you'll most readily find in antiques shops:

"Porcelain clocks have of late become very popular and are having a wonderful sale. The cases are made of one solid piece of porcelain, in irregular and fancy shapes, beautifully ornamented with raised work and colored/gold decorations. The porcelain case is especially desirable in addition to its beauty for the reason it will never become soiled. The finish is indestructible, and can be cleaned without any fear of damage. They have always been sold at very high prices, but we have made special arrangements by which we are able to sell them at a price which brings them within reach of anyone. In fact, everything considered, they are the cheapest clock made."

The porcelain clocks they pictured ran from $1.50 for a small one to $8.25 for a large mantel clock which struck the hour and half-hour. The cases for the most part were "imported"—you'll often find this type case marked Germany—but the movements were made in this country by the New Haven Clock Company, the Waterbury Clock Company, or by Ansonia. (*See also* Chesapeake Pottery.)

If it is an earlier, really elegant, porcelain clock you favor, you will find that, too—with looking. The clock case pictured was made by Wedgwood in blue and white jasperware, ca. 1820, and was fitted with a clock movement by Henry Marc of Paris.

COALPORT

Nothing about early potting was easy. To succeed, a man had to be artistically inclined, scientifically minded, and business oriented—and he couldn't loaf on the job. John Rose, who established the Coalport porcelain factory in Shropshire sometime between 1780 and 1790, answered all the requirements. Though his artistic originality is flawed by his persistent copying, he was in tune with the times. He was not the only one to copy, copy, copy to present-day confusion.

It is said Rose learned his trade as an apprentice to Thomas Turner at the Caughley Works; there was no finer teacher. In 1799, he began his acquisitions with the Caughley Works which he bought in that year. In 1800, he added the Swansea Works, and a few years later, Nantgarw. With the Swansea Works came William Billingsley, the artist-potter, bringing with him the secrets of the paste he had made at Swansea and Nantgarw. Billingsley died there in 1828. (*See* Crown Derby artists.)

Coalport's early specialty was a fine Dresden-like porcelain, the pieces highly colored, decorated with flowers in high relief, and often bearing the Dresden crossed swords mark. Soon Coalport was reproducing Sevres, even to the delicate pink known as Rose du Barry. Chelsea and Worcester and *their* marks were copied too.

Some of Coalport's work, of course, was original, and excellent in body and decoration. Needless to say, the pieces original to Coalport are the ones in museums and the ones that bring the highest prices today. "Coalport," "Coalbrookdale," "C. D.," and "C. Dale" are among their early marks, though often no mark at all was used.

Rose's own scientific contribution was a leadless feldspathic glaze for which he was awarded the Society of Arts Gold Medal in 1820. This he used for tea and fine dessert services, which he marked proudly, "Coalport Feldspar Porcelain."

After Rose died in 1841, the business went to his nephew; later it passed through many hands. For the middle history of the firm and its wares, which continued to stress the elegant, a good recent source of information is Godden's *Victorian Porcelain* (1961).

The company is still very much alive, and the fine china it makes today carries either the "Coalport" or "Coalbrookdale by Coalport" mark. (*See:* Salopian; Indian Tree Pattern.)

The porcelain teapot pictured, painted in colors and gilt, was made at the Coalport factory about 1820. It is now in the Victoria and Albert Museum in London. Its height? 6½ inches!

COLE'S POTTERY

See *Southern Highland Potteries*

COLONIAL CHINA

An unsigned column in the *Glass and Pottery World* for March 1895 comments on this subject, and we quote it here as much as anything to show the type of research and collecting done seventy-five years ago. The former hasn't changed much over the years, but who today could hope to find examples of old Delftware in Connecticut *frequently!*

"Nearly all old colonial ware was English. The settlement of New England occurred just about the time when pewter succeeded wooden trenchers; and while the Revolution was in progress, chinaware superseded pewter.

"One of the earliest mentions of china in America is in the Inventory of President Davenport of Harvard College in 1648—'Cheyny, £4.' Libson ware, which was an earthenware, was mentioned as early as 1656. A box of china was advertised for sale in Boston in 1732; in 1737, Peter Faneuil had a bountiful supply of glassware and china. There was practically no manufacture of fine pottery and porcelain in this country until the nineteenth century, and it was 1876 before any quantity was turned out. Potteries of coarse ware, however, were established at a very early date. John Pride of Salem was a potter in 1641.

"So it seems safe to say all china was imported. The first was doubtless old Delftware which is frequently found in Connecticut, where it was obtained from Dutch settlers in New Amsterdam. It is improbable that the Pilgrims brought over a few pieces of any sort in the Mayflower. The old Delft pieces are chiefly in the form of blue and white plates or platters, sometimes with yellow or orange color added.

"A well-versed collector, in searching through New England, has never found a single piece of Sevres, Dresden, or Berlin ware, nor any Italian or German pottery; nothing, in fact, but Chinese, Delft, and old English wares."

COLUMBIAN ART POTTERY
See *American Belleek*

COMARK POTTERY
See *Western Potters*

COPELAND
See *Spode*

CORDEY CHINA CO.
See *Cybis Porcelains*

CORK & EDGE

Though this trademark, with its spread eagle under the words "E Pluribus Unum," looks purely American, you'll never find it in your American porcelain and pottery marks books. It is one that Cork & Edge at the Newport Pottery in Burslem, Staffordshire, used on their molded "Babes in the Wood" pitcher illustrated here and no doubt on other special pieces. This earthenware firm operated as Cork & Edge from 1846 to 1860; as Cork, Edge & Malkin from 1860-1871; and as Edge, Malkin & Co., from 1871 to 1903. A variety of trademarks was used over the years; high grade ironstone tableware was their principal export product.

45

CORONATION SOUVENIRS

Anglophiles have a collectible tailor-made to their interests in coronation cups and other coronation souvenir pieces. It is not at all difficult to find pieces from the coronation of King Edward VIII, even though it never took place, for the wares had been out some months previous to his abdication. Though their production was immediately stopped when he abdicated and some of the pieces taken off the market, a great many were already in circulation. The beaker pictured is one of these. It was made by J. & G. Meakin, and bears the Official Design stamp of the British Pottery Manufacturers Federation. Similar pieces with the same design were made by other potters, some in fine and expensive chinas. This one is earthenware.

Souvenir pieces from later coronations—cups, mugs, ashtrays, and the like—show up frequently, but cups from earlier reigns in the 1800s take a little more looking for. For those who want to stretch the "Coronation" a bit, souvenirs from Queen Victoria's Jubilee are still around to fill a spot in such a regal collection.

COTTAGE OR CHIMNEY ORNAMENTS

Let the rich in their stately houses have their fine figurines from the porcelain manufactories of Dresden, Bow, and Chelsea. The poor, who liked things pretty, too, had Staffordshire ornaments to brighten their mantels and sideboards. "Flatbacks," meant to stand against a wall and decorated only where it showed, were turned out in prodigious quantities in the hundred years from 1760 to 1860, with the decade of the 1840s most prolific of all. Most of them were made in Staffordshire, but potteries in Scotland, Ireland, and Wales turned out their share. These hand-molded earthenware chimneypieces, hand-decorated in bright greens, blues, and orange on a creamy ground, or trimmed effusively in gold, offered a subject for every taste.

There were dogs for the dog lover—poodles, spaniels, greyhounds, setters, and pointers. There were cows and sheep; Scots Highlanders and their lassies; religious figures like John Wesley preaching and Elijah being fed by ravens. There were equestrian ladies and gentlemen; Josephine and Napoleon reclining on sofas; Gladstone and Pitt; grisly murder-house scenes; and inanimate clocks, bound to be right twice a day.

After 1850, the modeling was no longer done by hand; the colors became garish and haphazardly applied. They are still being made from the same old molds. *(See:* Bo'ness Potteries; Inanimate clocks; Staffordshire Dogs.)

46

COWAN POTTERY

Guy Cowan, who was teaching pottery in the Cleveland, Ohio, City schools system, opened his art studio in 1913, and persisted in it until 1920. Most of his studio wares were of the sculpture type, though he occasionally made vases and other decorative pieces. The several artists who worked there periodically over the seven years signed their pieces along with the company name, which was *always* used.

CRAVEN ART POTTERY
See *U.S. Art Pottery*

CROWN DERBY ARTISTS

The artists who decorated Crown Derby porcelains did not sign their work, nor did artists at other factories. But they had their specialties by which they were known, and their styles are identifiable. Many of their names crop up in records of other factories at various times, and experts are often able to put two and two together to come up with answers to ticklish attributions.

Litchfield in his *Pottery and Porcelain* gives the following list of Crown Derby artists and their specialties: Zachariah Boreman, landscapes, flowers, and birds; Will, landscapes; Brewer, landscapes and flowers; Bancroft, flowers and insects; William Taylor, Oriental subjects and flowers; Robinson, landscapes; William Corden, flowers; Stanesby, flowers; Haslem, figures and flowers; Cotton and Askew, figures; and Pegg, a Quaker, botanical flower subjects. William Billingsley who painted flowers, especially roses, is perhaps the best known of all.

Billingsley did more than the usual moving about. Among other factories he worked at were Worcester and Coalport, and at one time he was a potter himself at Nantgarw and Swansea. Some, at least, of his wanderings through England and Wales were due to a bigamy charge which relentlessly pursued him. On this account, too, much of his work was done under an assumed name. His beautiful roses, however, remained his own. (*See:* Derby; Nantgarw; Swansea.)

CROWN STAFFORDSHIRE

We see this mark so often on bone china in today's shops, we tend to think it an entirely modern ware, overlooking the fine print in the backstamp, "Est'd 1801." While the Crown name is fairly new—it was adopted in 1889—descendants of the same Thomas Green, who began potting for himself in 1833 at the

old Minerva Works in Fenton, are still running the business. The company has operated over the years under a variety of stylings—Green and Richards, Thomas Green, M. Green & Co., and T. A. & S. Green.

Early items tended toward miniatures—toy tea and dinner sets, small ornaments, and the like. Porcelain was made apparently from the start. By 1876, they had added adult-size dinnerware, vases, cutlery handles, and similar items. Their latticed bone china baskets, trimmed with sculptured china flowers, or sometimes filled with them, were brought out to mark the eightieth anniversary of the firm's founding, and were promoted with the slogan, "A May basket for every bride."

The May baskets and the miniature sets are still produced along with tablewares and incidental pieces. A great deal of this ware is exported to Canada, where American tourists are delighted to find it and bring it home as souvenirs.

The Crown Staffordshire "May Basket" pictured, filled with natural colored narcissus, primroses, pinks, pansies and rosebuds of china, was purchased in Nassau in 1958.

CROWN WORKS
See *Door Furniture*

CUP PLATES

In days when drinking tea was new and rather daring, when cups were handleless, and saucers deep, it was the fashion to drink it from the saucer. While this polite saucer-sipping was going on, the cup was genteelly rested in a specially provided cup plate, a little flat dish about three or four inches in diameter. Americans favored cup plates of glass, made here at home, but china ones, too, were used. Such Staffordshire potters as Adams, Ridgway, Wood, and others who participated in export wares, made them in their usual patterns. Especially nice ones to find today are those with American Views; in Spatterware; or printed with mottoes from *Poor Richard's Almanac.*

By 1840, cup plates were old style and many of them probably ended their days as play dishes for little girls.

The cup plate pictured, with its pseudo-Oriental scene, is transfer-printed in puce color. It is unmarked Staffordshire.

CUSPIDORS

Spittoons, as they were known before the refinements of the twentieth century decreed "Cuspadores" a more elegant name, were household necessities in days when snuff for the ladies and chewing tobacco for the men were *de rigueur* for all classes of society. Andrew Jackson's first official act as President is reputed to be the purchase of twenty spittoons for the White House. In Ulysses S. Grant's home in Galena, Illinois, built and furnished for him by grateful citizens of his hometown after the Civil War and now a national shrine, there is at least one spittoon in every room, barring only his daughter Nellie's bedroom.

The heyday of the spittoon was from the 1840s through the 1880s, though as cuspidors they were offered for sale in mail order catalogs by such companies as Butler Brothers and Sears Roebuck up to 1930.

Cuspidors were made of all sorts of materials—brass, glass, tin, iron, even plated silver, but china and pottery spittoons, easy to keep clean, were in abundance. Early types were of gray stoneware with blue decoration, of glazed redware, of Rockingham ware. Those made at Bennington, Vermont, were frequently marked. John Bell of Waynesboro, Pennsylvania, was another potter to mark his colorfully glazed spittoons.

For finer homes, there were cuspidors in luxury ware—Sevres, Meissen, Wedgwood, Spode; for lesser homes, Ironstone and majolica were elegant enough. By the 1880s, fancy spittoons of embossed Austrian china, delicately hand-painted, were popular. China cuspidors after the turn of the century were more cheaply made, tending to gaudy transfer decoration.

For collectors of cuspidors *per se,* the variety is wide and full of surprises. For the casual collector who is satisfied to have one or two examples around the house, cuspidors can be used handsomely for flower arrangements, unless, of course, the householders are still given to snuffing and chewing, in which case, spittoons are handy in their own right.

Cuspidors pictured are in Seaweed pattern majolica, and Rockingham ware.

CYBIS PORCELAINS

Cybis is a name Americans should recognize with pride,

for it represents, perhaps, the highest expression of ceramic art in this country. Cybis porcelain sculptures, still being made in Trenton, New Jersey, are not antique, though some early limited editions are now exhausted. Many of them go to private or museum collections. Their *Great White Heron* is in the American Consulate in Montreal; *Turtle Doves,* in the American Embassy at Rome. A ballerina, *On Cue,* is in the collection of Princess Christina of Sweden, and *Iris,* in Prince Philip's collection at Buckingham Palace. United States Presidents have chosen Cybis porcelains as gifts to heads of other nations.

Available to sightseers are the unbelievably natural *Flower Bouquet of the United States* at the Smithsonian Institution in Washington, D.C., a piece in which each state flower is represented—it made its first appearance at the 1964-65 World's Fair in New York—and *The Holy Child of Prague,* created for the National Shrine of the Immaculate Conception, also in Washington, where it occupies its own specially designed niche.

Boleslaw Cybis, a world-known Polish artist, was commissioned by his government to paint two *al fresco* murals for the Polish Pavilion at New York's 1939 World's Fair. On his way home, the news came that the Nazis had invaded Poland, and he turned back immediately to the United States. Here he has been ever since and is now an American citizen.

Turning to his first love, sculpture, for a livelihood, he opened a studio at Trenton and developed his work in ceramics. At first he made hand-painted plaster of Paris figures for sale in gift shops, but by 1942 he had founded the Cordey China Co., producing figures and vases decorated with hand-shaped accessories, such as ceramic flowers, porcelain lace, ribbons, and curls. A group of skilled and talented artists gathered about him, many of them, in those early days, displaced Poles like himself. The attractive gift shop figurines, wall plaques, flower decorated lamps, coffee sets, and similar items marked "Cordey," made from 1942 to 1950, are well within the range of the modest collector.

After World War II, when the gift shop imports from Europe and Japan were again available, Cordey production ceased and Mr. Cybis devoted his artistry to the outstanding porcelains, marked "Cybis," on which his fame rests. Illustrations of some of Cybis' major works are shown in a *History of American Art Porcelain* by Marvin D. Schwartz and Richard Wolfe (1967).

The 12-inch Dahlia pictured, with each segment of its 100 petals created individually, is an example of Cybis' exquisite flower work. This piece was limited to 350 copies, an edition now exhausted. In nonlimited editions, available in quality shops today, there are smaller flowers and a variety of charming animals, Madonnas, and children's heads and figures. Since many of them retail under $100, they are not out of reach. The limited editions, which include intricate birds and flowers, as well as figures, cost more but, of course, have more investment value.

DECK, THEODORE
See *Faience*

DEDHAM POTTERY

There'd be no mistaking Dedham Pottery even if it weren't distinctively marked with that name and a rabbit. It is an art ware, with turn-of-the-century beginnings, in a beautiful gray crackle glaze, decorated with bands of conventionally patterned flora and fauna in soft, slightly blurred cobalt. The patterns look almost as if they were stenciled; actually they were every bit hand-done. It was made in tableware and odd pieces.

Representative of its thirteen stock patterns are the Rabbit, Duck, Butterfly, Polar Bear, Iris, Magnolia, and Clover. The Rabbit was far in the lead. Among patterns that could be specially ordered, you'll find, with luck, elephants, swan, lions, crabs, turtles, and owls circling sedately around teapots and tea cups and bread and milk sets.

"Dedham Pottery" was the name the Chelsea Keramic Works took in 1895, when it moved, kilns and all, from Chelsea to Dedham, Massachusetts. The backstamp was adjusted to correspond with the new name. It was in Dedham that the crackleware was produced.

This pottery was always a family affair. In 1866, Alexander Robertson, an experienced potter from Scotland, established the Chelsea Keramic Works at Chelsea, Massachusetts. Two years later, his brother Hugh joined him, and in 1873, his father, James Robertson, came over to become a part of the growing concern. The company was then making beanpots, flower pots, simple vases and a rather ornate "Redware" or terra cotta. After James Robertson died in 1880, and Alexander went off to California in 1884, Hugh continued the business by himself. His particular interest was in perfecting a Sang-de-Boeuf and a craquelle glaze. His work

was excellent, but it was not profitable, and in 1889 the factory closed.

In 1891, a group of Boston businessmen who had purchased the Keramic Art Works, called him back to be manager of the Chelsea Pottery U.S. In 1895, the operation moved to Dedham, just the other side of Boston, and the name was changed to Dedham Pottery. The Chinese-like crackle stoneware Hugh Robertson made there was exceedingly popular.

Hugh died in 1908; his son William followed as head of the company; when William died, *his* son, J. Milton, continued to operate the business until 1943, when the Dedham Pottery closed.

Paul Evans, in *Western Collector,* May 1967, gives a comprehensive account of the Dedham Pottery and illustrates many of the patterns. The examples shown here, from his collection, are in the popular Rabbit pattern. *The Dedham Pottery* by Lloyd E. Hawes, Dedham Historical Society, is another research reference.

DELDARE
See *Buffalo Pottery*

DELFT

There is Old Delftware and the Delft we see in shops today. About all they have in common is the name, the color blue, and the place of manufacture—Holland.

The earlier Delft, made in the last half of the 1500s, was quite similar to Italian maiolica—a brownish earthenware body, covered with white enamel on which a polychrome decoration was painted and fired. The Dutch had learned the craft in Italy or from Italian potters in France and Belgium.

Toward the end of the century, while at war with Spain and Portugal, the Dutch captured several Portuguese ships with cargoes of Chinese porcelain. This was their first close look at Oriental wares, and they liked what they saw. After 1602, the newly-founded Dutch East India Company began to bring Chinese wares direct to Holland. Though Dutch potters did not know how to make porcelain, they adapted their processes so that their products at least looked like it, and they used Chinese-type decoration. They began to move about—to Germany, France, and particularly to England. It is quite probable more "Delft" was made in England than in Holland itself. (*See* Lambeth Delft.)

By this time, Holland potters had more or less concentrated in Delft, already an old city, rich and renowned for its breweries. De Porcelyne Fles (The Porcelain Jar), established in 1653, was one of some thirty potteries in the city. Over the years it was to become Joost Thooft & Labouchere, and is now the N. V. Royal Delftware Manufactory.

Though blue and white held first place in Delft decoration, other Oriental types, as they were introduced to the West, were given attention, particularly the red-blue and gold Imari wares from Japan and the "famille verde" from China.

But in the eighteenth century things went all wrong for Delft. Bottger in Germany discovered how to make real porcelain, and Wedgwood in England worked out a cream colored pottery body. Dutch potters, unable to compete with their local clays, closed down one after another. By 1813, only three remained. A few years later, De Porcelyne Fles was struggling on alone.

Then in 1876, Joost Thooft bought the factory and proceeded to revive blue and white Delft, revitalizing it with a hard white body and specially developed glazes. This is the Delft we recognize today on sight.

The new owners turned to Dutch scenes in decoration—landscapes, windmills, Dutch boys and girls. Other countries occasionally copied the color and decoration—you'll often hear of "German Delft"—but none ever equaled the brilliant glaze and color of the true Holland Delft.

Delft is made today in various qualities, from fine reproductions of eighteenth century pieces like the finger vases or quintals used at Colonial Williamsburg, to souvenir wares found in gift shops—little Dutch shoes, Dutch figures, windmills, cow pitchers, and other novelty items. Present-day Delft is clearly marked; Litchfield's *Pottery and Porcelain* lists a number of Delft marks of the seventeenth and eighteenth centuries.

DERBY
CROWN DERBY
ROYAL CROWN DERBY

While this well-known name in English porcelain goes back before William Duesbury bought the factory about 1755, nothing definite is known of its earliest days. Before moving to Derby to become a potter, Duesbury had been very successful in his china decorating establishment in London. Success followed him in his new venture. In 1769 he purchased the famous Chelsea Works, and the Chelsea-Derby period, when Duesbury kept both factories going, brought forth some of the finest examples of English porcelains.

In 1773, King George III visited the factory and, impressed, gave Duesbury the patent to stamp his wares "Crown Derby."

Duesbury died in 1786, at the age of sixty-two; the business went to his son, William Duesbury II, who teamed up with Michael Kean to run it. The second Duesbury died in 1796; Kean married his widow and continued the business. Artists Boreman and Billingsley left about this time, unable to get along with the new owner, so it was said.

William Duesbury III grew up, married the daughter of a wealthy London customer named Sheffield, and after Mr. Kean died, the firm became Duesbury and Sheffield.

Neither man was a potter, and in 1810 the business was sold to Robert Bloor, who had been their senior clerk. Bloor revived the Imari styles which had been popular around 1700, and which are still associated with Crown Derby decoration. He was more of a moneymaker than an artist, and the extra fine quality of the ware declined. Little good his money did him, for in 1828 he went insane and in 1845 he died. Without him, the business continued a downward course, but a small works in King Street was kept alive by a group of former workmen, using many of the traditional Derby patterns and figure models.

Salvation came in 1876 when a new company took command. Two years later they built a large new works on Camaston

Road. Business and quality revived to such extent that, in 1890, Queen Victoria appointed the company "Manufacturers to Her Majesty," with the right to be known as Royal Crown Derby.

Royal Crown Derby is again a giant in the trade; the story of its present-day work is well told in *Modern Porcelain* by Alberta C. Trimble (1967). For study of its early works, look for F. B. Gilhespy's *Crown Derby Porcelain* (1951) and *Derby Porcelain* (1961). Sections dealing with Derby in all the general books on British porcelains seem exceptionally full. (*See* Crown Derby Artists.)

DICKENS WARE

This was one of the art potteries made at Samuel Weller's plant in Zanesville, Ohio. Artist Charles Babcock Upjohn designed it, and it came out in the late 1880s. At that time, the Doultons in England were doing well with a line of figurines, tableware, and accessories depicting characters from Charles Dickens' works. Weller, ever alert to trends, remarked that if Dickens could create a character named Sam Weller, the least he could do was name a line after him.

The first Dickens ware, made for a brief time only, merely changed the background colors of the highly glazed Lowelsa ware from brown, shading to yellow, to dark green, dark blue or chocolate brown shading to lighter hues.

The second Dickens ware line is much sought today and pieces signed Upjohn are doubly treasured. This was decorated by the sgraffito method, the design being hand-incised and the background colors blended to beautiful shadow work. Glazes varied from a soft mat to a high gloss. Indian heads, monks, and fish were popular subjects of the decoration, all totally unrelated to Dickens.

The third Dickens ware line came out in 1904 or 1905. This was highly glazed with under-the-glaze slip painting, and it *did* have a Dickens character decoration, usually on the obverse of the piece, along with a raised disk telling who the character was and what story he appeared in. This is by far the rarest of Weller's Dickens wares.

Most Dickens ware is so marked, either incised with a sharp tool or impressed, though the third Dickens ware line is just marked "Weller."

The Dickens ware vase illustrated, from the collection of Lucile Henzke, is of the third type. The quotation on the reverse reads, "It was a still more exciting spectacle to behold Mr. Weller . . . immersing Mr. Stiggin's head in a horse-trough full of water. Pickwick Papers."

DINI CELLAI

This is a mark too modern for most marks books. It was used by Dini Cellai of Florence, Italy, and is found on many pieces imported to this country in the 1920s. Wall pieces, ashtrays, vases, and boxes were common products, light tan in color, some with gold decorations, often relief-molded. Some may also be marked "Made in Italy"; others no doubt depended for identification on paper stickers which got lost.

222   Marks Impressed

DOCCIA PORCELAIN
See *Capo-di-Monte*

DOOR FURNITURE

If you're looking for something unusual to collect, yet meaningful and of a certain artistry, think of porcelain door furniture—finger plates, knobs, keyhole covers, and the like. Some of these old architectural adornments were delightfully inspired. You'll more likely find them in junk shops than in antiques shops, though antiques dealers are buying up more and more architectural details from the many huge old Victorian houses which seem currently doomed for demolishment. Such items should still be on the inexpensive side.

One manufactory which specialized in porcelain door furniture was the Crown Works at Burslem, England, established about 1867 by Messrs. Gaskell, Son & Co., and later sold to Messrs. Lea, Smith & Bolton. This firm also made umbrella, parasol, and walking stick knobs of porcelain—another collecting thought for the individualist. Incidentally, you'll find porcelain cane and stick knobs made of Meissen, Chantilly, Bow, and Chelsea for long-ago dandies. They were still in style in the 1850s—several were displayed at the Crystal Palace Exhibition—and in the 1870s when the Crown Works were making them.

DORCHESTER POTTERY WORKS

In 1895 George Henderson went up to Massachusetts from Connecticut, where he had been managing a pottery in New Haven, to establish the Dorchester Pottery Works in Dorchester, a part of Boston. He was extremely successful with his stoneware jugs and jars of various sorts, and in 1914, the new kiln which he designed himself could hold enough ware to fill two and a half freight cars. In the 1930s, when twenty-eight potters were employed, the kiln was kept full and fired monthly. Industrial wares formed the bulk of his business, though he did make some decorated tablewares.

George Henderson died in 1928; his son Charles, who continued the business, in 1967. But the pottery still goes on, now under the aegis of Mrs. Charles Hill Henderson, who operates in limited production with three very talented workers. Concentration today is on decorated tablewares, handmade by the methods and with the craftsmanship of an earlier day.

It is still not too late to visit this nostalgic pottery and see for yourself how things were done—it's a revelation—and to pick up a charming piece or two of Dorchester pottery for your own use and pleasure. (*See also* Footwarmers.) The ashtray pictured, in blue and white, is signed by the artist, N. Ricci, along with "Dorchester Stoneware, C.H.H."

DOUGHTY BIRDS

The Royal Worcester Doughty Birds, among the finest examples of contemporary ceramic art, are true-to-life portraits of living birds in their natural surroundings. Dorothy Doughty, the gifted English artist who designed them for the Royal Worcester China Manufactory, produced the first of the series, *Redstart*

on a hemlock spray, in 1935. From then until 1960, thirty different birds appeared, sometimes three in one year, sometimes none at all.

Miss Doughty, at her studio in Cornwall, worked from living birds. On an American field trip in 1953, she spent three weeks getting close enough to the elusive oven bird to study it. Among others in her American series are the Scarlet Tanager, Parula Warbler, Bewick's Wren, and the Phoebe. Every model, each made in limited edition, bears the artist's signature and the marks of the factory. At a Parke-Bernet sale in 1961, the pair of cardinals pictured brought $2,400. Since then Miss Doughty has died, and her birds are even more highly cherished—and more highly priced.

Complete collections in this country are on display at the Findlay Museum, Chicago, Illinois, and at the Brooks Memorial Museum, Memphis, Tenn.

DOULTON & WATTS
DOULTON & COMPANY
ROYAL DOULTON

This is a continuing success story. It started in 1815 when John Doulton and John Watts acquired an interest in a little pottery in Lambeth, London, a neighborhood where twenty other small potteries were also making common stonewares. Today the Doultons are the only survivors of the group.

By 1826 Doulton & Watts owned their business outright and had moved to larger premises. They continued to expand. Several of Mr. Doulton's sons entered the firm, Henry eventually taking over the manufacturing end. For their first fifty years the company produced only brown salt-glazed stoneware, a light buff-colored stoneware, and terra cotta. (*See* Terra Cotta.)

In the late 1830s, Britian suddenly became aware of public sanitation. While all the speeches and arguments were going on—there was some opposition to glazed drain pipes and experiments were called for—Henry Doulton erected a huge factory equipped to produce drainage and sewage pipes on a large scale. When the Public Health Act of 1848 was passed, the company was ready for immediate production.

Mr. Watts retired in 1854 and the firm became Doulton & Company. Today the company owns several large factories, making drain and sewage pipes, electrical insulators, porcelain laboratory apparatus, sanitary fixtures, and other standard commercial products as well as artwares.

About 1862, Doulton came into a wider area of collector interest. At that time they began to experiment with finer clays and lighter shades of brown. The ornamental jugs they produced in salt glaze ware were at first decorated with sgraffito, but soon became more elaborate. They called them "Doulton Ware."

In 1873, they developed underglaze painting on biscuit and for years "Lambeth Faience" had great vogue. It was a fad for aristocratic and titled ladies to work at the art, and the excellent pieces they decorated were shown at special exhibits. The Lambeth Studios were consumingly busy, at one time employing 400 young ladies. In 1885, the Society of Arts honored Mr. Henry Doulton with its Albert Medal—the Prince of Wales himself came to the Works to present it—for "opening a new avenue for refined and artistic female labour."

In 1887, Doulton & Co. acquired the works of Pinder, Bourne & Co. at Burslem, Staffordshire. Here they began to manufacture the finest class of china. Their hard paste porcelains were decorated by world famous ceramic artists, many of whom signed their work. For their pottery they perfected beautiful and brilliant glazes—Sang de Boeuf, Rouge Flambe, Haricot, Peach Blow, Crystalline, Titanian, and Sung, the most gorgeous of all. Their "Persian" wares in pottery were delightfully designed by William Rowe. Pieces from this period, in both china and pottery, are well worth a collector's search. Doulton was always very good about marking their wares and usually the type, like "Flambe," "Titanian," appears along with the firm name. Porcelain and pottery mark books are prolifically detailed and make it easy to determine the approximate age of almost any Doulton piece.

Sir Henry Doulton died in 1897; the business continued under his son until 1899; then it became a limited company.

In 1901, the firm received authorization to use the word "Royal" in the description of their potteries and manufactures. You can buy new Royal Doulton figurines, dinner sets, little tobies and other oddments in almost any good china shop, or you can look in antiques shops for older pieces from the periods before and just after the company became "Royal." (*See* Jackdaw of Rheims.)

The plates pictured, from a set of twelve, are of the Lambeth Faience school, ca. 1880. They were purchased from the Cowden Castle estate in north central Scotland.

DRESDEN

Geographically Dresden and Meissen, in Saxony, were some twelve miles apart, but the backgrounds they furnished in the manufacture of the first European hard-paste porcelain unite them to such an extent that the porcelain itself is correctly called both Dresden and Meissen.

It seems that in the early eighteenth century, Johan Bottger, an apothecary's assistant in Berlin, began experiments in making porcelain of the sort that came from China. For his presumption he was suspected of alchemy, and to escape prosecution, he fled to Saxony. There he was promptly arrested by order of the King-Elector who thought there might just be something in this wild idea. Bottger was taken to Dresden and set to work to develop it.

In 1705 he was moved to a fortress in Meissen—everything was very secret—then, two years later, brought back to Dresden. By 1708, he appears to have produced the porcelain he was after. Early in 1710, the factory was set up in Meissen. Bottger was its first director. When he died in 1719, Haroldt or Herold succeeded to the post.

The earliest Dresden or Meissen products have always been much desired. Museums have almost all of them. An excellent book for details of the long production—1710-1894—is W. B. Honey's *Dresden China* (1934). For a short account, look in Litchfield's *Pottery and Porcelain* (revised by Frank Tilley, 1950). (*See:* Meissen; Augustus Rex.)

Illustrated is a Meissen, crossed swords mark, compote-centerpiece, in blue and white and gold. The eight figures at the base represent the Harvest and the Seasons.

DRESSER, CHRISTOPHER
See *Linthorpe Pottery*

DRESSER SETS

Along in the 1880s, matched dresser sets in milk glass were extremely popular. Such sets usually consisted of two large and bulbous bottles for toilet waters, or perhaps arnica and hamamelis, a large tray, and a complement of little boxes for salves and powder, and small trays for pins and whatever, and a long box for gloves.

In the hand-painted 1890s, these rather bulky milk glass sets, though not retreating altogether, gave ground to the new china dresser sets, dainty, delicate, and colorful.

A full-fledged china set might have, in addition to the large tray, a powder box, a hair receiver, small jars for creams, a pin.

tray, a hairpin box, candlesticks, and a ring tree. Sometimes a hatpin holder and a pair of small bud vases completed the ensemble. The whole set matched in decoration.

Not all sets were so complete; economical or less affluent ladies were satisfied with the essentials. Sets you find today may contain only a portion of the items mentioned and still be complete as originally purchased. Ring trees (illustrated) and hatpin holders were always available separately, and as many sets have been broken up over the years, individual pieces are more often found today than complete sets. (*See* Hair Receivers.)

DRUG JARS

Apothecary shops (drugstores to us) have been around for 4,000 years or more, and pharmacists have been using ceramic containers to store their drugs just that long. Alabaster ointment jars were used by Ancient Egyptians; earthenware by Romans; and the waisted type called albarello by Persians. Through the centuries albarellos, with their wide-mouth openings, were made everywhere—in Italy, France, Germany, Holland, England. The top was closed by tying a piece of parchment, or bladder, or cloth over the opening; a tag identifying the contents was attached. (*See* Albarello.)

The drug jars pictured are Viennese, and rare because Viennese porcelain makers seldom produced drug jars. (It would be much more likely to find one made by Wedgwood.) The example with spout and cover, resembling a chocolate pot, held medicinal syrup.

EAGLE POTTERY
See *Niloak*

EAST LIVERPOOL, OHIO, POTTERS
See:*Calendar Plates; Tea Leaf Ironstone; Laughlin, Homer; Great Western Pottery*

EASTER PLATES

From 1910 to 1935, Bing & Grondahl made a series of Easter plates. These were of the same size as their Christmas plates and of the same fine white porcelain decorated in underglaze blue. They were never as popular as the Christmas plates and fewer of them were made. Consequently they are much harder to find today. (*See:* Bing & Grondahl; Christmas Plates.)

Rosenthal has put out a few Easter plates in their fine Bavarian china, but the company is unable to recall just when. The example pictured, decorated in soft colors, is for 1915. Their Oberammergau plate, also pictured, honoring the presentation of the Passion Play, was the only one of its type issued until the 1970 Oberammergau plate came out. These are planned for European trade and only a few are exported to the United States. (*See* Rosenthal China.)

EGYPTIAN BLACK
(Wedgwood's Basalt)

Though a solid black stoneware, unrelieved by glaze, was

one of the earliest products of English potters, Josiah Wedgwood so perfected it that he is often considered its inventor. Certainly the formula he used was his own, and the black ware he made was the finest ever produced. He named it Basalt for the famous black basaltic rocks of the Giant's Causeway in Northern Ireland, and used it, with superb relief decoration, for his neo-classical style vases, boxes, tablewares, and busts. Other potters were quick to cash in on its popularity and began making "Egyptian Black" like all get-out. It's not anywhere near as popular today as it should be.

The so-called "Michael Angelo Vase," pictured, was inspired by one of that artist's sculptures and made of black basalt with applied Arabesque decoration by Wedgwood at Etruria in 1783. It is actually not a vase, but a lamp with three burners.

ELERS BROTHERS REDWARE

The Elers brothers, John and David, were among Dutch artisans who came to England in the wake of William of Orange. They were silversmiths, but they were also potters, and in Eng-

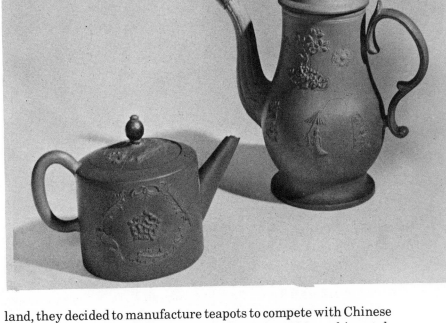

land, they decided to manufacture teapots to compete with Chinese imports. They opened a factory in Fulham in 1690, making redware, but soon moved to Staffordshire where they worked till about 1710. There seems to be no record of them after that.

The redware the Elers made was far superior to the heavy, crudely shaped and decorated slipware of the period. They were innovators. Using silver techniques, they improved the texture of the ware by turning it on a lathe instead of throwing it on a wheel; they used intaglio metal stamps to produce relief design; they copied the Chinese method of using hard firing rather than glaze to make the ware non-porous. They also introduced "chinoiserie," the most decorative of ceramic themes. Favorite motifs were peacocks, snails, Chinese figures, and prunus. When they stamped their work, they used an imitation Chinese seal or letters. Their colors ranged from a honey tone through brick red to chocolate. Examples of their work are now mostly in museums.

ELITE/LIMOGES
See *Bawo & Dotter*

EMPRESS CATHERINE SERVICE

Perhaps the most famous dinner service in the world was the 952-piece creamware set that Wedgwood and Bentley produced for the Empress Catherine of Russia in 1773-74. It was decorated with 1,244 views of Great Britain's rivers, lakes, ruins, abbeys, castles, and famous houses, beautifully painted by an army of decorators and artists. Since it was intended for casual use in Empress Catherine's country palace, *La Grenouilliere,* the palace emblem, a green frog, was incorporated in the border design.

Wedgwood had already won acclaim with the informal dinner service he had made for Queen Charlotte of England, whereby he earned the right to call his creamware "Queen's ware," but the set ordered for Empress Catherine created an even greater stir. Free-lance artists and important personages all over England came forth with sketches and paintings and suggestions for scenes to be used in decoration. Everyone wanted to be in on it, and many were.

The sample pieces the company made and sent to Russia for approval were decorated with enameled scenery in natural colors; the Empress deemed these too expensive and settled on a monochrome mulberry color, the only contrast being a bright green enamel frog in the garland design.

The set was a year or more in the making. Before it left for Russia, it was on display at the Wedgwood and Bentley showrooms in London. There the elite from all Britain flocked to see familiar scenes, often their own houses, pictured on the royal dinnerware.

As late as 1954, pieces from this set were on display in the Winter Palace at Leningrad. Should you be visiting Russia,

George Jones Parian sugar box, 3½ inches high, with matching gold-lined cup and saucer; ca. 1872.

Roseville "Rozane Royal" vase, ca. 1900; 14½ inches high. Roseville flower bowl, 10 inches diameter, and Mistletoe flower vase, ca. 1930; 6½ inches high.

Villeroy & Boch platter to Clover pattern dinner set, ca. 1900; 19 inches long.

Beatrix Potter Peter Rabbit figures on pottery tree stump. Clockwise: Hunca Munca, Benjamin Bunny, Tailor of Gloucester, Jemima Puddleduck, Sandy Whiskered Gentleman; the tallest is 5 inches high.

Left: Weller "Etna" vase; 10 inches high. Right: Weller flower vase, ca. 1930;
10 inches high.

we suspect you may still see them there. (*See* Queen's ware.)

Of the plates pictured, the one at the center bottom shows the decoration finally selected in monochrome mulberry with green frog. The others are trial pieces, executed in natural colors, which the Empress turned down.

EQUESTRIAN SERIES

Like their porcelain Doughty Birds Series, Royal Worcester's Equestrian Series is put out in limited editions, a procedure which greatly enhances the value of each edition as it is released. Miss Doris Linder, an English sculptress, is the artist. She modeled the Welsh Mountain Pony illustrated—it came out in 1967—at the estate of Lord Kenyon of Credington, Kent. This fiery little gray stallion, Coed Coch Planed, is the son of Coed Coch Madog, one of the most famous ponies of all times and whose blood runs through Welsh Mountain Ponies all over the world. Retail prices for these equestrian scupltures in porcelain range in the neighborhood of $500, but like the Doughty Birds they rise in value considerably the minute the 500th figure is finished and the mold is broken.

ETRUSCAN MAJOLICA
See *Majolica*

F

FAIENCE

Faience or Fayence, as a name for pottery, originated either from the town of Faenza in Italy or from Fayence in France; in both places maiolica, a tin-glazed earthenware, was manufactured in the 1500s. Later the term came to embrace all kinds of decorative earthenware. We usually think of it today as the gaily decorated, highly glazed, intriguingly shaped, peasant-type ware that comes to us from France, Italy, and Portugal.

In the early eighteenth century, especially in France, faience manufactories commanded the skill and taste of the finest sculptors and artists. (*See* Niderviller.) Toward the end of that century, as the demand for pottery rose among everyday people, workmanship declined. The fine early pieces, the statues and figurines and tablewares, so admirably molded, will be found today in museums or private collections, but nineteenth century examples are available, if not plentiful, from both France and Italy. Current pieces copy the old styles.

Of the French faiences, that made at Luneville in the Department de la Meurthe is perhaps the best known. Faience has been made there since 1723. The firm of S. Keller and Guerin acquired the factory in 1778, and Keller descendants carry it on. Their dinnerware patterns which feature a gay pink rooster decoration has been a favorite for years and years; you can see it modern-style in your china shop or department store today.

Luneville is well marked, and pieces without the "France" in the backstamp may be assumed to be before 1891. You'll find Luneville pieces in antiques shops in a variety of patterns and shapes—all charming. Recently we found a pair of hand-painted dog plates signed by the artist Onguene, pre-1891. Perhaps they were part of a larger set. One is illustrated here.

A shorter-lived faience factory is that of Theodore Deck in Paris in the last half of the nineteenth century. The pieces he made were well done and artistic; some of his plates were shown in the Paris Exhibition of 1878. His T. DECK incised mark is easily recognized.

In Italy, Nove Faience from Bassano, near Venice, is one to keep in mind. The factory here made faience from the seventeenth century well into the nineteenth, under a succession of owners. For a while—1762-1825—they worked with hard paste porcelain, but it is their faience which is best known. Their wares were usually marked Nove or Bassano, frequently combined with the name or initials of the current owner of the company; sometimes, with the owner's cypher alone. Consultation of marks books will give indication of age.

Our illustration shows a Nove Faience tureen, ca. 1870, hand decorated in natural fruit, with borders in *cafe au lait* tone. It is typical of Italian faience table pieces, past and present.

FAIENCERIES BRETONNE

See *Quimper*

FAMILLE ROSE

Five-color Chinese porcelains in which rose predominates, known as Famille Rose, relate to the reigns of the Emperors Yung Cheng (1723-1735) and Ch'ien Lung (1736-1795) of the Ch'ing or Manchu Dynasty. These rosy colors, derived from gold and ranging from light pinks to deep reds, had tremendous appeal to Europeans. Ch'ien Lung, particularly, encouraged trade with the West, and much of this ware was made to please Occidentals.

In Famille Verte, which was developed somewhat before Famille Rose, green predominates. This early ware enjoyed great vogue in Holland where it was conspicuously copied. There followed quickly Famille Jaune, with yellow predominating, Famille Noire, with black, and a similar decoration in which powdered blue was the dominant color.

FARMER'S CUPS

Giant cups that hold a pint or more are still being made, but today's buyers choose them more for flower arranging or waggish gifts than for coffee quaffing. The old ones—seek and ye shall find—were made in all kinds of pottery—plain white or colored Ironstone, Rockingham, Spatterware, blue printed ware, many with farm scenes, even in dainty hand-painted Austrian china. Some were affectionately lettered "Papa." Their age must be judged by the pottery itself.

While their ultimate destiny led them to the farm kitchen as a man's-size holder for coffee—and there are still old folks about who can recall, with awe, some hired man emptying a scalding cup in one draught—their original use was most likely for mush or bread and milk. Coffee was on precious few farm menus until after 1870, and some of these huge cups date earlier than that.

FENTON POTTERY

See *Bennington*

FISH AND GAME SETS

The hand-painted era, from the 1880s to the First World War, which was also the age of a "dish for every purpose," provided fertile ground for the Game plate. These appeared in a tremendous number of designs—deer, stag, quail, snipe, fish and more fish—all brightly painted in lifelike colors on splendid platters with plates to match. Game was still readily obtainable for the family table in those days, and often appeared on restaurant menus, so the plates were not just something pretty to have, they were definitely used.

Some were meticulously hand painted from scratch and signed by the artist, but most were factory decorated with decals, finished with quality handwork. A great many of them came from Germany and France, and were made of the fine porcelain so popular at that time. One collector, a huntsman, of course, has over 200 different platters, to say nothing of odd plates from broken sets.

The 18-inch platter pictured is marked "Austria." It is a thin china, featuring lifelike buck deer and doe, with a red flower border, green and gold scalloped edge, and was appropriate for serving venison steaks.

FLAXMAN, JOHN (1766-1826)

John Flaxman is remembered in ceramic circles for the pattern and groups he designed and modeled for Josiah Wedgwood, the first being a bas-relief of the "Dancing Hours" applied to a basalt vase. Copies of this were sent to London in September 1776. Flaxman was about twenty years old when he first began work for Wedgwood, and for the next twelve years he depended on Wedgwood for his livelihood. No complete list of his work there is extant, but it appears he was paid generously; records show he was given as much as two pounds ten for modeling a portrait for a ring, and six pounds sixpence for the drawing and modeling of each of the exquisite jasper chessmen for which he—and Wedgwood—were to become famous.

By 1789, he had begun to earn something in another branch of his profession—the sculpture of monuments to the dead. Here the finest qualities of his art are represented, and his memorial bas-reliefs are to be found in churches throughout England. Several are in Westminister Abbey. He was the first professor of sculpture at the Royal Academy of Art. In his day, he was called "the greatest of modern sculptors," and his work for Wedgwood was dismissed as "competent but dull." Shown is the jasper medallion he modeled, portraying Mrs. Wedgwood.

FLORENTINE CHINA
See *Gossware*

FLOWN BLUE

Flown Blue, Flow Blue, Flowing Blue—all names are equally acceptable for this sparkling stone china, decorated in rich blurry blue. It started its long run of popularity about 1825 when American Views were being made. It differs from that Historical Blue Ware in its body, which has a stoneware base; in its color, which is deliberately blurred; and in its decoration, which is of Oriental inspiration. It also stayed in production several decades longer. A chlorinated vapor, introduced into the kiln, caused the colors to spread and blur. Flown Brown and Flown Purple were also made; they proved less popular than the blue.

All Staffordshire potters made it. Meigh, using an impressed "Improved Stone China" as his trademark, called one of his patterns Troy. Podmore, Walker & Company trademarked theirs "Pearl Stone Ware," and made such patterns as Manila, Temple, and Corean.

The Alcocks used "Oriental Stone" as a trademark; their Scinde pattern was an all-time favorite. Wedgwood called his "Pearl Ware" or, from 1848 to 1860, just "Pearl" or "P." Knight Templar and the Chapoo plate (pictured) are Wedgwood patterns.

To the confusion of today's collectors, different companies sometimes used the same name on different patterns—but all names savored of romance and far-away places—Amoy, Hong Kong, Lahore, Pelew, Shanghai. Potteries in Scotland made their own versions, and in Holland, about 1850, Regout & Co., at Maastricht, brought out Siam, Timor, and others. (*See:* Petrus Regout; Martha Washington's States Pattern; Butter Pats; Wheeling Pottery.)

FOLEY CHINA

The name "Foley," which appears on many of the bone
china souvenir wares so popular in the 1880s, can confound collectors. And well it might, for "Foley" is not always the potter's
name. Foley China was made at the Shelley Potteries, Ltd., at
Longton, Stoke-on-Trent, a firm established in 1876 by H. Wileman and J. E. Shelley. In 1879, Mr. Wileman retired, and Mr.
Shelley remained as sole owner. His potteries used the trade name
"Foley" until 1912, when it was replaced by "Shelley."

Present-day Foley China is manufactured by E. Brain &
Company who have operated the Foley China Works, in Fenton,
since 1903.

FOOD MOLDS

Our forefathers were great ones for eating and drinking,
and the women spent an enormous amount of time preparing
food. So much labor was required, what with fireplaces and brick
ovens to be dealt with, flours and sugars and spices to be ground
or sifted, doughs to be kneaded, and game to be dressed, it's a
wonder the ladies had time to think of making things pretty.
But they did, at least when it came to their puddings and pastries.

Food molds, in which they baked their cakes and puddings
and crusty pastries or "set" aspics and jellies, were used freely
from the seventeenth century to the nineteenth. They were made
of all sorts of materials—silver, copper, tin, wood, glass, and even
iron, as well as stoneware, earthenware, and creamware. The

intaglio designs in the base which produced foods so handsomely decorated in relief were of great variety, from roosters, fruits, vegetables and flowers to geometric designs like the nineteenth century English Ironstone mold pictured. Potters in all European countries and in the United States made them, from country potters in Pennsylvania who turned out redware Turk's head molds for their neighbors to Wedgwood who made splendid ones for lordly tables. (*See* Jelly Molds.)

FOOT WARMERS

In days before central heating, feet could get as cold indoors as outdoors, and ye oldsters, for centuries back, kept foot warmers of one sort or another on hand for a frosty day. In colonial times, they carried foot stoves to church. In horse-drawn days, they tucked foot warmers under blankets and robes in sleighs. Women sewed in the parlor or washed up at the kitchen sink with their feet on heated slabs of soapstone.

The tank-types, filled with hot water, were wonderful warmers in bed. The earliest of these were of brass or copper, even pewter, but by the mid-1800s stoneware and pottery foot warmers took over. These were familiarly called "china pigs." Some were of stoneware, maybe with slip decoration, of mottled brown Rockingham, or of plain heavy cream colored pottery. At Bennington, Vermont, the potteries turned out fancy ones in flint enamel, shaped to the feet, toes and all.

The more conventional—and the most often found today—were cylindrical, usually with one flat side. Of this type, "Goodwill's Bed & Foot Warmer and Water Carrier," which is like a little keg with a wire and wood bail, was patented in 1895. Henderson's Patented Foot Warmer was made as late as 1920 by the Dorchester (Mass.) Pottery Works. (*See* Dorchester Pottery.) We have owned similar unmarked examples which were used well into the 1940s in a Veterans' Hospital in Maryland, and one marked "Medicine Hat, Alberta, Canada."

Betty Buckelew of Hattiesburg, Mississippi, owns one with a molded-on carrying handle of pottery across the top. It is marked on one end "O. K. Foot Warmer," on the other "Logan Pottery Co., Logan, O.," and on the side, below the stopper, "Pat. Appl'd For." The Logan Pottery was founded in 1902 by Charles Adcock and R. E. Stevenson, and closed in 1965, at that time being managed by two sons of Mr. Adcock. They made, in addition to foot warmers, stoneware beanpots, bird baths, ashtrays, jars, jugs, and such, though most of their business was in making red clay flower pots. For all, only local clays were used.

Enough potters produced foot warmers in wide enough variation over a long enough time span to make a goodly collection of different styles possible. Families who enjoy camping out will find one or two handy to have around for actual use.

FRANKLIN MAXIM MUGS

Benjamin Franklin, Printer, as he liked best to be described, was a diplomat, statesman, scientist, a man who did many things, and all of them well. He invented lightning rods, fireplace stoves, bifocals, and other pleasantries to make life easier. He originated the first police and fire departments in the country, and set up the Post Office in the way it should go. His able statesmanship in England and France served young America well.

His *Poor Richard's Almanack* (begun in 1793), like all proper almanacs, combined weather prognostications with witty observations. Franklin added moral maxims and lessons for youth. His almanacs sold at least 10,000 annually, and Staffordshire potters were quick to spread his wit and wisdom on children's mugs and plates.

"God helps those who help themselves," "A stitch in time saves nine," "Keep thy shop and thy shop will keep thee"—such were the proverbs our grandparents' grandparents read in the Almanack, learned from the mugs from which they drank, and passed on to their children. The sayings are now so much a part of our national idiom we seldom think who said them first. Surviving mugs and plates have mostly passed into collections, but they still show up often enough to keep us reminded that common sense, industry, honesty, and prudence are virtues that never hurt anybody.

FRANKOMA POTTERY

In addition to their Christmas plates, the Frankoma Pottery in Sapulpa, Oklahoma, makes other art pottery—dinnerware, vases, kitchen canisters, teapots, and similarly useful pieces. Though not as yet "collectible," outside of the Christmas plates, the pottery is of importance as a present-day expression of beauty in utilitarian forms.

John Frank, originator of Frankoma, went from Chicago, in 1929, to teach art and ceramics at the University of Oklahoma and to work with a geological survey unearthing Oklahoma clay deposits. In 1933, he started a studio pottery in Norman, where the University is located. There he experimented with native clays, glazes, and designs. In 1948, he moved to Sapulpa, near the source of the red-burning clay he had selected for his potting, and his studio became a small factory. It is larger now, and there is a showroom where visitors are welcome.

The glazes which Mr. Frank developed and blended reflect the colors of the desert and mountains of the Southwest, and are appropriately named: Onyx Black, White Sand, Brown Satin, Prairie Green, Desert Gold, Peach Blow, Woodland Moss, and Flame. For the Christmas plates the glaze used is called Della Robbia. The designs, too, are drawn from the Southwest, from wagon wheels and desert flowers and Indian art. (*See* Christmas plates.)

FROG MUGS

The rustic humor of eighteenth century potters delighted local pub crawlers and occasioned many a hoot of laughter when

an unsuspecting tippler found a frog in his mug. China it was, to be sure, and affixed to the bottom or the side, but startlingly lifelike at first glance. Such mirth-provoking joke mugs were made at Leeds, at Sunderland, at Nottingham, and other potteries.

The one pictured was made at Newcastle, ca. 1798. It is five inches tall, of cream-colored ware, transfer-printed. The frog is realistically mottled brown and green. (*See* Newcastle Pottery.)

FULPER POTTERY

In 1847, Abraham Fulper, a Hollander, became a partner in the Samuel Hill Pottery (established in 1815) in Flemington, New Jersey. He purchased the firm in 1860 and renamed it the Fulper Pottery Company. It remained in his family seventy years. Nineteenth century Fulper products were drain tiles, drinking dishes for poultry, stoneware bottles, jars, churns, and the like. Late in the century they brought out a Fulper-Germ-Proof-Filter, and by the early 1900s practically every railway station in the country had one of these stoneware water coolers. They were also used extensively in South America.

In 1910, Fulper entered the art pottery field, engaging J. M. Stangl as ceramic engineer. The Fulper doll head, made for a few years during the World War I period when imported dolls were off the market, is one of their most famous—and unusual—products. They also made a few Kewpie-type dolls during this period.

By 1929, Fulper had three factories, two in Flemington and one in Trenton, N.J. That year the larger of the Flemington plants burned, and according to Lucile Henzke in *American Art Pottery,* the major operation was moved to Trenton. Mr. Stangl acquired the company in 1930 which then became the Stangl Pottery. It is still in operation, specializing in distinctive hand-made tablewares. (*See* Stangl Birds.)

The smaller Flemington factory, no longer potting, is now used as a display and sales room. If you happen in the area, you'll enjoy stopping by to see present-day Stangl ware.

G

GALENA POTTERY

Always and forever there has been need of utilitarian pot-tery—jugs and crocks, bowls and jars. In our own country, the early potter followed close on every settlement, utilizing the clays of the area to turn out the humble everyday redwares that house-wives had to have.

For the potter proud of his wares, and for the housewife who used them, a location around Galena, Ill., was a fortunate one. Its native soil was rich in minerals, and the pots made from its clays were richly varied in color and markings. The plain lead-glazed ware from the Galena area was typically light pumpkin color, made handsome with yellow or cream color slip on the upper half, or with accidental dark spots of green or orange iron splashes from the firing.

From the 1830s to the 1860s, the potteries in this northwest corner of Illinois whirred busily. Today collectors are almost as busily hunting examples of this distinctive ware; and all through Jo Daviess County and surrounding areas, local historians are searching for forgotten pottery sites to dig in.

Wayne B. Horney's fine *Pottery of the Galena Area*, shows many illustrations in color and delves deeply into its history.

Pictured are a 10⅝-inch preserve jar, green with orange spots, in a typical Galena shape and a footed flower pot, glazed, in soft greens, yellow, and orange colors. The two handles have crimped tops.

GALLE POTTERY

Emile Galle (1856-1905) was the most renowned of French cameo glass makers and the foremost exponent of *l'art nouveau*, the "way out" style of his period. To find the familiar Galle signature on a piece of pottery can be somewhat startling to those who associate the name only with glass. Yet before he began his glass-making, Galle worked for a time with clay, and intricately shaped bowls, vases, plates, and the like bearing his signature, are still to be found. He worked with furniture, too, but both of these early diversions were so overshadowed by his glass triumphs, they are almost forgotten.

Galle's colorful heavy-glazed faience followed early rococo styles. Much of it was decorated like early Delft in design and color, showing Chinese and Imari influence, some in blue and white, some polychrome. The figurines he made and signed—cats, dogs, and grotesques among them—are delightful. This is one arena of ceramics where collectors of art glass, who like to have a piece for association's sake, vie with collectors of fine French faience.

The ceramic figures, Harlequin and Columbine, illustrated were done by Emile Galle about 1900; they are now at the Corning Museum of Glass, Corning, N.Y.

GAUDY DUTCH

Of all the early hand-decorated soft pastes, Gaudy Dutch with its rich coloring is the most spectacular. Made in England from about 1800 to 1825, it is actually a pottery imitation of fine Imari-type porcelains produced by Worcester, Derby, etc., which in turn were copied from the Imari wares of Japan. Some Gaudy Dutch designs are quite similar to the porcelain ones, particularly the Grape, War Bonnet, and Single Rose patterns.

In the making, the rich cobalt blue was applied to the biscuit, glazed, and fired. Then other colors—orange, yellow, green, red, pink, and shades—were applied on top of the glaze, and fired again. There is no lustre on any of the regular patterns.

Among well-known designs are Butterfly, Carnation, Sunflower, Dahlia, Oyster, Urn, and Zinnia; there are others. The Single Rose pattern is illustrated. Designs vary a bit, of course, from piece to piece, according to the individual decorator, but on the whole they are surprisingly uniform. (*See* King's Rose.)

Gaudy Dutch, by Eleanor J. and Edward G. Fox (1968) is a most complete book on this type ware.

GAUDY IRONSTONE
GAUDY WELSH

All these "Gaudys" tend to confusion, but Sam Laidacker unscrambles it thus in his *Anglo-American China, Part 1:*

"Gaudy Dutch (1800-1820). A soft paste pottery with blue under the glaze, other colors on top; no lustre.

"Gaudy Welsh (Swansea, 1830-1845). Similar but of translucent porcelain. Lustre is usually included with the decoration.

"Gaudy Ironstone (1855-1865). A heavy ware that is a mixture of pottery and porcelain clay, blue under the glaze, other colors on top, with or without lustre."

The lists of patterns and many illustrations given in *Anglo-American China* are marvelously helpful if you have pieces to identify.

The Gaudy Ironstone plate pictured is the "Blinking (or Seeing) Eye" pattern; it is marked "E. Walley Niagara Shape," with the English registry mark for 1856. (Edward Walley used several different marks on his wares, but the name "Walley" appeared in all of them.)

GEIJSBECK POTTERY

See *Western Potters in America*

GIBSON GIRL PLATES

The Gibson Girl, created by Charles Dana Gibson, burst on the waiting twentieth century in the pages of the original *Life*. Tall, aristocratic, and vibrantly beautiful, the symbol of American womanhood, she took the country by storm. She appeared everywhere—in Gibson's sketch books on parlor tables, in magazines (*Collier's* paid $1,000 apiece for 100 sketches), in advertisements, on catalog covers. She was embroidered on pillow tops, and burnt in wood on pipe racks. There were Gibson Girl shirtwaists, shoes, buttons—even corsets. And Gibson Girl plates.

These were made by Royal Doulton Co. of Lambeth, England, in 1900-1901, exclusively for the American market. A series of twenty-four plates, in 10½-inch size, was decorated with a

complete set of episodes from Gibson's portfolio, *A Widow and Her Friends*. They were of semi-porcelain, printed in underglaze black, with a petalled border of blue, and they portrayed that beauteous lady through her grief, into society again, and out, for with plate No. 24, she had become a nun.

Gibson Girl plates were distributed by Geo. F. Bassett & Co., 49 Barclay St., New York. The retail price was fifty cents. A small Bassett catalog (1900-1901) reproduced the twenty-four sketches used on the plates and urged ladies to look for these novelties in their local china shops.

Royal Doulton's second set was composed of twelve plates in 9-inch size, each centered with a different Gibson Girl head, printed in black, with a bowknot border of blue. Both sets are collectible today, though they may have to be assembled plate by plate. (*See* Doulton.)

GINORI

See *Capo-di-Monte*

GLASGOW POTTERIES

The first pottery of importance in Glasgow was the Delftfield, operating from 1748 to 1751. This pottery exported, presumably to America, Delft, brown-glazed Rockingham, black basalt, Queen's ware, and Derby porcelain. All of it was unmarked, and all of it was copied from English potters. If it helps in telling which is which, the quality of potting and decoration of the Scottish ware is considered to fall just a bit short of the average of the originals.

Campbellfield was another Glasgow pottery, best known for its considerable output of Staffordshire-like printed blue ware. This pottery was established in 1837 by John McAdam, but moved about for years under different managements. It took its final name, Campbellfield, from its street location in 1850. It closed in 1905. In its early phases, this pottery produced mainly brownware teapots and the like; the blue printed ware came along later. Their marks were "C. P. Co.," "Campbellfield," and after 1875, when the firm moved to Springburn, "Springburn" with a thistle, was added to the trademark.

The Glasgow Pottery (1842-1881) at Port Dundas was operated by two brothers, John and Matthew Preston Bell. Their trademark was, of course, a bell, either impressed or printed. Sometimes "J. & M. P. B. Co." appeared on the trademark. After Matthew's death in 1869, "J. B." or just "B" was used. Their printed wares included Willow pattern, Damascus, and Triumphal Car. For a few years they produced Parian.

In 1866, H. Kennedy started the Barrowfield Pottery in

Glasgow. His products were stoneware ginger beer bottles and jugs. There was nothing outstanding about his bottles except that he made so many of them at a time when ginger beer was extremely popular in this country—between the 1860s and 1880s, it was imported by the boatload—that Kennedy's Barrowfield bottles are always turning up here. Often they're found in such far apart places as Western mining camp digs and trash heaps in New England. They are buff colored, glazed with a deeper shade at the top. The mark of the company was a picture of a jug, with a ginger beer bottle on either side, under a ribbon reading, "Established 1866." (*See* Scottish Pottery.)

GOLF STEINS AND DECANTERS

The British were the first to develop golf as a sport, but by 1895, it had begun to be popular in Germany and in the United States. For trophies at tournaments, steins of pottery or porcelain, decorated with golfing motifs, came into being; then a few were produced for general sale to golf enthusiasts.

Golf steins and decanters were first made in England, then in Germany, then in the United States where Lenox was the most prominent producer. The pieces varied considerably in size, shape, and design; colorings ran to browns, greens, and blues. Occasionally English and German pieces were embossed, but the hand-painted decoration had the greatest vogue. Some steins were capped with silver, some had plain or pewter tops; a few had silver tops. Pewter-topped ones usually came from Germany; in World War I days when metal was scarce, they were made without lids. The golfing garb, the form of the players, and the clubs and balls as used in the painted decoration indicate their era.

Golf steins and decanters were never made in abundance anywhere. Outside of those made up for golf trophies, Lenox turned out at the most only a few hundred. Their rarest to find today is their triple-handled stein; their largest, a thirty-inch tall stein, which was made up in two designs, painted from drawings by Oliver Kemp, a Lenox artist. (*See* Lenox.)

The examples pictured, two decanters or liquor jugs, and a hand-painted stein, from the Jack Level collection, all date about 1895, but none are identified as to maker.

GONDER CERAMIC ARTS

See *Moss Aztec*

GORDON'S

See *Prestopans*

GOSSWARE

Should you see, sometime, somewhere, an odd-shaped miniature—pitcher, vase or urn—of delicate ivory-porcelain, decorated with a crest, and ask what it is, the answer will likely be "Gossware." The little piece may be plainly backstamped Arcadian China, Carlton China, Florentine China, or Nautilus Por-

celain; but because the Goss Potteries (Stoke-on-Trent, ca. 1858-1944) originated and made so many of these souvenir items, they are now credited with all. No others, though, quite equal the Goss quality.

These souvenirs, for British home consumption, were miniature copies of museum or historical jugs or urns. The stamp on the bottom identified them, such as "Model of an ancient Roman ewer found near Glastonbury," decorated with the Tothes coat of arms, or a "17th century Bellarmine jug found in Rochester," with a crest of the University of Liverpool. The decorations were usually decals, hand-touched with enamel. Thousands upon thousands of these novelties found their way home with vacationing Britishers and some, of course, with Americans on tour.

Goss Potteries made other artwares, too, specializing in fine porcelain floral jewelry and dress ornaments, powder jars, pomade boxes and scent dispensers for the great London and Paris perfume houses, and Parian of high order. Their Parian busts were especially well done. The Goss mark is either the name "W. H. Goss," or a falcon rising, or both.

GOUDA

Gouda, in south Holland, was a pottery-making area before 1700, and still is. Over the years Gouda potteries adjusted their output to contemporary needs, beginning with simple utilitarian wares and crude Delfts and moving through years of clay pipes to the Art Nouveau plates, vases, and novelties so sought by collectors today. Currently blue and white Delftwares are in production.

The chief manufactories are Plateelbakkerij Zennith, founded in 1749 by Van der Wants and still in that family; Goedwaagen's, founded in 1769, another family concern; and the Regina Art Pottery, started by one of the Van der Wants about 1898 in time to produce a great deal of Art Nouveau ware.

The early Art Nouveau pieces were usually dark in background, in high gloss, with floral decoration in bold purples, fuchsia, blues, orange, greens and turquoise. Later wares used a white ground, in dull finish, with the same bright decoration. These pieces are rich in color, a little gaudy, yet with elegance and individuality. A piece of Gouda Art Nouveau just couldn't be anything else.

There are a goodly number of backmarks, of course, but the word "Gouda" which appears in most of them will guide you. C. W. Moody's *Gouda Ceramics* is a good reference for marks and satisfying as a colored picture book of collectible examples. Gouda companies began Art Nouveau designs about 1885, kept them going until 1915, then later revived them. Some choice examples may be as late as the 1940s.

GRANDMOTHER WARE/BLUE CHELSEA

For reasons unknown, and no rhyme to them, this frosty-white ware with delicate laid-on sprigs of blue, was known for years as "Chelsea," or affectionately as "Grandmother's Chelsea." To call it "Grandmother" now is easy to understand. Almost every family owned a teaset of it sometime between 1830 and 1880. Until recently it has been common to find.

It appeared in earthenware, Ironstone, and porcelain—some porcelain sets *were* made at the Chelsea works, but not all. Shapes kept pace with contemporary chinaware styles; there are handleless cups and handled cups; 6-sided, 8-sided, and round plates; squatty teapots, graceful teapots, bulbous teapots. Color on the raised decoration ranged from the palest lavender-blue on early pieces to deep purple-blue on later ones. Sometimes a lustre wash was added, and occasionally other colors. The appliques were most often grape clusters and tendrils, but you'll find thistles used and various flowers, fruit in baskets and cornucopias, and wreath designs.

Many English potters made it; few marked it. Adams, Adderly, and Bridgwood & Sons were among those who did—occasionally. It is still being made and cautious present-day advertisers of current wares, to be clearly understood, call it "Blue Chelsea or Grandmother Ware." Today's ware is perfect; it has no flaws in the glaze, no black specks, no bubbles or rough spots around the sprigs, and the relief is somewhat lower than in old pieces.

GRANITE WARE
See *Ironstone*

GREAT WESTERN POTTERY
Early in the 1870s, John Wyllie, a Staffordshire potter, and his son, came to Pittsburgh, Pennsylvania, and set up a kiln, but soon moved on to East Liverpool, Ohio, where they acquired the two-kiln pottery of Brunt & Hill, then producing yellow and Rockingham wares and door knobs. In 1874, the Wyllies redesigned the pottery, which they called The Great Western, for the manufacture of Ironstone. They were among the first to make Ironstone in this country—some authorities say the very first —and they did so well with it that they soon added two more kilns. They operated with great success until 1891 when they sold the plant to the Union Potteries Company.

The Great Western boomed along with its area and region, making Ironstone, both plain white and colored, for every imaginable use. Among their products, nice to find today, were bread plates with mottoes, leaf-shaped and fish-shaped relish dishes, fluted compotes, valanced cakestands, dinner sets, tea sets, toilet sets, and parlor cuspidors.

Their trademark showed the flag shields of both the United States and Great Britain, with a crest of three feathers—the insignia of the Prince of Wales—above it, and "Stone China/J. W. & Son" below. (*See:* East Liverpool Potters; Ironstone.)

GRIFFIN, SMITH & HILL

See *Majolica*

GROSBRIETENBACH PORCELAIN

See *Limbach*

GRUEBY POTTERY

A lovely hand-crafted pottery to have and to hold—or just to look at—is any piece made by the Grueby Faience & Tile Company, founded in 1894 in Boston, Massachusetts. It is described as a hard semi-porcelain, smooth and satiny, with an opaque lusterless matt enamel glaze. Pieces are all impressed with the pottery mark—Grueby Pottery, Boston, U.S.A., Grueby, or Grueby, Boston, Mass. The monogram of the artist was often added. The usual colors are green-yellow and blue-purple, though yellow, blue, and pink were occasionally used. The decorations, in low relief, were often Egyptian-inspired, with long slender plant forms a favorite motif.

The ware was elegant enough to be sold at Tiffany & Co., in New York. In fact, Louis Comfort Tiffany's first glass lampshades were fitted to Grueby pottery bases. Later Mr. Tiffany made his own pottery lamp bases. (*See* Tiffany Pottery.) Besides the usual vases and decorative wares, Grueby made sculptured animals and statues. A set of their handsome architectural tiles, depicting the four Apostles, was used in the Cathedral of St. John the Divine in New York City.

According to Joseph F. Dinneen in *The Purple Shamrock: The Hon. James Michael Curley of Boston,* the Grueby Pottery was dissolved and the pottery sold to the Pardee Tile Company in 1919. (Mr. Curley was in partnership with Mr. Grueby in 1918.)

WM. GUERIN & CO.

See *Limoges; Jungle Book Series*

H

HAIR RECEIVERS

Hair receivers belong with dresser sets, and there they would have stayed, too, in this book, but for a conversation we overheard in an antiques shop recently. Two young women were looking at a dainty Dresden hair receiver. One said, "What a shame it has a hole in the lid." "Silly," said the other, "it's meant to be there. It's to hold violets."

No doubt people do use hair receivers nowadays to hold violets or any other short stemmed flower. But in ye olden days when grandma was a girl, hair was long, and 100 strokes of the brush was bedtime routine. The hair receiver was the receptacle for the "combings," all curled around grandma's forefinger and stuffed in the hole in the cover. All tidy and convenient. (*See* Dresser Sets.)

HAMPSHIRE POTTERY

The Hampshire Pottery (J. S. Taft & Co.) in Keene, New Hampshire, operated from 1871 into the 1920s. It began producing redware, moving on to stoneware and majolica, and later still to an art pottery of considerable merit. Most pieces are plainly marked, either "Hampshire Pottery" with or without "J. S. Taft," or "J. S. T. Co., Keene, N.H."

The art pottery, like that of Weller, Owens, and Roseville, though it resembles none of these, is just now coming into its own. Prices on it, though still not high, will be more so in the New Hampshire, Maine, and Massachusetts area where the name is better known and more honored than in other sections of the country. The same is true of Van Briggle pottery (*see* Van Briggle) which is more highly regarded in the Colorado-California area than in New England. Since almost all art pottery had wide sales distribution, it is often rewarding to shop for specialties away from their home base.

The eight-inch vase pictured is a soft green-blue, with off-white accents. The Hampshire Pottery also made a few souvenir wares in semi-porcelain. (*See* Souvenir China.)

HAND-PAINTED

From the 1860s through the first decade of the 1900s, china painting was an elegant accomplishment for young ladies. They studied under china painting "professors" when they could, or taught themselves from the several books and magazines devoted to the art. They filled their china closets with their works, and gave the "extras" away to friends.

A great deal of whiteware ready for decorating, delicate and dainty, in all kinds of fancy shapes and sizes, from pin trays to punchbowls, was produced by porcelain factories in Europe. Pieces marked Limoges were favorites. In this country, the Belleek factories in Trenton, N.J.; Knowles, Taylor and Knowles in Ohio; and others also produced for this profitable market.

Some of the work the amateurs turned out is very fine

indeed; some is extremely so-so. But talented or not, the ladies had a wonderful time at it, and left many pieces, often signed and dated, for us to use and enjoy today.

The pale blue bonbon dish illustrated, painted with garlands of roses and gold feet is a Limoges piece, signed with the initials of the lady who painted it at home.

HAROLDT or HEROLD
See *Dresden*

HART BREWER POTTERY
See *Toilet Sets*

THE HAVILANDS

The Haviland China story is filled with fathers and sons and brothers and nephews, some in France manufacturing porcelain, some in this country, importing and distributing it, and some of them financially engaged in both enterprises.

It began, you might say, in 1839, when a customer asked David Haviland, then a china dealer and importer in New York City—the Havilands had been in this country since 1650—to replace a broken teacup, unmarked. On his next buying trip to France he searched for a porcelain similar, found it at Foecy, and also discovered nearby the town of Limoges, already a thriving porcelain center. By 1841 he had a factory there of his own, Haviland & Co. The "& Co." was his brother Daniel, though Daniel—with three other brothers and assorted relatives—continued the importing firm, Haviland & Brothers, in New York.

David set Limoges on its ears with his innovations, particularly his wild idea of having his whitewares decorated right in Limoges, instead of sending them to Paris. He also introduced styles to please American taste.

When Daniel withdrew from the firm about 1865, David ran it alone until his sons Charles Edward and Theodore joined him. After his death in 1879, the sons continued it together, still as Haviland & Co., until 1892. Then Charles established his own firm, retaining the Haviland & Co. name, and Theodore had his firm, Theodore Haviland & Co. Charles died in 1923, and his son carried on until the firm was reunited with the Theodore Haviland branch of the porcelain activity.

So much for that branch of the family; their various backstamps can be found in any good book of pottery and porcelain marks, and their cherished china abounds on dress-up dinner tables and in grandmothers' cupboards across our land. (*See* Limoges.)

The Havilands, between them, produced several sets of dinnerware for the White House. The present Haviland & Co. (still of the family) began in 1970 to reproduce some of the Presidential plates Haviland had made. There will be eight in the series, one issued annually, all suitably marked as reproductions.

The Theodore Haviland & Co. demi-tasse pictured here shows the dainty flowered decoration and gold trim typical of Haviland china.

CHARLES FIELD HAVILAND

Back now to 1851, when Charles Field Haviland, the son of David's brother Robert, went from New York to Limoges to work for his uncle. He married there, in 1858, Mlle Louise Mallevergne, whose grandfather, Francois Alluaud, had founded the Alluaud porcelain works at Limoges in 1797. The next year, following his uncle David's example, he started a decorating shop, using the whiteware manufactured at the Alluaud factory. In 1876, he assumed management of the Casseaux Works, successors to the Alluaud pottery, in which his wife had inherited a share. When he retired in 1881, the Casseaux-Alluaud potteries were sold to E. Gerard Dufraisseix et Morel. The backstamp "Ch. Field Haviland" in a circle was his decorator's mark.

The firm of Charles Field Haviland & Company was something else again—a New York company, composed of CHF and Oliver A. Gager, established to import and distribute the products of Charles Field Haviland, Limoges.

HAYNES, D. F.
See Chesapeake Pottery

HENRIOT, JULES ET FILS
See *Quimper*

HENNECKE'S FLORENTINE STATUARY

If the imposing plaster Rogers Groups took the *haute monde* by storm, the plaster statuary made by C. Hennecke & Co., of Milwaukee, Wisconsin, made even greater inroads into the parlors and pocketbooks of less affluent beauty-seekers. Hennecke's statues were smaller, often using but a single figure, and were not confined as were Rogers' to genre subjects nor to a single finish. Rather he concentrated on bringing to the people the great art sculptures of the world, reduced to mantelpiece size, from the *Laocoon* and *Venus de Milo* to busts of Marcus Aurelius and

Nero, not neglecting such popular figures as Beethoven and General Grant. His genre subjects—the familiar "Playing Grandpa" and "Playing Grandma" pictured is one of his lesser efforts—inclined to a rather heavy humor, but were nonetheless engaging; and all were well done. Casper Hennecke had immigrated from Westphalia, Germany, and most of the modellers who worked for him had learned their craft in Europe.

His statuary, produced from 1881 to 1892 was much but not all of it marked, and was offered in eight different finishes, Florentine, a rich soft stone color, and Alabaster being the most popular. His Dark Bronze was also highly regarded. In addition to statuettes and the pedestals and wall brackets to set them on, he also made plaques for hanging with hooks attached, and advertised to make busts or medallions from photographs.

Hennecke's Florentine Statuary, Catalogue, No. 5, published in 1887, pictures upwards of a thousand of the figures the company produced. One of the most fascinating catalogs of all times, it has recently been reproduced by Betty C. Haverly. It was reviewed in *Spinning Wheel,* November 1972. (*See* Rogers Groups)

HEROLD CHINA CO.

See *Roseville Pottery*

HEUBACH BROTHERS

The Gebruder Heubach name and mark is best known to doll collectors since doll heads were their principal product. But there is no need for doll collectors to have all the fun, for this firm made other goodies, too. Their bisque figurines, made in the 1880s and later, are quite fine, and please collectors immensely because most of them are marked.

Moving into the 1900s, Heubach made glazed figurines. Some were elaborate and elegant enough to be mistaken at first glance for the subtly colored figurines from the Danish porcelain

Fig. One

Fig. Two

Fig. Three

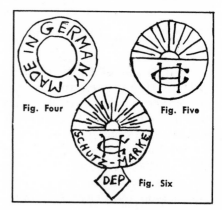

Fig. Four

Fig. Five

Fig. Six

factories. Others, like some of their small puppies, were just a high grade "cheap" novelty. A man we know carelessly tossed out a shoeboxful he had as a boy, thinking of them as "junk" because they had originally cost so little. There were in-between grades, too, with glazed figures, pin trays, and other novelties coming along in this century. While it would be nicest to have one of their handsome large glazed figures, any Heubach pieces would be welcomed by both doll and china collectors. The marks shown here are those which appear on the Gebruder Heubach pieces—on doll heads, bisques, figurines, and novelty items. The marks were used alone or in combination, stamped in red or in green, or impressed, but they'll be there in one form or another. (*See* Piano Babies.)

HILTON POTTERY
See *Southern Highland Potteries*

HOUND-HANDLED PITCHERS

Because it's such a pleasant thought, casual collectors may be inclined to credit their unmarked Rockingham hound-handled pitcher to Greatbach, the famous designer at the U. S. Pottery in Bennington, Vermont. While Greatbach did make his own version, potteries in England had made them earlier. A factory in Bohemia indulged in them, so did almost every potter in America. Very few are marked. Gracefully adorned with a dog handle, usually a greyhound, and with relief scenes of hunting or game on the sides, these jugs appeared in brown salt-glazed ware, in Parian, and Rockingham, in tall shapes and fat shapes.

The pitcher shown was made at Bennington, 1853-1858, probably by Greatbach. (*See* Parian for another illustration.)

HISPANO-MORESQUE
See *Italian Maiorca*

HISTORICAL BLUE PLATES (EARLY)
See *American Views*

HISTORICAL BLUE PLATES (LATE)

The historical calendar tiles Wedgwood made for Jones, McDuffee & Stratton so pleased that enterprising firm of Boston importers that, in 1895, they had Wedgwood produce for them a series of up-dated American View plates. These aped the earlier scenic plates, being of earthenware, blue and white printed, and using the traditional Wedgwood border. However, new and later

89

scenes were used and, of course, contemporary body, printing, and color. You need never worry about mistaking late for early.

In the booklet Jones, McDuffee & Stratton published for their 100th anniversary in 1910, wherein they claimed themselves "the largest wholesale and retail crockery, china, and glassware establishment in the country," they listed the titles of seventy-eight historical plates they had sponsored. The first was Boston Town House; the last, Union Station, Washington, D.C. In between were such distant scenes as Niagara Falls; the McKinley House, Canton, Ohio; and the Hermitage, Home of Andrew Jackson. Most, however, were of New England historical scenes or events.

Among later issues was a Longfellow series of six plates, depicting *The Children's Hour, Evangeline, The Village Blacksmith, Paul Revere's Ride, The Song of Hiawatha,* and *The Courtship of Miles Standish.*

Southern scenes appear on plates backstamped "W. H. Dubois, St. Augustine, Florida," and Western scenes on those stamped "Hunt Mercantile Co., Santa Barbara, California." Other special order plates were backstamped "Daniel Low & Co., Salem, Massachusetts." These names were all of retailers, who may have placed their orders direct or through Jones, McDuffee & Stratton. A Mormon Temple Block plate and a Pike's Peak plate were definitely imported by the Boston firm for Callaway, Hoock & Francis, sometime between 1901 and 1907, for names of both retailer and importer appear on the backstamp.

Though Jones, McDuffee & Stratton had control of these Wedgwood imports, competitors chipped away at it, and not until 1933 was the Boston firm free of others who also inscribed their plates "Sole Distributors."

The most persistent of their competitors was the Van Heusen Charles Company of Albany, New York. In the early 1900s, this firm imported an Albany Series of Wedgwood plates; three of the twenty-four are pictured here. After 1934, Ridgway, not Wedgwood, was making their blue plates, though the same Wedgwood border was used.

The Mellon Hewes Company, importers from Hartford, Connecticut, were in the race for a short time only, but you'll occasionally find a plate with their backstamp.

New York importers Rowland & Marcellus got their historical blue plates from S. Hancock & Co., Stoke-on-Trent, and published thirty-five of them from 1898 to 1900. The border they used, of fruit and flowers, was designed for them by their own artist, Morris Van Nostrand. (Van Nostrand, a long-time employee, later became owner of the Rowland & Marcellus china and earthenware importing firm.) After 1900, they used other potters, but the border remained the same until 1910.

Since this type "blue" plate persisted for many years—1950 had not seen the last of them—they are fairly plentiful today. Of course, if you are hunting one particular plate, you may run into difficulty, and Western and Southern views are rare. Most all have a long legend on the back, identifying the subject, the maker, the importer, and frequently giving the date.

These plates are nowhere near as expensive as the earlier American Views—in fact you could quite easily assemble enough to set an interesting table if you desired, and at a not unreasonable cost.

HUMMEL FIGURES

The first Hummel figures—endearing little boys and girls with round faces and questioning eyes—came out about 1934-35, made by the W. Goebel Porzallenfabrik of Oeslau, Germany. War years halted production, but by 1955 they were again on the market, and you'll still find them in delightful array in gift shops everywhere.

The artist behind them was a nun of the Franciscan Order, Sister M. Innocentia, who began life in 1901 as Berta Hummel. Her family, appreciative of music and art, encouraged her early

talent. In 1927, having finished her formal education, she entered the Academy of Fine Arts in Munich. There she met two Franciscan sisters who were also attending the school of Industrial Arts. In 1934 she took her own vows in the Convent of Siessen.

The sketches for the Hummel cards and figures which have enchanted the world were made within convent walls. The subjects she presented were the simple ones she knew best—flowers, birds, animals, and children remembered from her schooldays. Though she died in 1946, her royalties continue to help support her Order and its charities.

All authentic Hummel figures—there are imitations on the market—can be identified by the trademark "M. I. Hummel," indented on or near the base of each figure, and the trademark "V" which is stamped or indented on the underside of each figure. Present-day figures are marked on the base "W. Germany."

HYWOOD POTTERY

See *Niloak*

ILLINOIS POTTERS

The state of Illinois is a good hunting ground for nineteenth century crocks and jugs, inkwells, churns, and other common necessities in redware and stoneware. Unfortunately few are marked, and it may take specialized study to relegate your finds to the proper locality. The collections at the Illinois State Museum at Springfield will be helpful for study and comparison.

Though there were small potteries in Illinois earlier than 1836, quantity production got its start that year when John M. Ebey, a potter from Pennsylvania, set up a business in Ripley. The native clays were particularly propitious, and soon the Ripley area had a concentration of at least fifteen potters. One of them alone was producing 250,000 gallons each year and employing thirty-five men. Wares from Ripley went all over the state in peddlers' carts, and downriver as far as Louisiana by boat.

Another active potting center was Galena, in the northwestern corner of the state. (*See* Galena Pottery.) The Peoria Pottery was established before 1844; the American Pottery, in 1859. At Anna, Wallace and Cornwall Kirkpatrick, whose pottery was founded in 1859, made, in addition to the usual utilitarian wares, all kinds of unusuals—from dolls' heads to cemetery urns. They even showed a 25-foot-square model of a pioneer farm at the Philadelphia Centennial in 1876, complete with farm utensils and lurking Indians.

By 1900, most of these small potteries, and there had been a great many of them over the state, had disappeared. Some had not survived the hardships of the Civil War; others were felled by rising costs and difficulties in transportation. The larger potteries suffered less. Though the Allen Crockery Co., in Rockford, closed in 1895, the potteries at Crystal Lake, Dundee, and Morton, the Macomb Pottery in Quincy, the Ruckles Pottery in Whitehall, and the Western Stoneware Company at Monmouth (*see* Old Sleepy Eye) were among those to weather the century.

IMARI

Imari ware takes its name from the Japanese port of Imari from which porcelain made in Arita and neighboring villages was shipped. This area was already a center of earthenware production when, about 1616, the special clay needed for porcelain was discovered nearby. Arita potteries quickly switched to porcelain, making it for home use. Up to then, the Japanese had imported their porcelain from China and Korea.

This early ware, now called Ko-Imari (Old Imari), had great beauty. The paste was hard, fine, and very durable, pure white in color. The earliest pieces were modeled on Chinese blue and white wares or colored with enamels. Red was dominant, but other bright colors and gold and silver were also used. Since the various potteries of the area worked independently, many different shapes and patterns were produced.

By the end of the seventeenth century, Imari had assumed a character of its own. Highly decorative, often quite splendid, it reflected the taste of the rich Japanese merchants of the day. Dutch East Indies traders carried it West, and Europe fell in love with it. The Dutch at Delft imitated it; so did the Germans

at Meissen, the French at St. Cloud and Chantilly, and the English at Chelsea, Derby, Bow, and Worcester. Even the Chinese copied it.

By the nineteenth century, Imari had declined sharply. The colors were gaudy and the designs over-elaborate, often tasteless. Most of the large plaques and vases we see in Western collections today are of this later period; and it is this type, often in later, quite cheap wares, decorated in orange and deep blue, which we commonly associate with the term. While the gaudy late pieces are warm and rich in color and are decorative in both period and modern interiors, for elegance, Ko-Imari stands alone. (For further reading: *The Ceramic Art of Japan,* by Hugo Munsterberg.)

The square dish pictured is Ko-Imari, before 1820; the bowl, late 19th century.

"IMPROVED STONE CHINA"

See *Flown Blue*

INANIMATE CLOCKS

Whether Victorians hadn't money enough to buy real clocks or whether they preferred clocks that disdained time, there's no knowing; but they did, for some reason, mightily favor Staffordshire ornaments that looked like clocks or had a clock face somewhere painted on it.

A Philadelphia clock collector, who has amused himself by adding a secondary shelf of these inanimates, gathered up forty or more without half trying. All of them are different, though three Highland Piper groups show only slight variation; one has three pipes, one four, and a rare one, five (illustrated). This seems to indicate that different potters copied each other a bit, especially where popular designs were concerned.

These figures are unmarked, and while they are usually attributed to Staffordshire, many were made in Scotland. If the vent hole in the bottom is pricked in the form of an X, some collectors assert they were made by T. Rathbone & Co., in Portobello, near Edinburgh. (This applies also to other so-called Staffordshire flatback figures, especially the spaniels.)

Some of the clock figures are pale in color, decorated only with gold; others are gay with deep blue, coral-red, and dark green. Castles with clock dials are harder to find than figures, and generally less attractive. (*See:* Cottage Ornaments; Portobello Potteries.)

INDIAN TREE PATTERN

Almost every English and American potter has at one time

or another turned out a version of this conservative, elegant, and highly satisfying pattern. Coalport's "Indian Tree" dinnerwares have never been out of production since the early 1800s, neither have Minton's, nor Spode's. No one knows for sure which one originated it—possibly it was Thomas Turner at Caughley. Doulton, Copeland, and Aynsley also have made this pattern in porcelain. Burgess and Leigh of Burslem, after 1867, and Cartright Bros. of East Liverpool, Ohio, in 1880, were reproducing it in semi-porcelain and earthenware. John Maddock revived it in 1914 and 1921, and no telling how many other potters on both sides of the Atlantic have used it.

The central picture of the pattern, which covers most of the plate, is always the same, showing the gnarled brown trunk of a tree-peony with double peonies blossoming in various shades of pink amid green foliage. The design is pure Chinese, not Indian at all, though both cultures did widely use a symbolic tree-of-life in their art and decoration. Perhaps the Coalport people who advertised it as "Indian Tree" in 1801, thought a china China Tree too confusing.

The plate pictured, from a dinner set made by John Maddock & Sons, ca. 1921, is clearly marked "Indian Tree."

INKWELLS

In those unimaginable days before fountain pens and ball points, when eighteenth-century scribes wrote with quills and nineteenth-century writers with steel nibs, an inkwell was a common necessity. Today's collector has a wide selection in design and material. Even if he collects only pottery or porcelain examples, he'll find a goodly assortment, and in a wide price range.

Eighteenth century ink, by the way, came in a compressed block; nineteenth century ink, in powdered form; both had to be stirred up in water—a rather messy procedure.

There were elaborate inkstands of silver or porcelain for the wealthy; homemade inkwells, hollowed out of soapstone, for the poor; and in-between inkwells for all the voluminous Victorian writers of letters and keepers of diaries; substantial glass inkwells for clerks in offices.

Some early inkstands, both of silver and porcelain, were on trays, with racks for pens, and pounce pots for holding pulverized cuttlefish beaks or gum sandarac—this to be shaken on the unglazed paper to cover rough spots after an erasure. Pounce, so Amoret and Christopher Scott tell us in *Collecting Bygones,* means "perforated," and refers to the container rather than its contents.

The inkwell pictured is early Victorian, a little two-inch nest of yellow and orange sanded Staffordshire pottery, with a blue winged mother bird and two yellow nestlings perched atop.

There is also a beetle-like bug to which the birds are paying not the least attention. This is a type of pottery inkwell not uncommon, and still relatively inexpensive.

INVALID FEEDERS (PAP BOATS)

Invalid feeders or pap boats—shallow, long-spouted, handled cups for the introduction of nourishment into the mouths of babes and others incapable of feeding themselves, are ancient of days. Museum examples, most likely intended for infant feeding, may date from 1500 B.C. In more recent eras, feeders marked Spode, Davenport, Copeland, and Wedgwood often turn up. Many in plain white or with Delft blue decoration will be unmarked; some will say "Germany." Choice ones of majolica, Dresden, and Satsuma are known. When the Rockingham factory at Swinton closed in 1842, eighteen dozen "Feeding Boats" were listed in their closing sale notice.

All in all, these everyday items have been around so long and have been made in such quantity and so many qualities that there are plenty left for collectors. Most are still inexpensive. They are also surprisingly handy to have around the house in the event of broken legs, heart attacks, or other bed-confining misfortunes.

Pap, from whence came the early name, pap boat, was a mixture of flour or bread cooked in milk; also used in these feeders were preparations of gruel, cereals, and such, cooked in broth.

For widened collecting interest, covered medicine spoons might be included in this sick bed category. Since both invalid feeders and medicine spoons are found in materials other than china—silver, pewter, britannia, and glass—a collection can be quite diversified.

You might even consider adding pottery nursing bottles, provided you can find them; there are not many about. Comparatively few were made for the American trade; colonists and early settlers were more apt to carve a nursing bottle of wood or make one from a cow's horn than to buy a fancy one of pewter or "chiny." Pottery nursing bottles which show up in museum collections like that of the Mead Johnson pharmaceutical firm in Chicago have ornate transfer designs and are of a flat roundish shape. By the time ordinary people could afford to buy nursing bottles, glass ones were on the market.

IRISH BELLEEK

This exquisitely thin, lightweight porcelain has been made at Belleek in County Fermanagh, Ireland, since 1857. It is translucent in a cream-ivory tone, with a sort of seashell iridescent lustre. All kinds of articles have been made from it—teasets, figurines, centerpieces, baskets, and religious items. The designs and shapes frequently "follow the sea," with coral, sea-horses, seashells, and aquatic plants high on the popular list. Shamrock, too, has always been a favorite design motif.

The early Belleek mark, printed or stenciled in blue, red, brown, green, or black shows a wolfhound, tower, harp, and shamrocks. After 1891 a ribbon with the words "County Fermanagh, Ireland," was added, and about 1930, a circular mark in Gaelic. Marks from 1891 to 1946 were in black; from 1946 on, in green.

Don't be confused if you occasionally find the Belleek mark on heavier wares than the famous paper-thin porcelain. The factory has also made Parian; earthenwares, some transfer-printed, some painted or enameled; and a great deal of commercial pottery including telegraph-pole insulators and mortars and pestles for the drug trade. (*See* American Belleek.)

IRONSTONE

Charles Mason of Lane Delft, Staffordshire, patented the formula for Ironstone in 1813. It used a quantity of flint and slag of ironstone and produced a body heavier than porcelain, tougher, and more durable. Quite likely other experimenting potters had been making something similar before Mason's patent appeared. Afterward, all Staffordshire was bringing out wares marked with distinguishing non-infringing names like Pearl Stone or Stone China. (*See* Flown Blue.)

In decoration, Ironstone followed the current style. Much of Mason's earliest was in imitation of Imari, in reds, oranges, and blues, with snake handles on jugs. Others used it for transfer-printed blue ware, for scenic wares of lighter colors, for the flown blues and browns, whatever came into fashion.

Along in the mid-nineteenth century, the plain white, enlivened only by an embossed design took over. English potters by the dozens made hundreds of patterns for export; Meakin, Challinor, Forster, Boote, Powell & Bishop, and Anthony Shaw are among familiar Ironstone marks on English wares.

In the United States, where it was often called "White Granite," producers like Mayer Pottery Co., Great Western, Laughlin Bros., and Burgess & Co., of East Liverpool, Ohio; The American Crockery Company, Mercer Pottery Co., International Pottery Co., and the Etruria Pottery Co., of Trenton, New Jersey, were busily advertising their Granite wares by 1885, trying to keep ahead of British competition.

Cheap, thick and hardy, often embossed with wheat, berries, or leaves, it seemed just right for the farm kitchen. It's even been called "thresher's china." Then it went out of style, and thirty years ago, housewives were casually baking pies in old Ironstone plates. Today their daughters are wailing, "Mother, how *could* you!"

In *Old China,* Minnie Watson Kamm illustrates many Ironstone patterns, both white and decorated, and gives histories of their makers. (*See:* Cork & Edge; Mason's Patent Ironstone; Tea Leaf Lustre.)

The white Ironstone covered vegetable dish pictured is plainest of plain. Its chief interest lies in its backstamp, "Royal/Patent Ironstone/Burgess & Goddard," below the familiar English lion and unicorn seal. This firm was a manufacturer in Longton, Staffordshire. It was also an importer, with offices in New York City, for Staffordshire wares made at other potteries. In advertisements in the *Pottery & Glassware Reporter* from at least 1879 to 1884, they announced themselves U. S. representatives "of some of the most celebrated manufacturers of White Granite, Semi-Porcelain, Printed Ware and English China, including John Edwards, Wedgwood & Co. (this is *not* Josiah Wedgwood), S. Bridgwood & Son, G. W. Turner & Sons, Dunn, Bennett & Co., J. F. Wileman, Blair & Co."

Their 1884 advertisement was illustrated with vegetable tureens in Dunn & Bennett Co.'s "Marlboro," Wedgwood & Co.'s "Melton," Turner's "Phileau," and Bridgwood's "Lynhurst." All were in the "new square shape," and all, with the exception of Lynhurst, were pattern printed.

ITALIAN MAIOLICA

Maiolica was the Italian adaptation of the Hispano-Moresque pottery made on the island of Majorca, off the coast of Spain, in the fourteenth century. Hispano-Moresque wares, based on earlier Arabian pottery, were tin-enameled, decorated with metallic glazes; the ornamentation in lustre pigment was of a rich iridescent brown, sometimes relieved in blue.

The Italians, while using a similar tin-enameled body and metallic glaze, allowed themselves more latitude in decoration and color. They named their ware for the island of Majorca, and the first known example of it was executed by Luca della Robbia in 1438.

The period from 1538 to 1574 is considered the highest peak in Italian ceramic art. Elaborate vases and plates, many designed and painted by famous artists, were made to order as gifts for rulers and nobility. Each district, then as later, showed recognizable characteristics in design though some confusion arises through the occasional practice of potting in one district and decorating in another.

Practically all Renaissance maiolica is in museums, but later pieces of Italian faience have followed early designs, and the finer examples of later centuries are always desirable.

Pictured is a Renaissance bust by Andrea della Robbia, now in the National Museum of Florence.

IVORY CHINA

Around 1854, James Mcintyre, with W. S. Kennedy, acquired the Washington Works in Burslem, Staffordshire, an earthenware company established in 1843 by William Saddler Kennedy, which featured artists' palettes and other specialties. In 1860, the firm became James Mcintyre and Co.

One of Macintyre's innovations was the development of what he called "Ivory China." Some of this was lathe-turned and was often used in place of ivory. One of his lathe-turned specialties was a series of pepper and salt shakers with screw bottoms. This screw and top were of ceramic ware so hard and fine that it engaged tightly, providing a pottery shaker without metal or wood or cork. The mark on the bottom reads "Macintyre," often with a registry mark.

These are unusual to find, but they do show up once and again, and it's nice to know what they are all about.

JACKDAW OF RHEIMS PLATES

Amusing and sentimental collectibles—though neither plentiful nor inexpensive—are the Jackdaw of Rheims earthenware items produced by Doulton and Company from 1907 to the late 1920s. Charles J. Noke, then Doulton's art director, did the exceptionally fine drawings which decorate them.

"The Jackdaw of Rheims," a long dramatic poem by Thomas Ingoldsby, first appeared in the *Ingoldsby Legends,* published in 1840. Sixty years later it was still a favorite recital piece on the English Music Hall stage. If you've somehow missed this classic, it tells of a perky jackdaw who steals the Cardinal's ring, is cursed by the Cardinal in a truly rousing stanza, repents, and becomes so pious that he is canonized.

The Doulton series contains plates, large and small, pitchers of all sizes, tobacco jars, and all kinds of other useful forms. They are decorated in color under glaze with Noke's illustrations. Each piece shows a line from the poem in the upper portion, with ivy on a brick wall in the lower half. The date of manufacture is impressed on the bottom of each piece; for example, 4-07 indicates an April 1907 date; 5-22, May 1922.

Some of the later pieces were made in porcelain, somewhat paler in colors than the earthenware which collectors prefer. However, they are happy enough to take what they can find—so scarce are these pieces becoming.

The illustrations, from Chester Davis' collection, appeared in *Spinning Wheel*.

JACKFIELD

This is the name commonly applied to pottery (or even china) with a shiny black glaze. You will find it especially in teapots and in figures of cows, sometimes dogs. It is often red earthenware, covered with the sleek black glaze. The shiny cows may be plain, or with gilding; teapots may be further adorned with applied flower and leaf designs in the gayest of cozy Victorian colors.

True Jackfield ware, made in the Jackfield district of Shropshire in the early eighteenth century, and by Whieldon in Staffordshire at the same time, is more brownish or bronze than black. It's another thing altogether, though both wares go by the Jackfield name.

The Jackfield rooster, one of a pair, black with gilding, is of the Victorian era, made in Scotland.

JACOB PETIT

The background of Jacob Petit's porcelain operations is hazy. It is said he established a factory in Fontainebleau in 1795; it is known that his manufactory was at one time located in Paris. His forte seems to have been the copying of Dresden models and decorative styles. Litchfield writes in his *Pottery and Porcelain,* "The productions of this manufactory are not much sought after save by dealers, who buy them mainly for the American decorators' market."

This could be the reason why the name Jacob Petit is better known in this country than in France. If you go a-hunting, someone is sure to offer you a piece marked with "J. P." and the crossed swords of Saxony, or an unmarked piece attributed to him. Neither may have been made by Jacob Petit, but the candlestick-vase pictured definitely was. This is one of a pair, in tulip form, composed of blossoms in red, blue, and lilac tones. They are eight inches tall, and excessively rare. Derby in England also made similar tulip-form vases.

JAMESON & CO.

See *Bo'ness Potteries*

JAPANESE CHINA

See *Nippon*

JASPER WARE

If someone mentions casually he has a few pieces of Wedgwood, nine times out of ten he's talking of jasper ware, so closely are the two names associated. This fine unglazed stoneware, colored in blue, lavender, sage green, and other shades, and decorated with white sprigged-on bas-reliefs usually in classical scenes, was developed by Josiah Wedgwood in 1775. It is still being made by much the same methods in Wedgwood's fabulously modern plant at Barleston. It was popularly pleasing from the start.

Over the years it has been used for all kinds of ornamental and useful pieces—vases and plaques, teaware and chessmen, buttons and boxes and bottles, even ladies' shoe heels. Just as Josiah Wedgwood made other ceramics, other potters made jasper ware, notably John Turner and William Adams in Josiah's time. **Wedgwood pieces are marked.** (*See* Radford jasper.)

Along in the 1890s, quite a bit of German bisque came on the market, in pale blues, greens, sometimes pink, with white bas-reliefs of cupids, scrolls, heads, and such. This was inexpensive ware, seldom marked, made up mainly in plaques and small pieces like pin trays and boxes. It was sold as "German Jasper Ware."

The illustration shown under *Clocks* is the most familiar type of Jasper decoration. The Wedgwood wine cooler shown here in dark blue and white is a rare allover pattern, produced in 1850. It is 11½ inches high and one of a pair at the Buten Museum of Wedgwood, Merion, Pennsylvania.

JELLY MOLDS

We think of a ceramic jelly mold as a bowl of sorts with an intaglio pattern inside for shaping desserts. Remember the old Jello ads? In the late eighteenth century, say possibly from 1775 to 1825, an even more fanciful jelly mold was in style, used for fashioning a table decoration. Wedgwood made a great many, so did Turner, Neale, and others.

This was a two-part affair—a plain creamware container, usually wedge-shaped, but sometimes in obelisk form, and a smaller piece in the same shape, which fitted into it. The inside mold was often decorated to match a dinner or dessert set. The liquid jelly went in the large container, then the smaller one was pressed into it. When the jelly was set, and the outer container removed, there was a transparent jelly-covered centerpiece, with the design of the tableware showing through. It was never for eating. Examples may be seen at the Buten Museum of Wedgwood, Merion, Pennsylvania, or if you keep an eye open, you may find one for purchase at antiques shop or show.

JESUIT CHINA

Among China Trade porcelains made in the eighteenth century for export to European and American markets were occasional religious pieces, now designated as Jesuit china. They were probably first made for the Protestant Dutch, and only later were associated with the Jesuits. The rare example pictured is skillfully decorated with a Nativity scene in black and white, touched with gold. It was made at Ching-te-chen and decorated at Canton between 1750 and 1775. Recently it was presented to the Henry Ford Museum in Dearborn, Michigan, by Mrs. William Hughes Marshall of Milwaukee, Wisconsin, adding to the impressive Marshall collection of China Trade porcelain already at that Museum. (*See* Oriental Export Porcelain.)

JIM BEAM BOTTLES

See *Bottles*

JONES, GEORGE

So little majolica ware is marked that it is a happiness to find a piece that is, especially if it bears George Jones's cypher. The majolica he made at his Trent Pottery in Stoke, established in 1867, was especially fine and colorful, in the fanciest of designs —teapots, sardine dishes, ice cream platters, and all the rest. His mark was an intertwined GJ, often above a crescent device. In the latter part of 1873, "& Sons" was added on the crescent—we suspect with pride—and George Jones & Sons Ltd. carried on till 1951.

Besides majolica, which was extremely marketable in his time, George Jones began to make porcelain in 1872—he had worked at Minton's before setting up for himself—and continued in that medium to produce unusual and colorful and perfectly delightful pieces. Shown here is a covered box in Parian, gaily decorated with applied leaves, flowers, and extremely lifelike black and yellow bees.

JONES, McDUFFEE & STRATTON

See: *Calendar Tiles; Blue Historical Ware, Late*

J. JORDON

One of these fine days you may come across a jug or a vase or a pair of Rockingham flatback dogs that is marked "Jordon," or "J. Jordon," or "Jordon Ware/Clapham." They all look like eighteenth century wares, but they are nowhere near that old. In fact, these marks were used by J. F. Jordan, of the Clapham Common Brick & Tile Company, Clapham, near Worthing, Sussex, between 1918 and 1939. (Thank Godden's *Encyclopaedia of British Pottery and Porcelain Marks* for this useful bit of information.)

JUGS AND CROCKS

Potteries closely followed new settlements in the United States. Almost the first things the pioneer housewife demanded were crocks for her milk and butter, and for "putting down" her fruits and vegetables, and jugs for her vinegar and molasses. Since the early potter was dependent on local clays, and clays differed from place to place, each locality produced a pottery more or less peculiar to itself. We say "more or less" because similar clays might extend over large areas or a vein of unusual clay might run for miles. For example, a small pottery in Gonic, New Hampshire, in the early eighteenth century, turned out a redware

with a somewhat mottled glaze, indicative of a certain iron content in the clay which seems not to match with other New Hampshire clays. Yet in Alfred, Maine, at least thirty miles due east, a contemporary pottery was turning out redware with the same "Gonic" glaze. Who is to say positively which was which?

In the early 1700s, where local clays permitted, potters advanced to making salt-glazed stoneware which was less porous and which removed the possibility of lead poisoning present in the characteristic redware glaze.

By the mid-1800s, factories with access to proper material were making stoneware jugs and crocks not only for local trade but for shipping afield. Busiest were the potters in New England though their stoneware clay had to be shipped in by boat from New Jersey or Staten Island. Other prolific centers were New Jersey, New York State, Pennsylvania, Maryland, West Virginia, and Ohio. Frequently these gray or beige jugs and crocks, finished with a salt glaze, were decorated with designs in cobalt blue, some quite elaborately.

Of course, the decorated crocks are most desired today; those marked J. & E. Norton, Bennington, Vt., like the one pictured, are high on the want list. Any bearing the maker's name, either impressed or in stenciled blue letters, seem preferred to unmarked pieces unless the latter are especially well decorated or are unusual in respect to shape, intended use, color, or the like. Since jugs and crocks were made in quantity over a long period, it is not difficult to find pleasing examples to use around the house. (*See* Stonewares of Early America.)

JUGTOWN POTTERY

In the mid-1700s, a group of colonists from Staffordshire settled at Steeds, in Moore County, North Carolina. By 1750, Peter Craven had begun making plain "dirt dishes" to supply local needs. Over the years, other potters emerged. Whiskey jugs for Southern distilleries became their chief product. Toward the end of the nineteenth century some fifty potters were so engaged; and the area had long been known as Jugtown. The growing use of glass containers on the part of distilleries slowed down production; Prohibition put an end to it.

This is background history only, for it is the pieces made at the Jugtown Pottery, established by Jacques and Juliana Busbee, which are collectible today, particularly those produced between 1922 and 1947 when Ben Owen was their potter and Jacques the designer. The Busbees received a great deal of publicity for their folk craft revival, and Jugtown Pottery had a wide distribution all over the country. Many a tourist bumped over back country dirt roads to see the shop in operation, and take home a souvenir. After Jacques died in 1947, Juliana and Ben Owen ran the pottery until 1959, when Juliana sold it.

After that, Ben Owen established his own pottery nearby. His works, marked "Ben Owen, Master Potter," are collectible, too, and now is the time to make your selections—and to see his shop in operation.

The Jugtown Pottery opened under new management in 1960 and still continues, making the same type wares and using the same Jugtown mark.

The Busbees furnished two types of Jugtown Pottery; utility wares, authentically patterned from early pieces of the area—jugs, of course, crocks, pie plates, candlesticks, and the like—and Jacques Busbee's translations from Oriental shapes—vases, bowls, and jars finished with glazes he perfected. A Chinese blue glaze, ranging from light blue to deep turquoise, with spots of red-violet is one of his finest.

If you would like to learn more about this pottery and the pieces you should especially look for—several museums have already started collections—*Jugtown Pottery: History and Design,* by Jean Crawford (1964), published by John F. Blair, Winston-Salem, North Carolina, is the book for you.

The blue-lined, blue-decorated gray stoneware Jugtown pitcher illustrated is 3½ inches tall. There is also incised decoration about the top. The vase illustrated is redware with a dribbled turquoise glaze.

JUNGLE BOOK PLATES

Kipling's *Jungle Book* appeared in 1893, and ten years later it was still delighting children so much that the New York importer, Charles Strieff, had William Guerin & Company of Limoges, France, make up sets of plates with Jungle Book themes for American distribution.

Mary Bacon Jones of New York City designed them and copyrighted her six designs for "Children's plates," in Washington on June 15, 1903: Kaas Hunting (pictured); Mowgli's Brothers; Rikki-tikki-tavi; The White Seal; Tiger, Tiger; and Toomai of the Elephants. The sets were made in limited quantity, but there's still a happy chance you may meet one some day. They are plainly marked "William Guerin & Co., Limoges, France. Designed and copyrighted by Mary Bacon Jones."

KACHELOFEN (TILE STOVES)

K

As collectibles, these handsome heating structures are out of the picture. They are costly even in Europe where they are to be found, to say nothing of importing them and setting them up in working order. But there are a few about in our museums for you to look at and drool. The Metropolitan Museum in New

York has one of seventeenth century Swiss make; the Smithsonian Institution in Washington, D. C., has one from Scandinavia; and the American Swedish Institute in Minneapolis, Minnesota, (the old Turnblad mansion) has ten or more. These are from Germany, France, and Sweden—two have the Rorstrand label. They range from seventeenth century examples to one made to order in 1905.

The tile stove originated in Germany about four or five centuries ago, at a time when all available iron was being used for armor. It has been used in cold countries in Europe as late as World War II. In the beginning these elaborate heaters were for royal houses only, but over the years they became available to anyone with the price and the space to build one.

Massive and heavy, they were put together right in the house and remained a permanent fixture. They might be flat and oblong in shape, squat and round, triangular to fit a corner, or towering ceiling-high cylindrical pillars. Behind the gleaming tile facing was a maze of brickwork pipes and flues. Colorful facings ranged from early Delft blue and white tiles with simple patterns to the elaborate porcelain tiles made in France with delicate overglaze enamel painting, to the rich majolica tiles in the heavily elaborate designs favored in Germany.

The *Nurnberg Stove,* a children's story written by Louise de la Remee (Ouida) in 1882, is worth a sentimental reading.

The magnificent tile stove pictured is from seventeenth century Winterthur, Switzerland, constructed of individual tiles in pale yellow, enameled with Biblical scenes, soldiers, heraldic devices, Swiss scenery, and mottoes. It is 8 feet 7½ inches tall; 3 feet 6¼ inches wide. Notice the yellow lion feet.

KATE GREENAWAY'S "LITTLE PEOPLE"

Kate Greenaway (1846-1901), adored for her books and illustrations of children, disliked to draw feet and felt she did a poor job of them. So she put her chubby curly-haired boys into long fur-banded coachman's coats and her poke-bonneted little girls into long high-waisted party dresses, with only the tips of their shoes showing.

Like later-day Gibson Girls, her "little people" appeared everywhere on everything, from buttons and calico to wallpaper. Their quaint long garments were copied for real boys and girls, not only in England but on the Continent, even in fashion-fastidious France. Unfortunately copyright laws in her day were quite inadequate, and while manufacturers fattened on her dainty children, she herself profited very little from the constant forays into her designs and ideas.

Kate Greenaway figurines, in bisque and pottery, flooded the world. Her little boys and girls swung in swings, held matches,

sat on box tops, or stood beside flower baskets. A whole collection could be made of Kate Greenaway salts, little people with holes in their heads. Many were exact copies of her drawings and can be recognized in her books.

It is generally conceded these salts were made in Staffordshire, but by which potters no one seems to know. Apparently several were engaged in this piratical potting for there is great variety in their workmanship. It is said that some of the poorest examples were made in this country, a rumor that has never been tracked down. It was not unusual, twenty years ago, to meet these little shakers in proper pairs and inexpensive, particularly in the New England area. Today they're hard to find, and not at all cheap. Some are pictured here. Other Kate Greenaway ceramics to watch for are fireplace tiles; children's tableware—both Wedgwood and Minton made sets; majolica plates by the Royal and Imperial Porcelain Majolica Manufactory of Budapest; and many, many novelties, all with Kate Greenaway decorations.

For further reading: *Kate Greenaway,* by M. H. Spielmann & G. S. Layard (1905); *The Secret Door,* by Covelle Newcomb (1946).

KAUFFMAN, ANGELICA

Angelica Kauffman (1741-1807) was an artist who painted decorative pictures in the classical style. Born in Switzerland, she won recognition as a painter in Rome, then moved on to England. There she stayed fifteen years, painting portraits and historical and classical pictures, and cutting quite a social swath. Among stories about her is one that she married a servant in the belief he was a Count. After suitable tears, recriminations, and a financial settlement on her part, the marriage was annulled.

Her work was engraved by Bartolozzi, W. W. Ryland, Thomas Burke, and other leading engravers of the day, and original prints are still considered choice. She also designed for furniture inlays and porcelains.

She is mentioned here because many of her paintings were later reproduced on quantities of chinaware of varying degrees of quality. You will find handsome pieces, extremely well done, with hand touches added to the decal; in others, the decal seems slapped on, and crooked at that. Some pieces bear her signature, though she herself could not have painted them on the china. The popular period for this decoration, particularly on wares from Germany and Austria, was in the "hand-painted" era from 1870 to 1900, nearly a century after her death.

The marmalade jar illustrated (without its baseplate) was made in Austria—a quality piece of fine china, in rich turquoise blue and gold. The "handpainted" classical decoration in color showing Leander and Hero in the Temple of Venus is signed "Angelica Kauffman."

KENNEDY POTTERY

See *Southern Highland Potteries*

C. D. KENNY SOUVENIRS

Collectors of miniature items may find amusing the small stone bisque figures and ornaments in a two- to four-inch dimension which the C. D. Kenny Company of Baltimore gave away to its customers in many cities and for many years.

C. D. Kenny, dealer in teas, coffees, and refined sugars, and a great believer in advertising souvenirs, began operations with a single shop in Baltimore, Maryland, in 1872. By 1901, he owned fifty branch stores—in Washington and Georgetown, D. C.; Richmond, Norfolk, Lynchburg, Petersburg, Roanoke, and Danville, Virginia; Wheeling, West Virginia; Birmingham, Alabama; Atlanta, Georgia; Knoxville, Chattanooga, and Memphis, Tennessee; Pittsburgh and York, Pennsylvania; and Cleveland, Ohio. Through all of them his souvenirs were distributed.

Though many types of Kenny give-aways were presented, from elaborate tradecards to decorated tin plates, plaques, tea strainers, and toy alligators, the little white bisque figures seem to have been the most popular. Most had colored decoration, either glazed or unglazed with color painted on. Some were unmarked as to country of origin, others say Austria or Germany. *All* have "C. D. Kenny Co." incised on the base. There were parrots on vases, little girls on sleds, boys on boxes, monkeys on elephants, ladies on horseback, Indians in canoes, ad infinitum. These little figures are still plentiful, still inexpensive (though no longer give-aways), and are found in areas wherever Kenny stores existed.

The Kenny company turned to wholesale in 1934, thus ending the souvenir situation. Since 1940, the company has been a division of the Consolidated Foods Corporation in Chicago.

The Kenny souvenir illustrated shows an Indian girl in a canoe; brown and blue are the colors, under glaze. There is an Indian brave, too, just like her, except he wears no beads.

KEWPIES

The Kewpies were Rose O'Neill's dream babies. They first appeared, with their whispy topknots, cherubic faces, tiny wings, and fat tummies, in the *Ladies Home Journal* in 1909. They showed up soon after in *Woman's Home Companion* and *Pictorial Review*. Children who read their mamma's magazines screamed so loud for "a Kewpie to hold" that on July 15, 1913, Rose O'Neill registered her trademark for a bisque Kewpie doll. Two firms in Germany made the first ones: dollmaker J. D. Kestner, and toymaker George Borgfeldt & Company of New York, who had a factory there. Though Borgfeldt trademarked the Kewpies in Germany, France, England, and the United States, other companies, authorized and unauthorized, in this country and abroad, began quickly turning them out in various materials.

If you look for bisque Kewpies for your collection, try for the band: there is *Wag, the Chief* with a flag in his topknot; *The Army,* in soldier hat; *The Cook,* wearing an apron; *The Gardener; The Carpenter; "Careful-of-his-voice,"* wearing a head scarf;

"*Always-wears-his-overshoes,*" wearing you know what; *The Life Preserver; The Instructor,* with a Book of Useful Knowledge; "*Careful-of-his-complexion,*" in a sunbonnet; and clumsy little *Blunderboo.* Scootles, an elf-baby tourist to Kewpieville, is also nice to have. Kewpies may be marked "Rose O'Neill," or have a proper paper sticker, or both; the earlier ones will have tiny blue wings. While you're looking, keep an eye out for the charming china play dishes that Royal Rudolstadt in Prussia made and decorated with Kewpies.

KEYSTONE POTTERY

See *Bottles*

"KEZONTA"

See *Cincinnati Art Pottery*

KING'S ROSE
OYSTER KING'S ROSE

Though this colorful pattern from the first quarter of the nineteenth century lacks the characteristic blue of true Gaudy Dutch, it is so closely related in other respects that it falls in the Gaudy Dutch category. It is characterized by a prominent red-orange rose, off-centered in the design, with fuzzy yellow flowers, either red-fringed or with dotted borders. Sometimes a vine, or a sectional, or a solid pink border appears.

When a blue brush is added, bearing an outline in the shape of an oyster, it becomes "Oyster King's Rose." Few pieces are signed. (*See* Gaudy Dutch.)

KIRKPATRICK,
WALLACE and CORNWALL

See *Illinois Potters*

KNIFE RESTS

Knife rests of pottery, glass, or silver appeared in one form or another on all well-appointed dining tables of the long white damask tablecloth era. Large ones, placed near the platter, held the blade of the carving knife and fork when they were not in use. Smaller ones, usually in pairs, were at each diner's plate ready to rest the cutlery between courses. This "save your fork" dining custom, long out of style here, is still followed in France.

For pottery knife rests, the most common shape is a triangular bar about two inches long; glass ones usually look like small dumbbells; and silver ones of the 1880s and 1890s go all out for fanciness.

The Onion pattern knife rest pictured is bolster shape and was probably used with knives and forks handled in the same pattern or with a dinner set in Blue Onion. (*See* Blue Onion.)

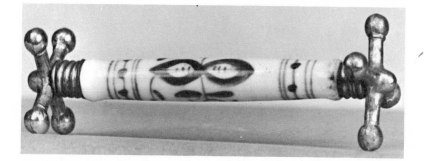

K. P. M.
(Königliche Porzellan Manufaktur)
(Royal Porcelain Company)

The familiar reddish-brown K. P. M. marks on fine delicately decorated porcelain—the imperial globe and cross, and the eagle, both with the letters K. P. M. below—are the ones we associate with the Royal Porcelain Company of Berlin. Though the eagle mark was used from 1823-1832 and 1844-1847 and the globe and cross mark from 1832 on, these are still called the "modern" marks to differentiate them from the earlier wares before industrialization took over.

The factory dates back to 1752 when William Kasper Wegeley, a textile manufacturer, obtained a monopoly of Berlin from Frederick the Great to produce porcelain. He lost the Royal patronage in 1757, and promptly gave up potting.

Five years later, in 1761, Frederick had Johann Ernst Gotzkowsky reopen the factory. Dresden was at that time suffering from the Seven Years War, and their pottery was at a standstill; it seemed practical to have a manufactory in Berlin. Almost immediately the K. P. M. initials were used as a mark, at first with a scepter, later with other symbols.

The various early marks of the Königliche Porzellan Manufaktur are included in porcelain marks books, but they really need not concern us too much as we will seldom find a piece available for purchase. If you should, you'll find it very beautiful—and very expensive. Since there have been many copyings, do get expert advice before buying. (*See* Lithophanes.)

111

KNOBS FOR CANES & UMBRELLAS
See *Door Furniture*

KNOWLES, TAYLOR & KNOWLES
See: *American Belleek; Calendar Plates; Lotus Ware*

L

LABELLE CHINA
See *Wheeling Pottery Co.*

LAMBERTON CHINA

In 1927, on the occasion of its 100th birthday, the Baltimore and Ohio Railroad blossomed out with new and special dinnerware in its dining cars. It was transfer-printed underglaze in blue; the border showed famous locomotives; the center views were of famous scenic points along the line. Each piece was backstamped "Scammell's /LAMBERTON / China/Patent applied for." Passengers were allowed to buy the plates, and anyone could buy other pieces at the B & O headquarters in Baltimore. These sentimental pieces are by far the most interesting of wares marked Lamberton.

The Lamberton Works in Trenton, New Jersey, had at least two owners before D. William Scammell took it over from the Maddock Pottery in 1892; Maddock had it from the Trenton China Company. The Maddock Pottery had made thin semi-porcelain dinner and toilet sets, marking their decorated wares "Lamberton," and their undecorated wares "M/China/L"—the "M" for Maddock and the "L" for Lamberton.

The Scammell Company produced two grades of dinnerware, marketed as Trenton China and Lamberton China. The firm discontinued its blue ware for the railroad during World War II and sold its blue china engravings to the Sterling China Company of East Liverpool, Ohio. The firm is not listed in Trenton city directories after 1954. Late B & O dining car dinner services, though of the same design, were made either by the Sterling China Company or by the Shenango Pottery Company of New Castle, Pennsylvania.

The scene in the B & O plate pictured is of the Gap at Cumberland, Maryland.

LAMBETH DELFT

From the mid-seventeenth to the early eighteenth century, English potteries, especially those concentrated at Lambeth, were busy making Delftwares to compete with those made in Holland. The first of these was the Delftware pottery established in Lambeth by a Dutchman, Jacob Jensen, who came over from Holland with a crew of trained Flemish workmen. English potters, using a similar thick white enamel of pinkish tinge on which to paint their decoration, usually in blue, achieved the general characteristics of the Holland Delft they copied.

The best English Delft was made at Lambeth, where at one time some twenty potteries were engaged in producing it. Likely there was as much Delft, if not more, made in Lambeth as in Holland. Drug jars, pots, and serving plates or chargers are among the pieces which have survived in greatest number. Most are in museums.

The pro-Jacobite Lambeth plate pictured, now in the Colonial Williamsburg collection, commemorates the First Uprising, showing Charles II in the Boscobal Oak after the battle of Worcester in 1651. (*See:* Colonial Chinaware; Delft.)

LANCASTRIAN POTTERY

See *Pilkington's Royal Lancastrian Pottery*

LANGENBECK, KARL

See: *Avon Pottery; Mosaic Tile Company*

LA SA

See *Weller*

LATE SPATTER (LATE SPONGE)

Recently people have begun collecting what they call Late Spatter, or sometimes Late Sponge—heavy, coarsely sponged blue and white mixing bowls, pitchers, butter crocks, toilet sets, and what have you, that were in common use till a short time ago.

The shape of the piece and its original use will indicate its age; slop jars, for instance, went out after World War I; custard cups lingered not much longer. While this ware is so distantly related to true and early Spatterware that it should hardly be mentioned in the same breath, we whisper it here. After all, it is collected, being exceptionally decorative and still inexpensive enough to be used with enjoyment. (*See* Spatterware.)

LAUGHLIN, HOMER

This pottery in East Liverpool, Ohio, is still in business, one of the largest plants of its kind in the country, but individual pieces or maybe even whole dinner sets from an earlier age can be found with looking. Try for their white or decorated Ironstones manufactured before 1900.

Homer Laughlin started out making yellow ware at Little Beaver, Ohio, in 1843, but nothing much seemed to come of that. He served through the Civil War, and 1867 found him buying and selling, but not making, the still popular yellow ware. Then he and his brother Shakespeare set out to import wares from Europe. But in 1873, the brothers went to East Liverpool, Ohio, and started potting on their own. Their white Ironstone came out in 1874, and soon they were making decorated stone china patterns as well. One of their decorated patterns, put out in 1886, was called Shakespeare; cardinal birds and cherry blossoms distinguished it.

Until 1893, the name of the company was Laughlin Bros. In that year Shakespeare withdrew from the firm, and it became Homer Laughlin, Successor to Laughlin Bros. In 1897, it changed again to Laughlin China Co.

At first, the Laughlins made translucent porcelain tablewares—something to look for—as well as earthenwares. They dropped the porcelain in 1889 and concentrated on high grade semi-vitreous earthenware. Several marks have been used over the years, one on their Ironstone wares had quite a British look—the word Laughlin with a large "L" embracing the British Lion and the American Eagle, obviously a round-about way of looking imported.

LEECH JARS

For centuries the popular remedy for congestions, swellings, and almost every other ailment known to man was the drawing away of blood, either by cupping, where the patient's skin was punctured and a suction cup applied, or by the application to the afflicted spot of live leeches, those aquatic blood-sucking parasites. In the sixteenth and seventeenth centuries, the barber-surgeon was even known as a "leech."

An advertisement in a Maryland paper in 1857, read: "Bryson Gill & Sons, Dentists, Cuppers and Leechers, No. 56 Sharp Street, near Pratt Street, Baltimore, where they keep always on hand a large supply of the very best Swedish leeches, which they will sell wholesale and retail. Terms cash on delivery. N. B. Cupping and Leeching by Mrs. Gill."

The barber-surgeons, the apothecaries, and other users kept their leeches in ventilated pots and jars expressly made for that purpose, and clearly labeled. Of these gruesome pots, Leeds, Liverpool, Sunderland, and Wedgwood contributed their share, as did various continental makers of majolica, faience, and Delftware. As late as 1890, Hagerty Brothers of New York were listing leech jars on their wholesale price lists of druggist's wares.

For finding a leech jar nowadays—say you're looking for a little gift for your doctor come Christmas—the likeliest place is among the discarded stocks of old drug or apothecary shops.

LEEDS

The Leeds Pottery was established in the mid-1700s and through many changes of ownership continued into the late nineteenth century. The most familiar of its products is its early cream-colored earthenware, similar to Wedgwood's Queen's Ware though of a yellower tint. The designs for their basket-pattern dishes, their openwork-edged trays and fruit baskets, their candlesticks, and utilitarian wares were chaste and simple, yet with an elegance. Many of these also resembled Wedgwood's.

Not all their creamwares were undecorated; some were transfer printed, and some were decorated in underglaze colors or overglaze enamels. A simple blue feathered edge on tablewares is characteristic and familiar.

Other wares were made there, too—whatever was in vogue —black basalts, shiny black Jackfield type ware, white and enamelled salt glaze stoneware, figures and groups a la Staffordshire, and lustered earthenwares. Early pieces are the ones to look for, and the factory was so productive over so long a period that they can be found.

In the late nineteenth and early twentieth centuries, some of the Leeds creamwares were reproduced. The reproductions are thicker in the potting than the originals, with a glaze that inclines to craze. Skip these in your buying, even if they are marked

"Leeds Pottery." For a late report on all about it—styles, patterns, shapes, markings, owners—look for a copy of *Leeds Pottery,* by Donald Towner (1963).

The Leeds creamware teapot illustrated is in the historic PVOR pattern, a commemorative piece honoring a Dutch monarch, ca. 1767.

LENOX CHINA

Walter Scott Lenox, born in Trenton, N.J., in 1859, learned the potting trade at Ott and Brewer and at Willetts Pottery in his home town. In 1889, with Jonathan Coxon, Sr., he formed the Ceramic Art Company, also in Trenton. In 1894, he bought out Coxon and operated the business under his own name until 1903 when the present Lenox, Incorporated was organized. The product was—and still is—Belleek, though the term "Belleek" was dropped in 1915 and it is now known simply as Lenox. Enough for dates.

At a time when imported china was "the thing," and some American potters were even stamping French marks on their wares in order to sell them, Walter Lenox determined to make an American product that Americans would buy, simply for its own high quality. His struggle was hardly begun when he was struck with paralysis, losing his sight and the use of his legs. Disdaining affliction, he turned to Harry A. Brown, then secretary of the company, and there developed between them one of the most affecting relationships of which American industry has record.

Lenox's mind remained brilliant, resourceful and active; he saw through the eyes of his alter ego. He continued to visit the factory regularly, directing the development of new products he could only feel.

In the beginning, he had made mostly ornamental objects, but before he died in 1920, a 1700-piece dinner service in Lenox was furnished for President Wilson, the first American-made dinnerware ever to grace the White House.

Pieces of it are pictured here; the rim is cobalt blue, the outer border of etched gold, and the President's seal in raised 24-karat gold. (*See* Washington-Wakefield Pattern.)

LESSORE, EMILE

Emile Lessore was a French artist who took up decoration of pottery as a hobby. When his beloved wife died in 1859 he sought to ease his grief by a change of scene and a new profession. He went to England where he associated himself with the Wedgwood factory as a decorator. The Watteau-like charm of his designs lifted the painting of pottery to a fine art.

His association with Wedgwood continued until 1875, even though he went back to France in 1863—he had found England much too cold and damp. Small designs he would send to the factory to be filled in and finished by others; larger, important pieces were shipped to him in France for execution. His work was signed—watch for his signature on vases, cream jugs, sugar basins, dessert plates, comports, ewers, and the like. A tray is illustrated.

LIMBACH

We find plenty of late German porcelains imported in the 1880s and 1890s, but outside of Meissen and Dresden or pieces represented as such, we do not often come across much early German porcelain. What little chinaware there was in the colonies, the early settlements, and the New Republic of America came from England or France, and we have no family treasure houses of "handed-down" German wares from that period.

Yet the late eighteenth and early nineteenth centuries saw many busy German porcelain manufactories. Gotthelf Greiner's plants in Thuringia were among the most prosperous—he had five of them. The Limbach factory, where he began operations about 1772, and his Grosbreitenbach works were his best known. He made figures of excellent order and dressy tablewares, and before operations ceased in 1896, his Thuringian factories had produced a goodly amount of porcelain.

Some of it is bound to show up in shipments of antiques from abroad, and some of it must already be on these shores,

brought over among their belongings by a host of political refugees in 1848 to 1850, business and professional people for the most part, who had money and possessions to bring.

There are various markings for the Limbach figures and earliest pieces; you'll need to consult a good marks book to identify them. But later Limbach and Grosbreitenbach tablewares seemed to have settled to the common use of a three leaf clover mark.

The Limbach pieces pictured are from a coffee set; they show fruits painted in natural colors on a shallow ribbed ground which is partial evidence of their Thuringian ancestry.

LIMOGES

Limoges, France, located about 230 miles southwest of Paris, has long been regarded as the chief porcelain center of Europe. Potteries in the town were making earthenware as early as 1736; after kaolin was found in the neighborhood in 1768, they changed wholeheartedly to porcelain. By 1840, there were thirty porcelain factories in the Limoges area; in 1882, there were forty-two.

United States importers, who had always dealt chiefly with England, "discovered" Limoges, you might say, with David Haviland. In 1842, soon after Haviland had established his manufactory in Limoges, the U. S. imported 753 cases of French porcelain as against 621 cases of English earthenware. In another ten years, the English were far, far behind; in 1852, the U. S. imported 8,594 cases of French porcelain, only 353 of English earthenware.

For over 100 years "Limoges" was backstamped on all quality porcelain pieces manufactured there; "France" was added after 1891. It was a place name only, and did not refer to any specific company.

However, should a piece of heavy earthenware with the mark "O.C. Co. Limoges" show up to puzzle you, this "Limoges" is a pattern name, used for tableware made by the Ohio China Co., East Palestine, Ohio, and selected, no doubt, to befuddle not only you but its original purchaser. (*See* Haviland.)

Identifying marks used on Limoges wares, as published in 1898, are given here. In a listing of 21 present day Limoges porcelain producers exporting to the United States, as compiled in *France Actuelle* (Dec. 15, 1967), the only lap-over names are Haviland; Robert Haviland & C. Parlon; G. D. A.; and Lanternier & Co.

Marks on porcelain made at Limoges; those which include "France" in the legend were used after 1891. Many of them do not identify the manufacturer, only the U. S. distributor.

1. "AE/CHF," used by Charles Field Haviland for wares distributed by Haviland & Abbott, New York; prior to 1868; "CFH/GDM," used 1882-1891. Circular stamp used on decorated ware.

2. "H & Co/L" is the mark of Haviland & Co.; on decorated ware they used Haviland & Co/Limoges.

3. Theodore Haviland, Limoges.

4. "H & C" is not a Haviland mark but one used on wares made by other Limoges firms for Hinrichs & Company, N. Y. Circle mark, from 1891.

5. Two marks used by Wm. Guerin & Co. on wares distributed in the U. S. by Charles Streiff, New York.

6. Limoges wares made for Levy, Dreyfus & Co., New York.

7. Limoges wares imported by the Pairpoint Mfg. Company, New Bedford, Mass., and distributed by them.

8. Limoges wares made for Lazarus, Rosenfeld & Lehman, New York.

9. Two marks used on wares made by A. Lanternier for George Borgfeldt & Co., New York, distributors.

10. "Elite" was used on Limoges wares decorated by Bawo & Dotter, New York, importers. (Later Bawo & Dotter established their own whiteware pottery, too, using the same mark.)

11. Three marks registered by Charles Ahrenfeldt & Sons, importers, New York.

12. Used on Limoges porcelains made for distribution by C. L. Dwinger, New York.

13. Mark registered by P. H. Leonard, New York, for Limoges wares imported for distribution.

14. Two marks used by the M. Redon pottery, Limoges, who had a New York distribution office of the same name.

15. Used on wares imported by L. Straus & Co., New York.

16. Used on Limoges wares imported by Vogt & Dose, New York.

17. Two marks used on porcelain made by Delinieres, on wares for distribution by Endeman & Churchill, New York.

18. Mark of Societie la Ceramique J. Pouyat, Limoges, a firm having its own distribution office in New York.

19. Used on Limoges wares produced for the Royal China Decorating Company of New York.

LINTHORPE ART POTTERY

A surprising number of art potteries have been inspired either by the desire to Improve the General Taste or to Help Out Local People. Many have succeeded in both purposes simultaneously. Some developed into long-lived commercial firms; others lasted only a few years.

The Linthorpe Art Pottery in Middlesborough, Yorkshire, resulted from a suggestion by designer Christopher Dresser to his friend John Harrison, a wealthy landowner in the district, that a pottery might alleviate some of the poverty caused by the slackening of the iron trade in that area. Why not use the red brick clay on the Harrison estate? Harrison fell in with the idea, and the pottery opened in 1879, with Dresser as its permanent art director.

Christopher Dresser (1834-1907) was by profession a botanist, lecturing at two London medical schools. He was also a designer in glass and metals, well ahead of his time in his concern with the functional. Occasionally you will find in an antiques shop some object bearing his mark, perhaps a silver teapot or a lacquered brass candlestick, which looks completely modern.

At Linthorpe, his use of brick clay was revolutionary—it was so common a material experienced potters had never thought to use it for other than tile, drainpipe, and cheap redware. He invented a new and spectacular method of glazing, which produced low-toned reds, mottled olives, browns, and yellows. The pottery specialized in incised and perforated wares and created many original shapes. No one piece was quite like another; even "matched" vases failed to match exactly. From the first, Linthorpe products, from small ashtrays to large decorative plaques, were of superior quality, comparing favorably with Wedgwood and Minton.

Financially the pottery did not fare so well. Dresser's famous glazes were expensive to make; his production costs were high. Still, when the factory closed in 1899, it had served its immediate purpose. It had provided work for local people until the iron trade revived. It had placed on the market art pottery of great distinction, unique in its glazes, for when Dresser died, the secret of his glazes went with him.

The multi-colored bowl-vase pictured is impressed "Linthorpe" across a lozenge.

LITHOPHANES

Lithophanes are porcelain transparencies in which the impressed design is brought out distinctly only when it is held against the sun or against artificial light. They were used mainly for lampshades, for plaques to hang in a window, for night lights, or in the bottoms of teacups and steins. Sometimes, in steins, the pictures were slightly naughty, but lampshades and plaques and light-screening shades or fans were eminently proper—copies of popular pictures of the day, genre scenes, or familiar portraits.

The patent taken out about 1828 by Baron de Bourgoin of Rubelles Faience Potteries, Seine-et-Marne, France, seems to have introduced these transparencies. Their early wares were marked with an applied tablet reading Rubelles, S & M. Later marks differed but "Rubelles" always appears as a part of them.

Soon factories in other countries were licensed to produce

lithophanes. A French company which marked theirs ADT, presumably A. DeTrombley, made some, as did Minton, Copeland, Wedgwood and others in England. But the best of the lithophanes, the most elaborate, and the greatest number were made in German factories, with the Royal Porcelain Company in Berlin (KPM mark) in the lead.

While a manufacturer's mark is frequently found on the rim of a lithophane, no artist seems ever to have signed his work, yet it was the artist who painstakingly sculptured the scene in

wax for the plaster cast from which the piece was made.

Lithophanes lasted no longer than kerosene lamps, and had begun to fall into disfavor some years previous to kerosene's fade-out. They are not at all common now, and far-seeing collectors who gathered them up in years past have a right to feel smug. New lithophanes, now being made in plastic or in a heavy porcelain, are easily distinguished from the old.

"LIVERPOOL BIRDS"

See: *Sadler & Green; Queen's Ware*

LIVERPOOL JUGS

Liverpool was a source of rich deposits of clay and marl, and from its earliest times—it was chartered by King John in 1299—some sort of earthenware was being made there. By the late eighteenth century, Liverpool potteries, like those in Staffordshire, were producing creamware or Queen's Ware. Light weight and smooth textured, it was ideal for transfer printing, the new process which Sadler and Green, two Liverpool potters, had just invented.

After the American Revolution, Liverpool became a regular port-of-call for American merchant vessels trading in Europe. Enterprising Liverpool potters bid for their trade by decorating creamware pieces with black and white transfers of patriotic American designs and inscriptions. Sometimes they colored the transfer by hand; occasionally they added a bit of gilt. What matter if they spelled a state's name wrong or used identical portraits for Thomas Jefferson and James "Maddison" when they expressed such un-British sentiments as "By Virtue and Valour we have freed our Country, extended our Commerce, and laid the Foundation of a Great Empire," and pictured an American soldier with his foot on the head of a British lion!

A great volume of these "American souvenir" wares were pitchers. Nearly all were melon-shaped, with graceful curving body, pointed lip, and strap handle. They might be anywhere from a few inches high to twenty; sentiments were always pleasing to Americans.

Before this colorful ware was overshadowed, about 1825, by the Staffordshire American Scenes, quantities had been brought to this country. Some of it is still around for lucky lookers and finders. For more about these jugs, see *Liverpool Transfer Designs on Anglo-American Pottery,* by Robert McCauley.

In 1972, a Brooklyn, N. Y. firm began bringing out a series of reproduction Liverpool jugs; they are 3-pint size, printed in black on white.

However distasteful Liverpool potters may have found the American sentiments they printed on their mugs, they did not let patriotism stand in the way of profit. The mug pictured, 5¾ inches tall, 3¾ inches in diameter, printed in reddish brown, honors Commodore Decatur, whose name appears above his portrait. On the banner beneath is "Free Trade & Sailors Rights," and at the base are given Decatur's exploits in the War of 1812: "Destroyed the Frigate Philadelphia 1814/Captured and brought in the British Frigate Macedonian 1812."

LOGAN POTTERY

See *Footwarmers*

LONHUDA

In 1892, W. A. Long, a druggist in Steubenville, Ohio, who had been experimenting with pottery glazes for several years, formed the Lonhuda Pottery Company, named for the owners —Long, W. H. Hunter, and Alfred Day. Like the Rookwood made under Miss Laura Fry's patent of 1889, Lonhuda featured underglaze decoration on a blended brown background.

Long exhibited his Lonhuda at the Chicago World's Fair in 1893. Samuel Weller saw it, liked it, and persuaded Long to come to Zanesville, Ohio, and locate at the Weller plant. Long stayed with Weller only a few months, then took himself and his process to the J. B. Owens company. He didn't linger there either, but soon moved on to Denver, Colorado, where he established the Denver China and Pottery Company, and went on making Lonhuda.

Back in Zanesville, Weller kept on with a Lonhuda-type ware which he called Louwelsa, and Owens kept on making it as Utopian. Miss Fry brought suit against Weller for infringement of her patent; Weller claimed that though the wares appeared the same, his process was different; the suit was eventually dropped. With such a mishmash, collectors can well understand why it takes a careful peer at the marks to distinguish these look-alikes—Lonhuda, Louwelsa, Utopian, and Rookwood.

LOSANTI

Along in the 1870s, about the time when titled and aristocratic ladies in London were having a go at decorating Doulton's Lambeth Ware, American ladies in Cincinnati were engaged in similar endeavors, and with much more enduring effect. One of them was Maria Longworth Nichols who later established the Rookwood Pottery; another was Mary Louise McLaughlin.

Miss McLaughlin remained more or less in amateur standing, experimenting with both pottery and hard porcelain. Eventually she had her own kiln, and did all her own designing and potting, even to firing the kilns. She was very good. She used Ohio clays for her Cincinnati faience, and one of her vases is now in the Philadelphia Museum.

After pottery, she turned to hard porcelain; Losanti ware was the result. She exhibited examples of it in the Paris Exposition of 1901.

She "retired" at fifty, satisfied that she could do what she set out to and content to tell others how to do it as well. Her books, *Pottery Decoration under Glaze* (1877), *China Painting; Pottery Decoration, Suggestions to China Painters,* etc., sold in great numbers and china painters all across the country were familiar with her name and methods. Her books are easier to find than examples of her work—and very nice to have, too, as adjuncts to handpainted china collections.

LOTUS WARE

Produced by Knowles, Taylor & Knowles Co., of East Liverpool, Ohio, between 1891 and 1898, Lotus Ware was so named by Col. John N. Taylor, then president of the firm, because of its resemblance to the petals of the lotus blossom. It has a peculiarly translucent bone china body with a soft velvety glaze, reminiscent of Belleek. The decoration, often figure work, is executed in enamel, built up over the glaze instead of under it, similar to pâte-sur-pâte.

Some exquisite pieces were shown at the Chicago Exposition in 1893, decorated in dainty colors with jeweled and openwork effects, some with raised coin-gold after the Renaissance style. Overglaze paintings of flowers, landscapes, or mythological subjects were always superbly done. China painting was then the rage, and some pieces were sold plain for amateurs to decorate; their work is not often as fine as the factory turnout.

The mark on Lotus Ware consisted of a circle enclosing the letters K T K Co. with a star and a crescent, above the words "Lotus Ware," usually printed in overglaze in green.

Knowles, Taylor & Knowles made other wares, too. In fact, they were among the first potters in the Ohio district to make Ironstone (1872); they also made quantities of semi-vitreous hotel ware, marked "KTK China." Lotus Ware was their most ambitious—and most costly—line. (*See* Calendar Plates.)

LOW TILES

It is surprising how little is known about Low tiles, considering their unusual beauty and the great number that were turned out between 1877 and 1907. Many of them are no doubt still intact in mantel and hearth facings or wall panels in the "best" houses of their period. Occasionally a loose tile or two with the Low factory mark will show up in an antiques shop, handsome enough for framing, and definitely *not* to be overlooked.

John Gardner Low, instigator of the company, had studied art in Paris as a youth; later he had been associated with the Chelsea Keramic Art Works. In 1873, he began his own experiments and in 1878, with the financial help of his father, the Hon. John Low, started his Art Tile Works in Chelsea, Massachusetts.

The decoration he devised for his tiles was unique, and effective enough to win him medal after medal in this country and abroad. It often involved the use of such natural objects as leaves, grasses, dried flowers, even fabrics, pressed into moist clay to produce an intaglio design, then somehow reversed to make a cameo effect for a pair.

Low's beautifully glazed "plastic sketches" in low relief, which were sometimes framed as pictures or inserted into box tops as well as being used architecturally or for stove decorations, included classical and oriental art motifs, allegorical representations of people, designs from nature, landscapes, and farm scenes.

Those designed by Arthur Osborne, and signed "A. O." are especially choice.

In 1883, John Farnsworth Low (John's son) joined the firm, so you'll find some tiles marked "J. & J. G. Low" and almost as many marked "J. G. & J. F. Low." The business was apparently carried on to 1902, though it was not liquidated until 1907. In addition to tiles, the company made a few inkwells in the 1880s, and also a few clock cases. For collectors these are rare finds.

Spinning Wheel magazine for March 1969 carried an excellent account of Low tiles by Mrs. Barbara Morse, a Low tile collector who has done her research well.

A plastic sketch, "The Wood Gatherer," by Arthur Osborne, is shown here. This is a large tile, approximately 8 by 4¾ inches, and developed in a beautiful bluish-green, almost turquoise, colored glaze. The legend on the back informs: J. G. & J. F. Low/ Art Tile Works/ Chelsea, Mass., U. S. A./Copyright by J. G. & J. F. Low, 1885. This was used as a central motif or for the corner sets in a fireplace facing, and also as a decoration on small iron parlor stoves.

LOUWELSA

See: *Lonhuda; Weller; Zanesville Pottery*

LOWESTOFT

How Oriental or Chinese Export porcelain ever came to be so widely called "Lowestoft" is anybody's conjecture; perhaps because Lowestoft on the Southeast coast of England was an unloading point for exports from the Orient; perhaps because the porcelain factory at Lowestoft, like others of its time (1752-1802), was copying Chinese wares to the best of its ability; perhaps just because some "authority" liked the sound of Lowestoft better. Whatever the reason, the misnomer has caused American collectors considerable confusion.

There was a *real* Lowestoft porcelain. It is a soft paste, with some twenty-percent bone ash, a formula quite similar to that used by Bow, and quite unlike that used in China. Early productions were painted in underglaze blue, with patterns showing the Chinese influence. Teawares and sauce boats comprised most of their early output.

When Robert Browne, Jr. succeeded his father in 1771 as owner of the pottery, he instituted some changes. He began to use overglaze enamels, and transfer printing under glaze. He made animals and figures, and copied Dresden, Worcester, and other porcelains, even to their marks.

Toward the end, the Lowestoft operation made a great many special event or souvenir pieces, like mugs and inkwells, inscribed

"A Trifle from Lowestoft," or from Bungay, or Wangford, or other local spots. Chaffers' *Marks and Monograms,* the new revised 15th edition, gives additional information.

LUNEVILLE

See *Faience*

LUSTREWARE

English lustreware was purely a commercial product, typically English, and not copied from the Continent or the Orient, though it retains the name of those earlier iridescent wares. Silver lustre, the first English type, was invented by John Hancock of Hanley, Stoke-on-Trent, about 1800, to give the poor man a chance for "silver" on his table. Silver resist decoration quickly followed, then came the gold, copper, and pink lustres in great profusion. Potters all through Staffordshire and Wales produced it, and pitchers, plates, bowls, teasets, goblets, salt dishes, puzzle jugs, and tobys bloomed in innumerable cupboards and shelves in that country and this.

Only two metals were used to produce the many variations. All the silver lustres were made from platinum. The copper, bronze, gold, yellow, pink, mottled pink, ruby, and deep purple lustres were made from gold. Gold over a dark background produced copper as well as gold lustre; gold on white or light backgrounds produced pink lustre in all its variations.

For resist lustre—silver resist (1805-1840) brings highest prices today—portions of the pattern were painted in with some

127

substance, like sugar and glycerine, which did not take the lustre when immersed in it. This was washed off when the piece was dry, leaving a design in lustre on a white or colored ground.

If lustre is your love or you want to pursue it, John and Baker's *Old English Pottery* is the book to own or borrow.

LYCETT, EDMUND
See *Tiles*

MAASTRICHT

In 1834, when Staffordshire wares were being imported to Holland at a great rate, P. Regout (Petrus Regout and Co.) established a pottery at Maastricht to manufacture the same type of popular wares, and to stem the tide of importations. He copied his competitors closely, even bringing in English workmen to show him how. Not only did he succeed in supplying Holland with English-type made-at-home earthenware dishes, but was soon exporting a few of them as well. Six large factories at Maastricht are currently busy producing ceramic wares, primarily for home consumption.

For all the number of Maastricht pieces backstamped with the P. Regout sphinxlike trademark we come across today—you can hardly find an antiques shops without at least one colorful small bowl or plate—practically nothing has been written about this company. Many marks books do not mention the name; Dutch promotion sources prefer to talk about their beautiful Delft. The only account of any substance that we were able to locate was in *Antiques Magazine* for March and April 1931. There, dating was established by the style of the backstamp, and the progress of the company was followed from 1834 to the time of writing. Illustrating the study were examples of historical scene plates

Sevres covered urns, ca. 1800; 16 inches high.

Victorian Trinket Box, ca. 1880; 4¼ inches long. Cottage or Chimney Ornament, Staffordshire fireman, ca. 1840; 4 inches high. Bacchus, Staffordshire, ca. 1870; 6¼ inches high.

Quintal, Leeds-type finger vase, ca. 1810; 8¾ inches high. Imari, shell-shaped relish dish, late 19th century; 11 inches long.

Stangl Pottery Birds, cock and hen, ca. 1950; cock is 9 inches tall.

which closely resembled those made in Staffordshire in the 1830s and 1840s.

The plate pictured is almost identical in both design and body to some hand-painted underglaze English wares, particularly those made by Adams from the 1850s on. The colors are red, blue, and green, with the "cut sponge" flowerets in purple. The same pattern was put out by Villeroy & Boch at Wallerfangen over a long period of time. Who copied whom is the question?

MACOMB POTTERY
See *Illinois Potters*

MADDOCK POTTERY
See *Lamberton China*

MAJOLICA

Majolica is a ware of such distinctive personality that people either like it very much or can't abide it; there's no halfway. This coarse and heavy earthenware, colorfully lead-glazed and design-molded, appeared on the ceramic scene about 1851. It took its name, though nothing else, from Maiorca, a tin-glaze ware made in fifteenth century Majorca—a ware too remote now for more than museum appreciation. (*See* Italian Maiolica.)

Victorians adored Majolica, and loaded their dining tables with colorful sardine dishes, decorated with fish; leaf-shaped relishes; ice cream platters, like straw hats tied with ribbons; oyster plates adorned with seaweed; pitchers and teasets in no end of imaginative shapes, from fish to cauliflower. There were Majolica urns in the parlor, umbrella stands in the hall, jardinieres in the conservatory.

Considering the quantity of Majolica made, surprisingly few potters marked their wares. In England, Wedgwood and George Jones were among those who did. In this country, Griffen, Smith and Hill at Phoenixville, Pennsylvania, marked their Etruscan Majolica (1870-1890), and D. F. Haynes at the Chesapeake Pottery in Baltimore marked his Avalon and Clifton wares. All marked pieces are considered choice.

Among other American companies to make Majolica were the Mayer Pottery Mfg. Co., Trenton, N.J.; Morrison & Carr, New York City; James Taft's Hampshire Pottery, Keene, N.H.; and George Morley & Sons, East Liverpool, Ohio.

By the early 1900s, Majolica had run its course. What little was produced after that, mostly for premium give-aways, was poorly made and pale in color. Rickerson's monograph, *Majolica, It's Fun to Collect,* is excellent for study. (*See:* Jones, George;

Clifton Ware; Chesapeake Pottery; Hampshire Pottery; Sarreguemines.)

The teapot and stand illustrated is finely modeled, but unmarked. It is a rich cobalt blue, the raised flowers are pink; foliage, twig handle, and twig rim of trivet in natural colors.

MARBLEHEAD POTTERY

With all the current excitement about American Art Pottery and everyone scurrying around to pick up lovely pieces before the prices rise and rise, you are going to run into many a backstamp you've never seen before and can't locate in any marks book available to date. One such may be that of the Marblehead Pottery—a sailing ship flanked by the initials "M" and "P". Not only is this pottery most attractive—some of it is quite elegant —but it has an unusual story. Dr. Herbert J. Hall, a physician in Marblehead, Massachusetts, started the project in 1904, as therapy for some of his patients. The work went so well in its experimental stages and the techniques in glazing and decoration developed so successfully that the pottery soon became a commercial venture as was the case with Arequipa. (*See* Arequipa.)

Arthur E. Baggs, a chemist, who had been the work supervisor of the pottery, purchased it in 1915. The usual products were vases, bowls, flower containers, teapots, candlesticks, and the like. The designs were simple; the colors, limited mainly to old blue, a tobacco brown, wisteria, soft yellows and greens and grays. Some pieces had incised outline decoration, sometimes they were molded, sometimes painted. Flowers, birds, little animals, fruit, and marine designs like seaweed and seashells were the common decorative motifs. The glaze most often used was a soft matt finish though some were semi-gloss. Their pitchers, with old ships in medallions painted on the sides were most attractive.

130

Unusual were the many "to order" pieces they made. They advertised that their "Experimental Department" was set up to take care of special orders and that they could make many "odd pieces not available elsewhere."

The pottery operated until 1936, and as it apparently did some business by mail order as well as through wholesale outlets, Marblehead pieces should show up almost anywhere in the country.

MARBLES

Through the ages schoolboys in spring have played with marbles, from the clay pellets of Ancient Egypt through the intricately spiralled glass marbles from nineteenth century Bavaria to present day glassies from the Five and Ten.

The height of marble production in Nurmberg, Bavaria, then the toy center of the world, was in the late 1870s and 1880s, when more than 100 varieties were being manufactured there—of different materials, different sizes, and different decorations. The "crockery" marbles were the common ones, the "commies." Made from clay, these were rolled into balls in the palms of the hands —little children often worked at this operation. They were dried a bit in the air, rolled again, then set on tiny 3-legged tripods in an oven to bake. Sometimes the tripod marks show darker than the rest. The usual colors, burnt on, were shades of blue, brown, and white. Sometimes a painted design was added.

While crockery marbles in themselves cause no great stir, every marble fancier wants a few of them to round out his collection. Year by year they are getting scarcer and scarcer.

MARIESBERG

See *Rorstrand*

MARTHA WASHINGTON "STATES" PATTERN

In the days of our early Republic, as in earlier times, the gentleman of the house took care of all purchases, including interior furnishings and decorations. Gifts of china or objects of art were presented to him rather than to his lady. So it was an event when Captain Vanbraam of the Dutch East India Company, a naturalized American citizen and a long-time friend of George Washington, presented Martha Washington with a forty-five piece set of china in 1795. He had had it made for her on one of his voyages to China, and it is a fine example of Oriental

Export ware. Pieces of the set are on display at Mount Vernon.

The design features the MW cypher and a gold sunburst, a green and gold chain about the border in whose fifteen links appear the names of the states then in the Union, and a blue snake, tail in mouth, encircling the rim. *Mount Vernon China,* a booklet published by the Mount Vernon Ladies Association and on sale at that mansion in Mount Vernon, Virginia, tells the complete story.

From time to time there have been reproductions of this pattern. The plate pictured (top) was authentically copied in porcelain from an original in the Smithsonian Institution by the Shenango China Company in New Castle, Pennsylvania in 1932. In limited edition, it was sponsored by the Quota Club International, Inc., to mark the George Washington Bicentennial. The history of the pattern is given on the back of the plate. Haviland & Company also brought out a limited edition in 1969.

An earlier reproduction was put out in 1876 for the Centennial Exposition in Philadelphia by Samson of Paris, and another in 1893 for the Chicago's World Fair by the same company. These imitated the original Oriental Export porcelain; the Shenango and Haviland plates copied the design on modern day porcelain.

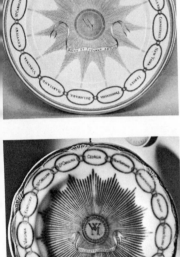

More familiar is the Flown Blue adaptation (also pictured) which appeared sometime in the nineteenth century, perhaps for the Centennial in 1876. It persisted for several decades and had wide distribution throughout the country. Some plates, in semiporcelain, were even given away as premiums by business concerns.

If you find one, check the backstamp. If no country of origin appears, you may assume it was made before 1891; if it is marked "England," it should date from 1891 to 1900; if "Made in England," it's after 1900. No country but England seems to have been involved with this Flown Blue adaptation. Potters seemed reluctant to stamp their names on these pieces, which could indicate that several of them used the same pattern. (*See:* Flown Blue; Oriental Export; Samson.)

MARTIN WARE

The Martin brothers of Fulham, England—there were four of them—produced some distinctive and artistic glazed stonewares, in designs classical and grotesque, from 1885 into the twentieth century. The pieces they fashioned with individual care and artistry are now being quietly collected in England where they are better known than in this country. Luckily a few pieces have strayed in this direction and for the moment are not outrageously expensive.

Robert, the eldest Martin, started the pottery in the converted stables of his parents' home in Fulham. He had previously worked for a stone cutter and for a sculptor and was the genius and mainstay of the business. Walter, the second brother, when he joined the enterprise at the age of fourteen, had already served a year or two at the Doulton factory as a color boy. By the time the other two boys were old enough to join their brothers—Edwin as decorator, and Charles as business manager—the premises were outgrown, and the whole family, with the pottery, moved to Southall. A showroom was opened at High Holborn, and the business prospered. It started its decline in 1912 when Charles died, and ended with the succeeding deaths of the other brothers.

The feeling that you get from Martin ware is that the potters must have enjoyed making it. The glazes they used were usually browns and stone colors—yellow, slate blue, gray-green. Decorations were often black and white sgraffito type. In their grotesque designs they tended toward the macabre, decorating their vases and jugs with hideous snakes and writhing creatures, and evil-omened flowers. Their long-beaked Martin birds, wild eyed and sinister, were their most popular figures. These often appeared as tobacco jars—just the thing for Papa's smoking room. The one pictured is typical. It is signed "R. W. Martin" and dated 1899.

The Martins were proud enough of their lively work to scratch their signature on most of it. The earliest pieces were marked "R. W. Martin, Fulham"; later ones, "Martin Bros. London and Southall."

MASON'S PATENT IRONSTONE

The formula for the Ironstone Charles James Mason of Lane Delph patented July 23, 1813, called for "slag of ironstone pounded and ground in water, in certain proportions, with flint, Cornwall stone and clay, and blue oxide of cobalt." The resulting chinaware was considerably heavier than porcelain, cheap, and durable. It lent itself well to copper engraving. Mason designs followed the earlier Oriental patterns and were characterized by the rich reds and blues of East Indian ware. Other manufacturers immediately brought out their own versions, or copied Mason's.

For forty years, the Mason family held the patents, then, in 1848, sold the business to Francis Morley, who continued to use the same molds and designs. When Morley retired in 1862, Geo. L. and Taylor Ashworth took over the firm. They, too, kept on using the best of Mason's patterns, continuing them into the twentieth century.

Since both Morley and the Ashworths not only used Mason's original molds and decoration but sometimes used the Mason name or the old Mason crown along with their own distinguishing marks, collectors should take special care to distinguish between the early Mason ware and later productions for there is a difference

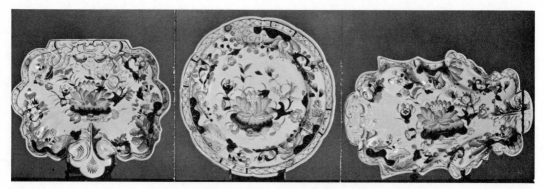

in the quality of the body and workmanship, and consequently in value. Godden's *Encyclopaedia of British Pottery and Porcelain Marks* is particuarly helpful in listing and dating the variations in marks.

McCOY POTTERY

The McCoy name is always turning up on attractive pottery to confuse collectors. Is it old or new? Ken Deibel, a collector from Dallas, Texas, tells us that the Nelson McCoy Pottery Company, Roseville, Ohio, was started on a small scale by Nelson McCoy, Sr., in 1910. He died in 1945 and his nephew, Nelson Melick, who had been in the business for twenty years, took over as president. When Mr. Melick died in 1954, Nelson McCoy, Jr., took his place. It became one of the largest artware manufacturers in the U. S. However, it was purchased by the Mount Clemens Pottery Co., Mount Clemens, Michigan, in 1967; Mr. Nelson McCoy, Jr. continues as president and general manager at the plant at Roseville, Ohio.

A marking in script may indicate the earlier pieces. Eventually the McCoy mark will disappear; all new items being produced are marked MCP, the initials of the new parent company.

There was, however, an earlier McCoy Pottery where several higher quality art lines were produced. Paul Evans, a West Coast collector and researcher, clears up any confusion. The J. W. McCoy Pottery, he tells us, was organized by James W. McCoy (Nelson's father) in 1899 in Roseville, Ohio. Among the art lines he produced were Mont Pelee, a dull black lava-type pottery with an occasional bright or iridescent spot (1902); a matt green art line of vases, jardinieres, cuspidors, fern dishes, and umbrella stands (1906); the Loy-Nel-Art line in standard brown glaze and in matt green with embossed or incised decoration (1908); and Navarre, from Owens molds (1912). George S. Brush had joined the firm in 1908 and in 1911 it became Brush-McCoy. McCoy's son, Nelson, had organized his own company the year before, and was making stoneware kitchen ware. He did not branch out into mass-produced artware until 1926. Both firms

134

were located in Roseville, and both prospered. Brush-McCoy continued with new art lines and also did a huge business in standard yellow cook ware and blue-banded yellow bowls. In 1925, the Brush-McCoy firm name was changed to the Brush Company. So today there are no McCoy firms in business. Though the later artwares of either company were rarely of high quality, they are attracting increased collector attention as mass-produced industrial artware.

The globe-shaped cookie jar pictured is from the Nelson McCoy Pottery. The mark is incised in script, and the plane used as a knob is the type in operation about 1948. The jar is ten inches high, brightly colored with turquoise blue oceans, red and yellow continents, and a gold standard.

MCINTYRE, JAMES & Co.

See: *Ivory China; Moorcroft*

McLAUGHLIN, MARY LOUISE

See *Losanti*

McNICOL, D. E. CO.

See *Calendar Plates*

MEADERS' POTTERY

See *Southern Highland Potteries*

MEDICINE SPOONS

See *Invalid Feeders*

MEISSEN PORCELAIN

Meissen porcelain, with its even, brilliant glaze, unsurpassed finish, and sharp, bright colors has ever held world-wide reputation for excellence and value. Produced by a process discovered by Johann Freidrich Bottger, under the patronage of August II Elector, it was first made in Dresden, Saxony, about 1708.

Later the factory moved to nearby Meissen, the place names giving the ware an interchangeable nomenclature.

The secret for making porcelain spread, and soon Meissen models were being copied by Sevres, Worcester, Bow, Chelsea, and Derby. In 1731, Meissen adopted as their distinctive mark the crossed electoral swords, to be placed on all their wares made for market. About this time, painted figure subjects and relief ornament became leading features.

The miniature chocolate pot pictured has lovely applied

flowers, leaves, and insects; it belongs to a set which consists of matching covered sugar, creamer, and four cups and saucers. (*See* Dresden.)

THE MERRIMAC CERAMIC COMPANY

In New England as in Ohio, a host of small art potteries came and went in the turn-of-the-century years. The Merrimac Ceramic Company of Newburyport, Massachusetts, established in 1897, was one of these, lasting but a short time and never reaching commercial proportions. The pottery marked its wares "Merrimac," and though its work was not particularly unusual, little enough of it was produced to make finding a piece a minor event for those who aim for a comprehensive collection of American art pottery.

METTLACH

During the French Revolution, the Abbey of Mediolacum (meaning "between the lakes," later shortened to Mettlach) in the Saar Basin, having weathered the vicissitudes of a thousand years and more, was plundered, the monks driven out and the lands confiscated.

In 1809, Eugene Francis Boch, who had learned potting in his father's establishment at Sept Fontaines, purchased the ruins and the lands from the government for the purpose of starting a pottery of his own. The area abounded in hard coal, and one of the government's conditions of sale was that Boch use hard coal in firing his kilns. This was an entirely new procedure, for up to then, wood firing was the accepted method. Boch developed the necessary techniques, and Mettlach became the first pottery in Europe to use coal firing. Nicholas Villeroy, whose pottery in nearby Wallerfangen had been busy since 1784, followed suit. The two men, in 1836, joined forces as Villeroy & Boch.

Mettlach attracted a great colony of capable workers. The company supplied housing, offered training in potting, and encouraged experimentation. It was a potter's paradise. By 1851, the Old Abbey was completely restored, and the company began to use the incised Old Tower trademark on their wares.

Steins and other stonewares with bas relief decoration were always the specialty of the house. In 1860, a ware called Chromolith was developed, in which the ornamentation was inlaid into the body of the articles in colored clays, giving the effect of cloisonne enamel work. At first this secret process was used only on steins, tankards, and chalices, but by the beginning of the twentieth century, it was being used for wall plaques, vases, punch bowls, jardinieres and pedestals, teasets, toilet sets, umbrella stands, and such. Tablewares in so-called "Inlaid Stone Ware" were introduced just before 1914 when Mettlach production was curtailed by the war.

Another Mettlach "first" was design print under glaze on stoneware from especially designed copper plates. This you'll find used for steins, too.

The Mettlach works were destroyed by fire in 1921, and production was never resumed. All records of the company were lost in the fire, but occasionally company catalogs come to light. One, for 1899, has been used as the basis of *Mettlach Steins and Their Prices,* a paperbound, by R. H. Mohr.

The 2½-litre stoneware wine Krug illustrated (numbered 2085 on the base) is buff color top and bottom, blue with white relief figures in the middle portion.

The Inlaid Stone Ware pieces were either terra cotta and sage green like the plate pictured or Delft blue and light tan on cream. The finish was matt. (*See* Villeroy & Boch.)

MILLINGTON, ASTBURY & PAULSON

See *Zouave Pitchers*

MINTON'S

Thomas Minton established a pottery at Stoke-on-Trent in 1793, having prudently purchased land in Cornwall with rich deposits of kaolin and Cornish stone from which he could draw raw materials—enough to keep him supplied for twenty years or more. About 1796 he began making his now famous porcelain.

Minton's early porcelains have been somewhat neglected by collectors. They were generally unmarked and, more often than not, were attributed to some other maker—Coalport, Derby, Swansea, or Worcester. Minton's finest early decorators—Thomas Steel, Joseph Bancroft, and George Hancock—had formerly worked at Derby. Minton himself had been an engraver for Spode and Wedgwood. Add to that, Minton's copied the Dresden crossed swords mark on some of its finest floral encrusted pieces. It was enough to confuse anyone.

Happily the present existence of several early factory pattern books enables accurate identifications. In his *Illustrated Encyclopaedia of British Pottery and Porcelain,* Geoffrey Godden shows several pages from the pattern books and illustrations, some in color, of pieces correctly identified from them. He promises, soon, a book or two (now in preparation) devoted exclusively to Minton's wares of the pre-1850s and the post-1850s. After 1862, all Minton's wares were clearly marked; Godden's *Encyclopaedia of British Pottery and Porcelain Marks* lists Minton's works chronologically.

Not only was Minton's famous for its porcelain, but also for its majolica, its Parian, and its pâte-sur-pâte (*see* Solon, Marc Louis), and its bone china. The story of Minton's current output is told in Alberta C. Trimble's *Modern Porcelain* where many of its presently procurable patterns are pictured. (*See* Indian Tree pattern.)

The Minton washbowl and pitcher, pictured, in early Ironstone, resembles closely the Imari-type decoration used on Mason's Patent Ironstone wares. Orange and cobalt blue are the predominating colors.

MOCHA WARE

Mocha ware belongs to the banded creamware family which was originated in England in the late 1790s, most likely by Benjamin Adams of Greengates. Banded creamware was thin and light, with bands of orange and other bright colors top and bottom. Mocha ware had decoration added between the bands—incredibly feathery ferns and lacy trees and seaweeds. No design exactly duplicated another—each was as individual as an ink blot.

The ware took its name from its resemblance to moss agate from Mocha in Arabia, where coffee comes from. One early method of obtaining this airy design was, after the ground color had been laid and was still moist, to turn the piece upside down, dot it at intervals with a brown color evolved of tobacco, printer's ink, and water, and let the dots dribble.

Many potters made Mocha—and made it right up to 1914. Early pieces included mugs with strap handles and foliated ends, pitchers, pepper pots, bowls, covered dishes, and occasionally teapots and cups and saucers.

After 1840, Mocha ware became heavier in body, white in color rather than cream, and with round handles instead of strap handles. Some English authorities will tell you it was made only in England. They must never have heard that Edwin Bennett, around 1850, was making Mocha ware, with bands of crudely spattered slip, in Baltimore, Maryland, U. S. A.

The Mocha mug illustrated has a tan ground and varicolored bandings; and is decorated with rooted "seaweed." It is English, ca. 1830.

MOONLIGHT LUSTRE

Moonlight Lustre is one of the names given a style of overglazed decoration for pearlware in which pink, gray, brown, and other color stains were combined to form a splashed-gold marbled effect. The result, in which pink, purple, and ruby are the predominating colors, is exceedingly rich and glowing.

While various potters in the early 1800s, exploiting the new lustering process invented by John Hancock at the Turner potteries at Lane End, produced their own versions of this ware, none made it as extensively nor with greater artistry, nor so meticulously marked as did the Wedgwood firm, at that time headed by Josiah Wedgwood II. The best of Wedgwood's Moonlight Lustre was produced between 1805 and 1820; Josiah II, himself, called it "Holy-door marble."

Collectors of Wedgwood, as well as collectors of lustre, like to have at least one example of this type ware. Since several potteries, including Spode whose splashed pink lustre came out slightly before Wedgwood's, Wood & Caldwell, and Shorthose and Company, were all making similar pieces at the same time, it would be unwise to attribute a piece to Wedgwood unless it is impressed with the Wedgwood factory mark.

Much of this Wedgwood ware is now in museums or in private collections, but there are enough occasional pieces about to keep a determined seeker on the *qui vive*. This is not a decoration that takes kindly to soap and water, so if you are fortunate enough to own a piece or two, wash it gently and infrequently—eschewing soap and detergents. Bright sunlight fades it, too. The cabinet is the place for it. *Old English Lustre Pottery,* by John & Baker has a chapter on it.

The illustration shows a Wedgwood pearlware Moonlight Lustre potpourri jar, with perforated inner lid, ca. 1810, from the Buten Museum of Wedgwood, Merion, Pa.

MOORCROFT

Moorcroft pottery, originated in 1913 by the late William Moorcroft in Burslem, England, is still being made by his son, Walter Moorcroft. This ware, while hardly antique, is true hand work—thrown on the potter's wheel, then decorated. The exceptionally high temperature at which the colors are fired give it unusual brilliance. An early advertising folder announces Moorcroft's appointment as Potter to Her Majesty Queen Mary, and notes that its tableware "is found in Royal households and many of the finest homes in the world."

The mark MOORCROFT/BURSLEM, impressed or printed, was used from the beginning. The W. Moorcroft signature was registered as a trademark in 1919, though it had been previously used on articles decorated by William Moorcroft when he worked at James Mcintyre & Co., Ltd., (Mcintyre, since 1928, has been making only electrical wares.) Walter Moorcroft continues the same signature mark, and also uses the painted initials W. M., both in addition to the printed mark MOORCROFT/MADE IN ENGLAND.

MORAVIAN POTTERY

The pottery made by the Moravians at their Watchovia Settlement in Salem, North Carolina, is something to know about even if you never see a piece outside of a museum. It is a slip-decorated redware, puzzling because its decoration does not fit in with concepts of Pennsylvania German ware of the same type. In fact, the pottery the Moravians made is more closely related in decoration to the styles and traditions of northern Italy than to any other European locale.

The Moravians were originally from Bohemia, followers of the Great Reformer, John Huss. They got into Germany when they were seeking religious refuge and were given haven on the extensive estate of Count Zinzendorf. From there, the Count, converted to their missionary philosophy, led the band to William Penn's colony in Pennsylvania where he founded Bethlehem and Lititz.

In 1766, some of his followers migrated to North Carolina to found the Watchovia Settlement in Salem. They developed a considerable craft center there, where silverware, pewter, iron-work, furniture, and clocks were fabricated as well as their distinctive pottery. Pottery production ceased about 1830. Examples of all their crafts are to be seen at the present restoration, Old Salem, Inc., and anyone interested in Moravian pottery is urged to study the exhibits there.

MORAVIAN POTTERY & TILE WORKS

Dr. Henry Chapman Mercer founded this factory in Doylestown, Pennsylvania, in 1898, and began making decorative wall tiles. This was a studio operation and the handmade tiles produced there—Dr. Mercer designed them all—ranked with the best in the field. They came to decorate such diverse structures as the Capitol in Harrisburg, Pennsylvania, Mrs. Jack Gardner's Palace in Boston, Massachusetts, hotels in Cairo, Egypt, and the gambling casino at Monte Carlo. Except for the name and Mercer's first tile designs, inspired by old Moravian stove plates, his richly colored, matt-finished tiles had little in common with the pottery made by early Moravians in Pennsylvania and North Carolina. Dr. Mercer died in 1930; the factory was continued for a decade or more by his assistant. Now, as the Mercer Museum, operated by the Bucks County Commission, it is well worth visiting as an example of an early 20th century industry and for the handsome tilework incorporated in the building.

MORTAR AND PESTLES

Often overlooked among Josiah Wedgwood's showier contributions to the ceramic world are his utilitarian innovations. Not the least of these are his hard porcelain mortars and pestles still in use today.

The mortar and pestle was known to primitive man, and from the time of written history has been associated with pharmacies. Descriptions of sixteenth century pharmacies show a great array of mortars in various sizes, used for the grinding of herbs and powders. While the larger sizes were made usually of bronze, often intricately carved, smaller sizes might be of marble, agate, or glass as well as metal. Some were of lignum vitae. No one seems to have thought of using stoneware or porcelain for this purpose until about 1780 when Joseph Priestly, the English chemist, proposed the idea to his friend Josiah Wedgwood.

In the Wedgwood and Bentley catalog of 1799, hard porcelain mortars and pestles, listed along with inkstands and eye cups, presented Priestly's argument: "The Mortars will be of great Use of Chymists, Experimental Philosophers and Apothecaries, as well as for Culinary Purposes; not being liable like metals or marble to be corroded by Acids or other Chemical Menstrum."

So correct was Priestly in his thinking, and so sensible was Wedgwood in the mortars he devised that the same type is being made today, some by the present Wedgwood company, some by other concerns. Over the years, the "Wedgwood mortar" has become a generic term, and when U. S. State Boards require pharmacies to have in possession from one to three sizes of "Wedgwood mortars," as many State Boards do, they are specifying the type, not necessarily ones made by the Wedgwood firm. Any comprehensive collection of mortars and pestles should contain at least one of the Wedgwood-type, preferably an old one bearing the Wedgwood mark.

The mortar and pestle illustrated, which is only 1⅜ inches

tall, is one reputed to have been made by Wedgwood for Joseph Priestly in 1779. It is now in the Buten Museum of Wedgwood, Merion, Pa.

MOSAIC TILE COMPANY

The Mosaic Tile Company of Zanesville, Ohio, was organized in 1894 by Herman Mueller and Karl Langenbeck who had been working together at the American Encaustic Tiling Company. This company, too, became large and prosperous, vying with the American Encaustic as the world's largest tile producer. Like its rival, Mosaic made handsome tiles for floors and walls and also indulged in a long list of novelties. Bookends, statuettes of dogs and buffalo, cigarette boxes, and the like are to be found—some of them advertising pieces. Happily both tile and novelties are marked with the Mosaic name and trademark. To look for particularly are the 3½-inch hexagonal portrait tiles made during the World Way I era. There were four of them—Woodrow Wilson, Abraham Lincoln, William McKinley, and a Pilgrim Father—the heads in white relief on a Wedgwood blue ground. Tile pictured is from *Baby's Own Opera* set. (*See* American Encaustic Tiling Co.)

MOSS AZTEC

In 1897, when Samuel Weller deserted his flowerpot business in Zanesville, Ohio, to manufacture artwares, two of his former workmen, John Peters and Adam Reed, took it up. They prospered and in 1901 were incorporated as Peters and Reed. About 1905, they, too, took a turn at artware and hired Frank Ferrell who had been with Weller as designer and salesman. He stayed with them two years before he moved on to Owens. For Peters and Reed he developed a pine cone design, "made of reddish clay with raised design, sprayed with green paint which was then wiped off from embossings and backgrounds." This was an adaptation of the pine cone design he had made for Weller who had turned it down and which Roseville later used so successfully. The same technique was used for other patterns, too, and was called "Moss Aztec."

In 1920, Harry S. McClelland bought Peters' stock and changed the name to Zane Pottery. Moss Aztec was continued in production and sold well until 1926, when they changed from reddish-brown clay to white. Mr. McClelland died in 1931. His widow, Mrs. Mabel McClelland, ran the business until 1941, when she sold it to Lawton Gonder; he operated as Gonder Ceramic Arts until 1957.

MOSS ROSE

See *Wheeling Pottery Co.*

142

MOUNT CLEMENS POTTERY CO.

See *McCoy Pottery*

MUSTACHE CUPS

Beards and mustaches became the style for American men along in the mid-1800s. Up to that time, except for the earliest explorers and settlers, men were clean-shaven. None of the signers of the Declaration of Independence and none of the Presidents until Lincoln wore either beard or mustache. But the mid-1800s were rugged times and men chose to look in tune. Mustaches came in with the military during the Mexican War, the beard with the Gold Rush. Men of all walks of life succumbed to the vogue which lasted some thirty-five years. By 1885, the beard was on its way out; the mustache lingered into the 1890s.

There were certain disadvantages to the mustache, especially at meals; and the mustache cup, with a bar across the top, came along to keep it out of the coffee. There were mustache spoons, too, and mustache glasses, all designed for the purpose of keeping that hirsute ornament neat and tidy.

Mustache cups, common a few years ago, are harder to find today, and correspondingly higher in price. Most of them were very fancy, particularly those of the 1890s. Some have applied flowers and much gold, some have raised lettering, like "Remember Me," some are elaborately hand-painted—all of them types of decoration which seem to indicate they were not cups the men bought for themselves, but were rather presented them by doting females who like things shipshape.

The mustache cup pictured was given to her father for Christmas in 1879, by a little girl in Springvale, Maine: it cost a quarter. Though it is just about as plain as they come, it is bright and gay. The cup and saucer are a bright green; the medallion, yellow set on white, shows a hand-painted young lady with birds in her blue hat.

NANKIN CHINA

See *Canton*

NANTGARW

The short-lived Nantgarw (pronounce it Nantigrew) China Works in Nantgarw, Glamorgan, Wales (1811-1814 and 1817-1822), was owned by William Billingsley, the flower painter of Derby and Swansea porcelains, and his son-in-law, George Walker. They made a fine translucent porcelain, and among their productions was a service for King George IV—"the pattern was a green vase and a single rose on every piece, and every rose different." From this, one will readily perceive the skill and artistry of the painter Billingsley and the grade of china produced.

The marks used at Nantgarw were impressed in the body of the china. NANT-GARW, and underneath, "C. W." for "China Works" (some pieces have been found with "China Works" written out) and also the word "Nantgarw" in red. The initials sometimes have been read as "G. W.," and assumed to stand for George Walker, though no pieces have turned up with the name spelled out.

Nantgarw pieces are, of course, collector items—and choice ones. For illustrations of various pieces and further study, see *The Pottery and Porcelain of Swansea and Nantgarw,* by E. M. Nance (1942) and *Nantgarw Porcelain,* by W. D. John (1948).

The superb quality 10-inch plate pictured is impressed, "Nant-garw, C. W." It dates about 1820, and is now in the Victoria and Albert Museum collection in London. Ornate Nantgarw wares like this are believed to have been sold in the white to London decorators who painted them to city tastes.

NAPKIN RINGS

Napkin rings came on the American scene about 1860, and by 1865, seem to have been in fairly high demand. By 1880, extremely elaborate ones were being made, and by 1890, you'd look a long way to find a dinner table set without an individual ring for each member of the family. Most of them were of silver or silver plate, including the fancy novelties. A few were of glass, either cut or pressed; fewer still were of china, late comers to the fashion.

Still there are enough china napkin rings about to make a search for them worth while; even today they dress a family table in an unusual and attractive manner. You will find more of porcelain or bone china than you will of earthenware; many will be hand painted, sometimes by amateurs, sometimes at the factory. Some will be conventionally round, others oval in shape; some will be made in Germany, some at Limoges, some in this country, some in Japan. Decorations are usually delicate and refined in a manner suited to the fine napery of the cut glass, silver, and Haviland era. We've never seen an "un-pretty" one yet. But we have seen a Staffordshire number with a little Kate Greenaway girl sitting atop. That's one to look for!

The napkin ring illustrated is unmarked, but probably German; "Souvenir of Florida" is inscribed on the back. The color is orange, with applied white orange blossoms and green leaves.

NAST A PARIS

Besides numerous pieces of his porcelain, for which Nast is best known, the Louvre in Paris owns a piece of his bisque, *L'Amour et les Graces;* he is represented at the Victoria and Albert Museum in London by a graceful basin and ewer; in this country, cups and saucers with his signature are to be seen at Mt. Vernon among George and Martha Washington's effects.

The porcelain manufactory of Jean Neponucene Herman Nast, on the rue de Popincourt in Paris, between 1785 and 1817, turned out richly decorated table services, toilet articles, covered cups, bowls, boxes, and the like. His porcelain was of extreme whiteness, and his decorations, following the popular style of the day, were chiefly remarked by delicate sprig patterns, exquisite flowers, and graceful borders. Rumor, quite unfounded, has it that he designed the cornflower pattern he used so often, and which was widely copied, for Marie Antoinette, whose favorite flower it was.

Many of his pieces are unmarked; those which are, bear "Nast a Paris" in red or black, or the letter "N."

NAUGHTIES AND POTTIES

Along in the late 1800s and continuing into the 1900s, there was a slight flurry of naughty bisques, when innumerable figurines of children, puppy dogs, and pussy cats, seated on chamber pots, were cheaply made and cheaply sold as souvenirs at fairs, bazaars, and other such festivities. Sometimes the potty was used alone, usually in china, decorated with ribald sayings in the bottom.

More elaborate bisques were less obvious, but slightly more risque. The example pictured, for example, is a turtle-shaped box with lady's head and feet. Remove the cover, and the lady's bare bottom is exposed. Another version of this turtle lady shows her

with the exposed parts covered with a "Teddy Bear," a pun in bisque which helps to date the fun.

Earlier examples of this trend include the glazed pottery Victorian trinket boxes whose covers showed "naughty" scenes—there is one with figures of a man and woman crawling into bed with the notation "Last one in bed, turn out the light."

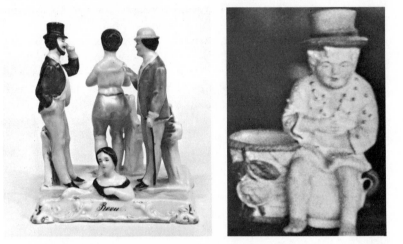

These examples of questionable taste of all periods have been gathered by collectors over the years until they are no longer particularly easy to find. The bisques are still inexpensive when they do show up. The Staffordshire-type naughties which have long been in the same price range as other elaborate Victorian trinket boxes are now moving sky high. A rare one, previously unrecorded, titled "Review," showing two men ogling two women bathers, brought close to $2,000 at a 1973 sale at Christie's in London!

NAUTILUS PORCELAIN

See *Gossware*

NEWCASTLE POTTERY

Early in the nineteenth century, the Newcastle Pottery in Northumberland was as well known as the potteries at Leeds and Liverpool. Here was made a good, low-cost earthenware which looked a bit like Leeds, and was often transfer-printed like Liverpool wares. For some reason unknown, the name did not linger in memory. Now comparatively few people recognize it at all, and Newcastle wares are variously attributed to Leeds, or to Liverpool, or to Wedgwood whom they imitated to the extent of marking some of their wares "Wedgewood," trusting that extra middle "e" to fool the centuries.

Printed earthenware mugs seem to have been a Newcastle specialty; at least, more accurately marked mugs have turned up than any other type of vessel made there. Two in the Brighton Museum are pictured in Godden's *Encyclopaedia of British Pottery and Porcelain;* one laments Nelson's death in 1805; the other shows the Duke of York and Mrs. Clarke "Burning the books of Curious Arts," ca. 1809.

The one we show in illustration is the exterior of the Frog Mug pictured under that heading. Ca. 1798, of creamware, transfer-printed, it is clearly marked Newcastle Pottery. The legend on its face records a timely event: "A South East View of the STUPENDOUS Iron Bridge built over the River Weare at Sunderland by Rd. BURDON, Esq. M. P. Begun 24 Sep 1793. Opened 9 August 1796." A harmless looking mug for a frog to hide in, wouldn't you say?

NEWCOMB POTTERY

Newcomb Pottery is Louisiana's own, established in 1897 by women art students at Sophie Newcomb College in New Orleans (now part of Tulane University). The clay they used came from St. Tammany's Parish, and the natural designs they chose to decorate their experimental wares were straight from the Deep South—magnolia, jasmine, cypress, long-leafed pine, and the like.

Though the pottery operated only as a studio, its wares were distributed through agents all over the country. You do not have to live in Louisiana to find a piece of this hand-thrown ware, incised and molded by hand in the appearance of low relief. The glaze is generally a distinctive "Newcomb" blue, actually a combination blue-green, with designs in contrasting shades of yellow, white, and pink. Most of the pieces were matt finished. Some used a semi-transparent "misty" glaze. High gloss glazes were used only before 1910; these are the hardest to find today. All pieces are well marked.

The studio closed in 1940. The Newcomb Guild, established that same year to supplant it, closed operations in 1952.

Lucile Henzke's *American Art Pottery,* gives satisfying Newcomb details.

The vase illustrated, from Mrs. Henzke's collection, is 6 inches tall; the decoration, believed to be by Sadie Irvine, though unsigned, shows moonlight through trees bowed down with Spanish moss.

NIDERVILLER

A faience factory was started about 1754 in Niderviller, in the French department de la Meurthe, not far from Luneville.

Factories in both towns began by making faience. About 1765, Niderviller decided to produce hard paste porcelain, and with the assistance of Paul Louis Cyffle of the Luneville factory, who was a celebrated modeler, produced some fine examples.

Some years later, one of Cyffle's artists, Charles Gabriel Sauvage (called Lemire), left Luneville to work at Niderviller, and it is for the fine biscuit porcelain figures he made there that Niderviller is remembered. There was nothing outstanding about their porcelain dinnerwares nor the faience which they never stopped producing, but Sauvage's biscuit porcelains were exceptional.

Several changes of ownership and corresponding changes in marks took place between the time the factory opened and when it closed around 1830. It is not likely you'll need to bother with remembering marks, for Niderviller is museum material, especially the figures.

The biscuit porcelain statuette, pictured here, is attributed to Charles Sauvage Lemire and Niderviller. It commemorates the signing, in 1776, of the treaties of commerce and alliance between France and America against Britain, in which France recognized America's new independence. Louis XVI and Benjamin Franklin are the participants. The Metropolitan Museum in New York now owns it. (*See* Luneville.)

NILOAK POTTERY

Between 1910 and 1946, while the Niloak Pottery existed, a steady stream of tourists stopped off in the little Ozark town of Benton, Arkansas, to watch the potters at work and to bring home as souvenirs swirl-patterned bowls, vases, pitchers, and novelties molded from the multi-colored native clays.

Charles Dean "Bullet" Hyten first saw the potting possibilities in the vari-colored clays of Saline County's hills and began experimenting with them. By mixing different colored clays in layers, then letting the centrifugal force of the potter's wheel do its work, he produced an unusual artware, depending for decoration on the soft natural browns, blues, and reds of the native clay. No two pieces were just alike.

For his method of using clays, he obtained a U.S. Patent, and his hand-thrown, hand-finished ware, called Niloak's Mission Pottery, was marked with the patent number and an art-lettered "Niloak" from September 1910 on. Niloak, by the way, is "kaolin" spelled backwards.

At its peak, Niloak produced an annual 75,000 pieces, with six potters, including Hyten, working. Prices ranged from 50 cents to $50, depending on the size and intricacy of the piece. Since there were sales outlets all over the United States and Canada, as well as thousands of souvenir-toting tourists, there's no telling where anyone may come across a Niloak novelty, smoking set, umbrella stand, even a clock.

To keep the factory going during the Depression, Mr. Hyten introduced a line of castware, glazed in various high glazes and semi-matt finishes in solid and drip colors. This less expensive ware was called "Hywood," and was first marked "Hywood/Niloak." After the factory changed hands in the mid-1930s, the Niloak name alone was used. The Mission ware was discontinued in 1942; in 1946 the pottery closed.

The Niloak Mission ware vase pictured, in browns, cream, and blue with a waver of pink, is from the collection of the Frank R. Smiths, who were among Niloak visitors from Maryland in the 1920s.

Hyten also operated the Eagle Pottery, a few miles north of Benton, which his father had operated before him. Here he made commercial stoneware—jugs, crocks, churns, flowerpots, and such. This was an entirely separate concern, but was continued by Mr. Hyten into the late 1930s.

NIPPON

Nippon, which appears in the backstamp of so much Japanese china of the last seventy-five years, is not the name of the manufacturer, but of the country of origin. It means "Japan," from the Japanese name Nihon, which is approximated in English by "Nippon."

There were many china manufactories operating in Japan in the last quarter of the nineteenth century, and more by the beginning of the twentieth. After 1891, when it was obligatory to include the country of origin in the backstamp, "Nippon" appeared, often with, but sometimes without, the Japanese trademark of the maker. "Japan" was officially substituted for "Nippon" after 1921.

A stepped-up movement toward china for export, particularly to the United States, began about 1875. *An Illustrated Catalogue of the Japanese Exhibits at the Foreign Exhibition in Boston, Massachusetts*, in 1883, lists the porcelain factories which displayed their wares. Among them were Koransha, in Arita; Hizen, reorganized in 1875, making Imari ware; Seiji Kuaisha, also in Arita, also recently reorganized, and also working in the Japanese style; Kiriu Kosho Kuarsha, of Tokio (The First Japanese Manufacturing and Trading Co.) which had established a wholesale and retail branch in New York City in 1877, importing from its own factories in Japan; T. Nobata, Yokohama, who manufactured and decorated "new" Satsuma and Makudsu ware at his own factory, as well as decorating plain pottery from Satsuma and from the Ota factory where Makudsu ware was made; and Matsushima-Ya, Imura & Co., of Yokohama, established in 1874,

who decorated porcelain with mineral colors in imitation of old wares.

Nippon Toki Kaisha began making Noritake china in 1904 in Nagoya. Other, lesser-known companies were springing up all about to take care of the American trade, for around the turn of the century colorful Japanese china was very popular here, particularly the hand-painted pieces which were less expensive than similar pieces from Germany and Austria. The Japanese touch that crept into the decoration added to its piquancy. Chocolate sets, cups and saucers, tea plates, hatpin holders, nut dishes, and other small novelties sold like hot cakes at summer resorts, particularly at beaches and boardwalks.

These wares are suddenly becoming popular again, after a rest of nearly fifty years. Collectors, unable to decipher the manufacturer's mark if there is one, seem content to class them all as "Nippon," and to judge individual pieces, not by maker, but on their own merit. Some of the pieces are exceptionally well done, and with the number of factories involved, there is a great variety of "Nippon" to choose from.

The hand-painted Nippon vase illustrated is quite handsome with its white, green, yellow and pink flowers and raised gold trim. Though the maker put his mark, a maple leaf, on the base along with "Nippon," he is unidentified. (*See* Noritake.)

NODDERS

Two centuries ago, in the marts, shops, and cubicles of London, collectors were going wild over Chinese porcelains as made at Meissen or Dresden, at certain new factories along the Thames, and in France. Pagods were their chief quest—grotesque Buddhas, Gods, and patron Saints of the Celestial Empire, all exquisitely fashioned in the Chinese taste and style, and cunningly fitted together so the heads would nod and the hands gesticulate.

So, from the Chinese originals, used in temple, palace, and home shrines, came the European porcelain replicas—the Pagods, which we call Nodders.

From these early and elegant examples—the one pictured was made at Meissen, modeled by J. T. Kaendler, ca. 1735—the nodders moved on through smaller and daintier figures in porcelain and bisque, sometimes Oriental in feeling, sometimes not, to reach a culmination in nodding papier mache grotesques and caricatures used in shop windows of the 1880s, and children's toys in the 1890s.

NORITAKE

Noritake china was first produced in 1904. The manufacturer was Nippon Toki Kaisha, and the location of the factory was at Nagoya, Japan. The company is still in operation, still making excellent popular-priced dinner sets, as well as incidentals. One of the early dinnerware patterns, no longer in production, is "Azalea." For some years, the Larkin soap company included dinner sets in this pattern on their premium lists; it was sold in stores, too, and was extremely popular. Pieces of "Azalea" are not particularly easy to find these days, for many people who "remember Mama's" are collecting it.

Noritake China will be marked "Noritake," sometimes with "Nippon" as the country of origin, sometimes with "Japan." Nippon should never be considered synonymous with Noritake, a popular misconception. (*See* Nippon.)

The old Noritake dinnerware patterns illustrated have very American names: Sandra, Roselace, and Colby.

NORTON POTTERY

See *Bennington*

NOVE FAIENCE

See *Faience*

NURSING BOTTLES

See *Invalid Feeders*

OBERAMMERGAU PLATES

See *Easter Plates*

OCCUPATIONAL SHAVING MUGS

Occupational shaving mugs appeared on barber shop racks in the 1880s. Men in all walks of life took pride in their personal mugs and carefully selected from the barber's supply catalog the design they wanted painted on them to represent their callings. Doctors, dentists, draymen, undertakers, railroad brakemen, even tobacco packers had stock designs to choose from. Come-lately occupations like telephone engineers and "typewriters" required special orders.

The mugs, of heavy white china, were for the most part imported from France or Germany, then decorated in shops in New York or Chicago where armies of artists stenciled names in gold and either made freehand occupational designs or added freehand flourishes to decals. Orders came in from all over the country.

Eventually sanitary regulations removed the shaving mug from the barber shop, and the electric razor supplanted its use at home. Now it's a collectible, and a haughty one, too. (*See* Shaving Soap Boxes.)

The "typewriter" shaving mug, pictured, is marked "TV/Limoges," and is signed by the artist, V. Price.

In 1953 and 1954, the John Hudson Moore Company, purveyors of men's toiletries, put out their line of Sportsman shaving soap in old style shaving mugs with occupational designs. There were at least twenty-two occupations represented, and at an additional charge, the owner's name could be added in gold. Most of the mugs have "Sportsman" incised in the base; some repeat the mark in gold and add a flying mallard. Others carry the John Hudson Moore name or that of their successor, the Lambert Company. We are told the pottery which made them is out of business and the molds have long since been destroyed. While Sportsman mugs are finely done and can be considered collectible, they are not in the class with the truly old occupational shaving mugs and should not command anywhere near as high prices. (*See* Shaving Soap Boxes.)

OHIO POTTERY CO.

See: *Calendar Plates; Limoges*

OLD PARIS

Old Paris porcelains embrace the wares of many minor

china manufactories and independent potters in Paris and the close suburbs, which sprang up in considerable numbers from 1760 on. Some lasted but a short time, others for several years. Many of the owners of these small factories, particularly in the earlier period, had served apprenticeship with Sevres, and their pieces show charm and excellence in workmanship.

Sometimes a maker's mark is found under the glaze, but most of these potters did not identify themselves with their wares.

The dish shown was made about 1830 by the pottery Schoelcher. It is transfer printed, a decoration on Paris porcelain credited to an innovation by Christopher Potter at the Rue de Crussol Works, ca. 1790. Potter was an Englishman who had probably learned transfer-printing at Liverpool. The hard-paste china he made in Paris, he called *Prince de Jalles* or Prince of Wales.

OLD SLEEPY EYE

Sometime, somewhere, if you keep your antiques eye open, you'll come across a piece of rather common-type pottery, white or buff, decorated in cobalt blue with an embossed Indian head, tents and trees or cattails and waterlilies. Most likely the piece you find will be a pitcher, though it may be a mug, or a vase, or a sugar bowl, perhaps a cuspidor. It will probably be marked "WSWC/Monmouth/Ill.," for the Western Stoneware Company, if it bears any mark at all.

The Indian has a gash across one eye—in some pieces it shows more than in others. He is Old Sleepy Eye, and in the earlier pieces, his name may appear in the design.

Old Sleepy Eye whose Indian name, Ishtaba, meant Eyelid Drooping, was born in Minnesota near the present site of Mankato. He belonged to the Lower Sisseton Sioux of the Chansdachikana band, and between 1820 and 1825, he was made a chief. As such, he signed the treaties of Praire du Chien in 1825, St. Peters in 1836, and Traverse des Sioux in 1851. He died at the age of 80 while visiting in Roberts County, South Dakota.

The town of Sleepy Eye, Minnesota, was founded in 1872 on the shores of the lake where the old chief spent most of his life. (About 1910, his bones were brought back to the town and a monument erected over them. It still stands, down near the railroad depot.) The Sleepy Eye Flour Mill (1880s-1921) was the industry of the town. At its peak this was one of the largest flour mills in the country, and souvenirs advertising it were legion. The Sleepy Eye pitchers were among them. These were put right into the sacks of flour until the U. S. Government, contending pitchers were cheaper than an equal weight of flour, called a halt.

The first of these pitchers—they came in five sizes—were made by the Weir Pottery Company of Monmouth, Illinois. In

1906, six potteries, the Weir Company among them, combined to form the Western Stoneware Company. The new firm continued to make Old Sleepy Eye items off and on for general sale until 1937. A production run in 1952 was made on two sizes of steins, in an allover chestnut glaze rather than in the usual cobalt blue. The Western Stoneware Company is still in business in Monmouth.

Old Sleepy Eye pieces are *not* found in museums, but in antiques marts, in second-hand stores, in country kitchens, and private collections. They are not at all rare, nor particularly old; they were cheaply made. Yet they have two things collectors favor: they have personality and meaning—and they are scarce enough to make hunting for them fun.

OMAR KHAYYAM POTTERY

When O. L. Bachelder of the Omar Khayyam Pottery at Candler, Buncombe County, North Carolina, died in 1935, he had been making pottery for more than sixty years and had achieved national recognition among American ceramists. His pottery was carefully modeled, hard, strong, and finished with excellent glazes which he had worked out through long experimentation. He had two kick-wheels and two kilns.

As an individualist he was unconcerned with mass production. Even if his work itself had not been so outstanding, his attitude toward it and his feeling as an artist and craftsman as expressed in a statement he made upon opening his pottery at Candler is enough to make one long to own a piece. He said:

"Here we have come and in the virgin forest and the fields of the mountains have builded our home and our shop. Nature had provided at our door a fine clay, richly impregnated with mineral oxides, which produces a pottery of great beauty. The ever-changing and shifting colors of the mountains in this Land of the Sky seem to have found expression in the many colored shapes produced. Commercial methods of rapid production and duplication are ignored. Each piece produced is a work of loving care. The potter's wheel, ancient of days, the head, a pair of hands, and a small piece of wood for smoothing are the only tools and in our kilns the various shapes are fired."

We have no illustration of any of Mr. Bachelder's pieces, but Allen H. Eaton, in his *Handicraft of the Southern Highlands* (1937) compares his work with that of Mr. W. B. Stephens, some of whose pieces are illustrated here under Pisgah Forest Pottery. Mr. Eaton considered the Bachelder pieces superior.

ORIENTAL EXPORT PORCELAIN

Chinese Export Porcelain, or China Trade Porcelain, as

well as Oriental Export Porcelain are the names now accepted for the ware which, until quite recently, went under the poorly conceived name of Oriental Lowestoft. It was made in quantity in China in the 1700s and early 1800s, and richly decorated to special order after designs sent out from the West. American market pieces bore such patriotic designs as eagles, Armorial devices, monograms, or cyphers, as well as Biblical scenes, floral designs, even pictures copied from engravings.

Armorial and presentation pieces are most eagerly sought by collectors.

Cups and saucers, plates, tureens, tea caddys, and platters in wide variety are still to be found, though most of the choicest pieces have already been gathered into collections, many in museums. (*See* Martha Washington States Pattern.)

For further reading and handsome pictures to look at: *Chinese Export Porcelain for the American Trade, 1785-1835,* by Mudge, and *China Trade Porcelain,* by Phillips.

The elephant candlestick illustrated is unusual. He is grayish-beige flecked with green, and very fierce of eye. Trappings and candlestick feature yellow and green. The Armorial cup and saucer are more typical.

"ORIENTAL STONE"

See *Flown Blue*

OTT & BREWER

See *American Belleek*

OVERBECK POTTERY

Four Overbeck sisters, Margaret, Elizabeth, Mary, and Hannah, established the Overbeck Pottery in their house in Cambridge City, Indiana, in 1910. It continued until the last sister's death in 1955. They made functional jars, dinnerware, and tiles, and decorative figurines, bowls, and vases. Each piece was unique, and a great many were commissioned. One collector had them model statuettes of his parents in their favorite chairs with the family dog at their feet.

Hannah, it seems, was the principal designer; Elizabeth was the technician; and Mary did chiefly designing and glazing. Margaret, who was the instigator and inspiration, died shortly after the pottery was started.

Though the brown glazes of Rookwood, Weller, and Roseville were immensely popular at the time they worked, the Overbecks preferred to use soft blending colors—blue, turquoise, dove gray, and other soft colors. Their most characteristic glaze was a semi-matt; often in two harmonizing shades of the same hue. Glaze inlay in combination with incising and carving was the usual decoration. The pottery mark is the monogram OBK with the initials of both designer and potter.

Examples are on exhibit at the Cambridge City Public Library. The 11-inch tall vase pictured is a deep cream, decorated with blue antelopes, rose circles, and brown foliage.

OWEN, BEN

See *Jugtown Pottery*

J. B. OWENS POTTERY CO.

J. B. Owens built a stoneware factory in Zanesville, Ohio, in 1891, and in 1896, he began to make art pottery, competing with Samuel A. Weller, who was already established in that field. Owens produced art pottery for only ten years before he turned to the more lucrative manufacture of tile, but they were busy years. His 1904 catalog, according to Norris Schneider, in *Zanesville Art Pottery,* measured an elaborate 14 by 20 inches and contained 800 items.

Owen's *Utopian* duplicated Weller's *Louwelsa,* which in turn, duplicated *Lonhuda.* His *Lotus* was similar to *Utopian,* but with lighter backgrounds. He also brought out *Cyrano,* a white lace design on black ground; *Henri Deux,* with designs cut in moist clay and the incision filled with decorations in color; *Feroza,* a metallic lustre to compete with Weller's *Sicardo; Mission,* in a matt glaze with church and landscape scenes: *Red Flame,* decorated with an embossed flower design covered with red glaze; and others.

All the Zanesville potters were very helpful to today's collectors by marking most of their wares clearly with their own name, and often the name of the ware. (*See* Zanesville Art Pottery.) Henzke's *American Art Pottery* is also an excellent reference.

The little swirled vase illustrated—it is 3½ inches high—is Owen's *Utopian;* the glaze is a rich brown, with brown and yellow flowers painted underglaze.

OZZO CERAMICS

See *Boehm Birds*

PAIRPOINT, LIMOGES

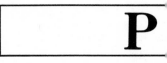

The backstamp "Pairpoint" above a crown, with "Limoges" below it on a fine, exquisitely hand-painted china piece will occasionally turn up to puzzle collectors who think of Pairpoint in connection with glass or silver—never with china. Yes, it's the same Pairpoint Corporation. They used this mark on fine chinawares which they imported from Limoges and decorated in their own decorating shop in New Bedford, Massachusetts, in the early 1900s. The mark was discontinued in 1909.

PAP BOATS

See *Invalid Feeders*

PARIAN

"Statuary porcelain" they called it when it first came out about 1840—this hard paste unglazed porcelain, made to resemble pure white marble. Then they gave it the permanent name of Parian, for marble from the Greek Island of Paros. Statuary porcelain brought classical culture to Victorian drawing rooms in the form of lightly draped ladies, usually copies of famous works. Hiram Power's *Slave Girl* was a great favorite; so was Venus de Milo.

Benjamin Cheverton invented a machine to reduce measurements of large statues to table size; sometimes his name appears on early pieces along with that of the original sculptor.

Who made Parian? Minton's and Spode (Copeland) were in at the beginning; Worcester, Goss, and Ridgway followed. Wedgwood brought out their own version, called Carrara. In the States, the U. S. Pottery at Bennington, Vermont, was making Parian of highest order by 1850.

As the yen for classicism diminished, Parian appeared in

smaller, less formal pieces—figures of children, singly or in groups; portrait busts; wall plaques; vases and ewers, hung with carved grapes and leaves and tiny tendrils, sometimes poised against a blue ground; little covered boxes; pitchers; anything at all that lent itself to the dignity of "marble." Parian was a proud ware, with a proud name, and the artists who designed for it and the workmen who crafted it, almost always did it justice. You'll find very little poorly made Parian.

Illustrated is a Parian hound-handled pitcher of English make. The Parian plaques, designed about 1887, by an itinerant artist named Priestman, and the jug, also 1887, were made by the Bennett Pottery in Baltimore, Maryland.

"PARISIAN GRANITE"

See *Booth's*

PASTILLE BURNERS

Pastille burners, cottage-style, were a conceit of the early nineteenth century. In these little ceramic houses and summer pavilions, dripping with vines and flowers, with moss on their detachable and perforated roofs, were burned pastilles—a concoction of powdered willow-wood, charcoal, benzoin, fragrant oils, and gum arabic—to sweeten the air.

Such was the popularity of these cozy cots that potters made them for night lights, banks, tea caddies, tobacco jars, and watch-holders as well as for pastille burners. The ones most sought, whatever their purpose, are those made in porcelain from 1820 to 1840 by Rockingham, Coalport, Worcester, and Derby, and in earthenware by Felix Pratt. These dainty cottages still have tremendous "sweet-william and hollyhock" appeal; they're expensive, but occasionally on the market.

The illustration shows, not a porcelain pastille burner, but a pottery money box, five inches high, gay in its colors of blue, yellow, ochre, green, and black. Felix Pratt made it, and though it is more crude than the bocage-covered china cottages, it is still in the luxury bracket. (*See* Prattware.)

PATCH BOXES

In the elegant days of Louis XIV when gentlemen wore extravagent periwigs and ladies built coiffures two-feet high, the beauty patch for milady's cheek was a titillating novelty. The French called them "flies," these wee black "court plaster" patches, cut in crescents, moons, and more intricate shapes, and a *boite a mouches* to hold them was an essential accessory.

Boites a mouches were mentioned in French writings as early as 1647. In England, a quarter of a century later, they became "patch boxes." Ned Ward, in 1698, wrote of the ladies: "By help of paint, powder, and patches, they are of waxwork complexion," and Henri Mission in that same year told of counting fifteen patches on a "swarthy wrinkled phiz."

The periwigs, the fantastic coiffures, and the extravagant laces and ribbons of the 1600s went soon out of style, but beauty patches remained in fashion for more than two centuries, and have never been completely discarded. Patch boxes continued to be made into the twentieth century.

These small and delicate containers were made in all sorts of material—enamel, gold, silver, brass, and porcelain. They were round, oval, oblong, or intricately fashioned in shapes of musical instruments, hearts, baskets, and figures. You'll find examples of porcelain patch boxes made at Worcester, Sevres, Chelsea, Capo-di-Monte, Meissen, and Dresden, and in late nineteenth century Carlsbad. Patch boxes make an intriguing collection, but for an inexpensive one, you should have started thirty years ago!

Though the elegant early patch boxes are understandably on the expensive side, late nineteenth century examples with colorfully applied flowers and other decorations, are still relatively inexpensive, though not nearly as plentiful as they were a few years ago. Patch boxes pictured are enamelled on porcelain.

PATE-SUR-PATE

Pâte-sur-pâte (paste on paste) is a process of ceramic painting which builds up, by brush strokes, in transparent slip a cameo design, usually in white, so fine and so delicate that the diaphanous quality of drapery is achieved. This is all hand work, an intricate building up of thickness on thickness according to the design, and it requires consummate artistry.

Originated in China, pâte-sur-pâte was used at Sevres about 1850. It was brought to perfection by Marc Louis Solon

at Minton's in Staffordshire. Solon, who migrated from his native France to England in 1870, worked at Minton's for more than thirty years, devoting his time there almost exclusively to the production of pâte-sur-pâte.

Solon's classical designs in white, usually on a dark blue background, were choicely prized by contemporary connoisseurs. At the famous Mary J. Morgan sale in 1886, where a huge Webb cameo glass covered jar brought $405, a pâte-sur-pâte amphora vase by Solon brought $2,900; a pair of his large pâte-sur-pâte vases, $8,100. His pieces are usually signed M. L. S. or Miles.

The luxury is usually followed by the staple, and in the instance of pâte-sur-pâte, the staple was the so-called Mary Gregory glass, where the decoration was cheaply imitated in opaque enamel. (*See* Solon, Marc Louis.)

The pâte-sur-pâte amphora pictured, made by Solon for Minton's, is deep green with white painting, 25½ inches high. The subject is an allegorical hunting and trapping scene; on the reverse is a composition of frolicking Amors.

PATRIOTIC WARE

Round about in various antiques shops are presumably a few plates and teaware pieces bearing the backstamp "Patriotic Ware/ADAMS Tunstall/England/Est. 1657." The central design is the Great Seal of the United States in full color—blue band, red and white stripes, green olive branch, and pink ribbon bearing motto. The border consists of alternate red and yellow leaves, separated by black triangles with a white triangle in each. The style of the Adams backstamp indicates that the ware was made after 1895, but no later than 1920.

Various collectors have suggested that these were souvenir pieces put out for McKinley's inauguration in 1897. They could be, of course, but more likely they were sold in and around the nation's capital as souvenir ware of Washington, D.C. Other Adams' plates of a souvenir nature use the same busy border, as one showing the Arms of King Edward VII (ca. 1901) as the central motif, and another showing the Old Spanish Arms, St. Augustine, Florida.

PAUL REVERE POTTERY

The Paul Revere Pottery operated from 1912 to 1942—in Boston, Massachusetts, until 1915, then in neighboring Brighton. The pieces made there were simple—pitchers, bowls, vases, cups and saucers, children's mugs, and the like. Though handmade, well-designed, and tastefully glazed, there was nothing particularly distinctive about them. They looked like what they

Majolica pitcher with eagle decoration, 10½ inches high; cup and saucer in corn pattern; covered sardine dish, base 7¼ x 6½ inches; all ca. 1870-1880.

Lustrewares. Gold Lustre teapot, "Made in England," ca. 1895; 5½ inches high. Silver resist pitcher, ca. 1825; 5½ inches high.

Buffalo Pottery, Deldare Ware in Fallowfield Hunt pattern, 1908; diameter of plate 9 inches; pitcher 9 inches high. Frog mug, ca. 1810; 4¾ inches high.

Mason's Patent Ironstone coffee pot, ca. 1830; 9 inches high. Ashworth plate in the same pattern, ca. 1880; 8½ inches in diameter.

were—high grade giftware of the period. It is the social history behind them that makes the ware interesting to collectors, especially those who like a story attached to their finds.

Mrs. James J. Storrow, civic-minded, wealthy, and imaginative, took an active interest in the reading groups from the North Bennet Street Industrial School in Boston which were under the direction of the North End Branch of the Boston Public Library. She was especially concerned with the high-school age Saturday Evening Girls. She followed their careers after they finished school and provided a vacation camp at West Gloucester for those who were working.

In 1906, Edith Guerrier, the librarian who supervised the groups, and her friend Edith Brown, an artist, conceived the idea of a pottery for the Saturday Evening Girls. Mrs. Storrow sponsored it. In 1912, the group was ready for commercial operation. Mrs. Storrow provided a house on Hull Street not far from the Old North Church where the signal lanterns were hung for Paul Revere. When neighbors objected to the smoke from the kiln, she built an attractive plant—a house really, designed by Edith Brown—in Brighton. Some thirty Saturday Evening Girls, after graduation, were regularly employed there under the direction of Miss Brown.

For the most part the wares they made depended on glazes for decoration. Among the colors they used were eggshell, gun metal, red, yellow, maroon, brown, and various shades of green and blue. Some popular children's pieces were made in blue and greens with animal borders in white.

The pieces are not uniformly marked. Most show PRP, either by itself or with the month and year figures or the initials of the maker. Some have the pottery's trademark—Paul Revere on a galloping horse.

The wares sold readily all over the country, mostly through gift shops. However, the cost of making far exceeded the price that could be asked, and the pottery was always subsidized to some extent by Mrs. Storrow. After Miss Brown's death in 1932, the workers kept the plant open another ten years. Mrs. Storrow died in 1944.

Many examples of the ware may now be seen at Storrowtown Village, a restoration on the Eastern States Exposition grounds at West Springfield, Massachusetts. The story of the pottery and the Saturday Evening Girls is told in a now rare little pamphlet, *The Paul Revere Pottery,* and by Ruth Fouts Pochman in *Spinning Wheel* for November 1963.

The illustration shows pieces of Paul Revere useful wares from the collection of Miss Sarah M. Usher.

PAULINE POTTERY

In the late 1870s, Mrs. Pauline Jacobus, whose husband

was on the Board of Trade in Chicago, decided she wanted to make pottery. Her husband approved, and she went to Cincinnati to learn how at the Rookwood pottery. By 1880, back in Chicago, she was holding ceramic classes of her own. Her clay was shipped from Ohio, and at first she had to send her pieces to Cincinnati to be fired. As soon as she had a small kiln of her own, she began to produce commercially. Kimball's in Boston, Tiffany's in New York, and Marshall Field & Co. in her own city were among her customers.

She solved the problem of transporting clay from Ohio by moving to Edgerton, Wisconsin, where there were excellent clay deposits. Her husband, as enthusiastic in the project as she, also promoted a pottery there, making porous cups for batteries for the Bell Telephone Company. John Sargeant came from Cincinnati to build a kiln which they both used. Thorwald Samson of Denmark was engaged to prepare the pottery forms. At one time twenty men worked under Mr. Jacobus, and thirteen women under Mrs. Jacobus. When Edwin Atlee Barber wrote his *Pottery and Porcelain in the United States* in 1893 the Pauline Pottery was the only one in Wisconsin mentioned.

Mr. Jacobus died in 1891, and both potteries were closed. Then in 1902, Mrs. Jacobus purchased the kiln, moved it brick by brick to her own property, and was again in business. Her endeavors ended for good in 1905 when her house in which she conducted her potting burned; she went to live with a married daughter; she died in 1930.

Collectors have a hard time identifying Pauline Pottery. Being of an experimental turn of mind, Mrs. Jacobus made pieces in so many styles, from Wedgwood and majolica to Chinese and Meissen, that no one type, with the exception of her beautiful peacock-colored glazes, seemed exclusively hers.

Of course, there is no mistaking pieces marked with her usual crown with "Trade Mark" above it, or with an imprinted "Pauline Pottery," but there were as many pieces with no mark at all. On some, "Edgerton Art Clay" appears or just the artist's name, like "N. H. Mears," for Helen (Nellie) Mears, a well-known Wisconsin sculptor, or "Th. Samson 1899." Some were simply marked "Made for M. F. & Co." (Marshall Field).

Study of collections at the Neville Museum, Green Bay, Wisconsin, and at the Wisconsin State Historical Society Museum in Madison indicate the remarkable variety of Mrs. Jacobus' truly outstanding designs and glazes as well as the number of identifying marks she used. The story of the Pauline Pottery and its talented owner is well told in *Wisconsin Heritage,* by Bertha Kitchell Whyte (1957).

The ewer illustrated, from the Neville Museum, has a predominately blue and gold border design and natural color garlands on a cream ground. The decorator, Eugenia A. Hutchinson, marked it with her initials "E. A. H."

"PEARL STONEWARE"

See *Flown Blue*

"PEARL WARE"

See *Flown Blue*

PEORIA POTTERY

See *Illinois Potters*

PETER RABBIT PIECES

See *Porter, Beatrix*

PETERS & REED

See *Moss Aztec*

PETRUS REGOUT

See *Maastricht*

PEW GROUPS

In the earliest period of salt glaze manufacture in England, so-called "pew groups" were made—small statuettes in which two figures sat on a high-back bench similar to a church pew. Often, though not always, they were decorated with bits of black or brown slip or with small dabs of cobalt blue. Pew groups were the only pre-1790 salt glaze pieces in which any color was used.

It is unusual to find an early pew group for sale today. Most of those extant are in museums where they can at least be looked at and studied. The one shown is at the Fitzwilliam Museum in Cambridge, England. Here, brown clay slip is used for color. The bench arms are long rolls of brown and white twisted together. Texture, as in the man's ribbed stockings and the pew top, was accomplished with a knife.

PFALTZGRAFF POTTERY

This stoneware manufactory in York, Pennsylvania, is remarkable for having been operated continuously since 1811, always by Pfaltzgraffs or their descendants. From 1811 to 1913, stoneware for agricultural, industrial, and domestic uses was made. The blue decorated crocks, jugs, pots, and other utilitarian pieces from this period are the ones of interest to collectors. On most of them the Pfaltzgraff name appears, usually impressed, though the initials will vary with the different owners; others are impressed or blue-stenciled "The P. S. Co. York Pa." for the Pfaltzgraff Stoneware Company.

Red flower pots became their chief products from 1913 to 1942 when their Heritage Stoneware was introduced. This up-to-date oven-proof, dishwasher-safe, chip-resistant blue-decorated stoneware is now being made in wide range of articles, from mugs to jugs to teapots and tureens. Many gift shops and most department stores carry it, and people who like an Early American look for their dishes but not at Early American prices, buy it.

The jug pictured is a recent commercial type made up by Pfaltzgraff for the Frankfort Distillers to hold Henry McKenna Kentucky bourbon in 1½-gallon and 1/5-quart sizes.

PIANO BABIES

In the 1880s, when the up-to-date parlor displayed bisque figures on the mantel, the well-dressed piano wore a bisque piano baby. These dainty infants, some quite small, others almost life-size, bare or half bare, crawled, sat, lay on their tummies, rolled on their backs, played with their toes, cried, or smiled. They added one more sentimental touch to a room filled with bric-a-brac and lessened the tedium of piano practice.

Perhaps the finest piano babies were those made by the German Gebruder Heubach. They were always extremely fine grained bisque, superbly modeled, and practically all of them, like everything else that left the Heubach factory, was decisively marked. Other makers, even though they were as particular in their work, were not as particular in their markings. Many did not bother to mark them at all.

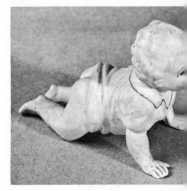

Elizabeth Coleman in *Dolls, Makers and Marks* identifies the brothers Heubach as Jean Paul and Ernest Christian Conrad. The Heubach firm itself was established in 1820, but the brothers did not come into the picture until much later. Their factory was in Lichte, near Wallendorf, not far from the Bavarian border; their specialty was bisque dolls and doll heads, though frequently, to our joy, they ventured into bisque figurines. The best of their early piano babies have a closed base, with only a small hole, pencil point size, near the mark.

Of recent years there has been a flurry of piano baby reproduction. Watch out for finger- or fist-size holes in the bases—they are suspect. Better still, watch *for* the old Heubach mark. (*See* Heubach Brothers.)

PIANOFORTES

Tiny china pianos, doll-house size, are hastily mentioned here as something you can collect if you're so minded. They've been about for several centuries—and still are made—as dainty bibelots for the musical or delightful rewards for a favored grandchild's well practiced scales. They're not exactly tokens, for the early Sevres and Dresden pieces may cost a pretty penny, but lesser and later models, though still old, in bisque or Staffordshire as well as porcelain, are not prohibitive in price.

The piano pictured is a Meissen-type in blue and white, 6 by 4 by 9 inches—a monstrous size compared to most you'll find.

PICKARD CHINA

Pickard, Inc. began in Chicago, in 1897, as a decorating establishment. The company employed most excellent artists and supplied them with the finest of whiteware to paint, much of it imported from Bavaria. Quality jewelers all over the country stocked their wares and, as gifts for the bride, Pickard's exquisitely hand-painted demitasses, bowls, relish dishes, pitchers, and other useful items vied with cut glass and silver. Their allover gold decoration was delightfully suited to Golden Anniversaries, though brides seldom waited fifty years to enjoy it.

In 1938, the company moved to Antioch, Illinois, and began

to manufacture the china they painted. Pickard, Inc. is still in business, still delighting brides—and their mothers—with fine tablewares in contemporary fashion.

Pieces from Pickard's decorating period, which are now among the collectibles, will often carry the backstamp of the china manufacturer as well as that of Pickard. Often, too, the name of the artist will appear. Among signatures to look for on pieces prior to 1920 are: E. S. Challinor, who did florals and scenics; Podlaha and Hessler, who specialized in stylized patterns; Vokral, known for his fruits and nuts; Marker, for scenic work; Klippon, for flowers, particularly roses; James, for Dutch Provincial type decorations; and Leonard Kohl, who was adept at all types.

The pitcher illustrated is in the Aura Argenta Linear pattern, ca. 1910-1920, hand decorated by Mr. Hessler. The lower portion is covered with plain gold; the conventional flower design is in silver.

PIE BIRDS

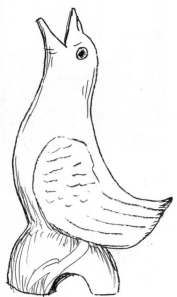

No one has to be an ancient to recall a piebaking mother or grandmother rolling a little cornucopia of brown paper and sticking it into the center of a fruit pie just before it went in the oven. The hot juice bubbled up into the cornucopia instead of out the slits in the piecrust; when it cooled, it came back down into the pie where it belonged. If she had no brown paper handy, maybe she used a few sticks of macaroni.

The ceramic pie bird was a refinement on this principle. In kitchens given to gadgetry a hollow china bird, about four inches tall, with open beak and open base, and prettily colored under glaze, took the place of the brown paper cornucopia or the macaroni. Either because these dainty birdlings seemed a foolish expense to multiple pie bakers or because they broke and were tossed aside, there are not many about today.

A collector in Pierce, Nebraska, Mr. L. D. Martelle, who drew the picture used here, has found only nine in about that many years. All were purchased in different localities in the mid-West.

A grandmother in Rocky Ridge, Maryland, still mourns one she broke as a bride—it was dark blue with black wings and yellow beak. The only written reference we have found was in "Prairie Winter," by Margaret Creal in the *Ladies Home Journal*, December 1965. Describing a childhood winter in Grenfall, Saskatchewan, she wrote:

"At lunch we had thick soups and stews, and even the dessert was hot—rice pudding, upside-down cake, deep-dish plum pie with steam puffing sweetly from the bird's beak in the middle of the dish."

From her account the early 1920s could be the date of its

use in her family. Mr. Martelle, who also remembers them from childhood, dates them between World War I and the mid-twenties, but no later.

The photograph shows what Mrs. William Montgomery of Hanover, Pennsylvania, who owns it, calls "a pie chimney." It was brought from England as a present to her mother about 1898, and was used in meat pies to control the juices and effect the rather large hole in the top crust usual to English meat pies. It is white semi-vitreous china; the legend on it reads, underglaze in blue: "Roe's Patent Rosebud" in the circle, and beneath it, "Wm. Whiteley Ltd/Universal Providers/ Bayswater.W." Whiteley appears to be the supplier, not the potter.

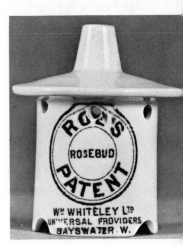

PILKINGTON'S ROYAL LANCASTRIAN POTTERY

If we lived in England instead of the United States, we would see more of Royal Lancastrian Pottery, and know more about it. Knowledgeable critics have said that some of the "most outstanding art pottery of the Western World" was made at Pilkington's between 1903 and 1938, and A. V. Rose, Tiffany's ceramics expert, called its spectacular Lancastrian Lustre ware the "finest lustre pottery ever made." Even though its distribution in this country was considerable—Tiffany & Company in New York was its chief outlet for thirty-five years—examples here are not plentiful.

The Pilkington Tile and Pottery Company was founded in 1892, near Manchester, England, headed by William Burton, formerly with Wedgwood. By 1900, it was probably the largest producer of decorative tiles in England. Today, as Pilkington Tiles, Ltd., it is still doing a thriving business.

From the beginning, Burton had art pottery in mind, and by assembling the finest of designers, chemists, and craftsmen to work on this project as well as on the tiles he was ready by 1903 to launch Lancastrian pottery, named for its home county of Lancashire. In 1913, when it was granted a Royal Warrant by King George V, it became Royal Lancastrian.

Their first chemist, Abraham Lomax, was responsible for most of the unusual glazes which made Lancastrian famous and won it such high praise. Their Lancastrian Lustre ware, decorated in Hispano-Moorish style, which came out in 1905, was the most famous of all. Many important artists designed for Lancastrian; their names and marks are included in Chester Davis's article on the pottery which appeared in *Spinning Wheel* for March 1970; he also discusses the various glazes in some detail.

World War I caused a slowdown in operations, and though some excellent pieces, both Lustre and matt glazed, were made in the 1920s and chemist Arthur Chambers developed a handsome

new "Lapis Ware" in 1928, the earlier momentum was gone. The pottery ceased production in 1938. It was revived briefly in 1948 to produce small items only, like bowls, ashtrays, and tableware. In 1957, it closed for good. Royal Lancastrian ware will never be made again, but you can see an extremely fine collection of early pieces at the Manchester Museum in England.

The shaded green and russet vase pictured is in Vellum-type matt glaze, with a blue lining. R. Turncliff was the designer in 1905. It is 10¾ inches tall.

PINDAR, BOURNE & CO.

See *Doulton*

PISGAH FOREST POTTERY

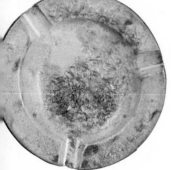

The Pisgah Forest Pottery, at the foot of Mount Pisgah in Arden, North Carolina, not far outside of Asheville, was a continuation of the Noncommah Pottery started about 1900 by Walter B. Stephen and his mother, Mrs. Andrew Stephen, in Shelby County, Tennessee, near Memphis. Walter Stephen moved to North Carolina in 1914 after his parents had died.

Mr. Stephen was a constant experimenter and produced some truly fine porcelain glazes, his beautiful turquoise crackle glaze and his crystalline glazes being his finest and most important. He also made what he termed "freehand cameo," with the decoration resembling Wedgwood's sprigged-on jasper, though his was built up by applying the porcelain paste layer by layer with a brush. The subjects Mr. Stephen chose were mostly American, such as a Buffalo Hunt, a Covered Wagon, or pine trees which he often did in white on a sage green background.

Mr. Stephen and Mr. Bachelder of the nearby Omar Khayyam Art Pottery were great friends, according to Allen H. Eaton in *Handicrafts of the Southern Highlands;* he says their glazes were somewhat alike, though Mr. Stephen's products were not so hard, and that he tended toward lighter shades. (*See* Omar Khayyam Art Pottery.)

After Mr. Stephen died in 1961, at the age of 86, the pottery has been continued by G. G. Ledbetter and William Case who had long been associated with Mr. Stephen.

Besides the fine glazed pieces, the crystallines, and the cameo-ware, which every collector would like to have and hold, the pottery made (and still does) the usual jugs, vases, teapots, and candlesticks that all the potters of the area were making. Situated as it is, in a scenic vacation land, thousands of tourists from every state in the Union have visited the pottery and taken home examples.

Pieces are marked "Pisgah Forest Pottery," sometimes with

a crude scratching of a potter at work. Many of the crystalline and cameo pieces are marked "Stephen"; those, of course, are what everyone hopes to find. Neither of these has been made since Mr. Stephen's death.

The illustrations, from the collection of Mrs. Lawrence Duvall, of Washington, D.C., show a piece of crystalline, and one of the Covered Wagon cameo pieces; note that the latter is marked "Stephen" in the design.

PLASTER PLAQUES

Plaster figures (*see* Chalkware) were common enough in the early 1800s. As examples of folkware, they are desirable antiques today. Plaster plaques of the mid-century were a Victorian refinement—at least they were of the same basic material—striving for fine art. Such sculptured pictures got a tremendous boost when the artist Frederico Juistini of Lucca, Italy—he signed his works "Justin"—exhibited some of his plaques at the Crystal Palace Exhibition in London in 1851.

One of these, depicting St. Louis leading his army against the Saracens, is shown here. This and one similar, representing St. Louis bearing the Crown of Thorns to the Sainte Chapelle in Paris, are now in the Victoria and Albert Museum in London. Both are plaster, covered with an electro-deposit of silver. Many copies of these were made and widely distributed. They show

up now and then, sometimes confusing collectors with their silver coating.

By the 1900s, plaster plaques had become everyday affairs,

sentimentally conceived, commercially made, and cheaply priced. (They're still inexpensive.) No silver covered them, but sometimes a rubbed-on brownish paint relieved the whiteness of the bare plaster. Most familiar of subjects were cherubs in various poses, often heads without bodies. Almost everyone over fifty recalls their sweet faces and chubby shoulders protruding an inch or two from their plate-size plaques. They hung in dens and living rooms and front halls, and children and old maid aunts adored them. If they fell off the wall, they usually broke, and never had to be dusted again!

PLYMOUTH POTTERY

Unlike the Rowantrees Kiln and Brookcroft Pottery, which were also founded by women within the past forty years, the Plymouth Pottery in the Sparrow House at Plymouth, Massachusetts, has not expanded along commercial lines. It has remained a quiet "for fun" group of interested and talented amateurs who have managed over the years to turn out a great deal of attractive low-fired redware.

Plymouth pottery was first made in 1936 in State-sponsored classes taught by Katherine L. Alden, a master craftsman of the Boston Society of Arts and Crafts. Out of these classes, the Plymouth Pottery Guild evolved, composed of eligible pupils who wanted to keep on making pottery and to sell some of it.

State-sponsorship ended in 1961, but weekly classes have continued, and the Guild remains active. It is a co-operative and maintains its shop and kiln in the Richard Sparrow House, Plymouth's oldest, built in 1636-1640, which Miss Alden owns.

Most of the pieces are made by hand or on the wheel. Many of the shapes and designs are reminiscent of early ware, but one-of-a-kind small figures and garden items are also made up, and their special order wedding and baby plates are in demand. Local red clay is used, and until recently the ladies ground it themselves. Now they have it prepared for them, though they still compound their own specially developed glazes.

The Sparrow House is open to tourists from June to October; in the winter months, the potters make up their stock for the coming summer. Writes Miss Alden, regretfully, "A few of the first classes are still interested, but production totals are slipping. We are not getting any younger."

All of which leads us to suggest to collectors of pottery that now is the time to add an example of Plymouth Pottery, even if you have to go to Plymouth to get it—and stand by while it's being made! The mark is a circular "Plymouth Pottery" impressed, with a picture of a birdhouse across which are the words, "Sparrow House."

The small Pilgrim figure pictured is one of Miss Alden's

individually modeled (not molded) pieces. In *The Folk Arts and Crafts of New England,* by Daniel Foley with Priscilla Lord (Chilton Books publishers), some of her flower pots are pictured, similar to those made by some unknown potter 150 years ago.

POILLON POTTERY

The mark of this small and short-lived pottery is two P's joined together, one being upside down. It was located in Woodbridge, New Jersey, and examples of its work were exhibited at the St. Louis Exposition in 1904. This will give you an idea of the time it was in operation.

PORSGRUND

The Porsgrund Porselaenfabrik in Porsgrunn, Norway, went into operation in 1885 under the aegis of Jeremiason Johan, a local ship owner who found it practical for his ships carrying lumber to England to bring back suitable clays. The early product was a fine porcelain in choice table and decorative wares. At first it had mainly local sales, but between 1900 and 1910, a considerable amount of it came in to the United States. World Wars and political upheavals in Norway itself changed the export picture, and only recently has Porsgrund re-entered the American market.

The present product is no longer luxury porcelain but a more utilitarian, "for everybody" porcelain, well designed and distinctively decorated. In Norway, Porsgrund porcelain is used in many of the *de luxe* hotels, and in most hospitals. Fine artists are at work there, and their signed pieces are worth collecting for the future. In the meantime, you can use them with pleasure and pride. Norway House in New York City is one spot you'll always find pieces.

The mark of the factory is an anchor flanked on each side by a "P," usually with "Porsgrund" above and "Norway" below. After 1954, the numeral "54" was added to the mark.

PORTOBELLO POTTERIES

Portobello, a small town near Edinburgh, was a brickmaking center in the eighteenth century. In addition it supported two potteries, Benjamin Walker's, who made pictorial tiles, and Scott Bros., who went in for good quality dinner and tea wares. Scott also made a limited amount of local redware, decorated in yellow slip, including animal and bird figures. These are much treasured today. Marks, when applied, were "Scott" over "P. B."; when impressed, "Scott Bros." (This should not be confused with another Scott Bros. mark used at the Southwick Pottery in Sunderland at a later date.)

In 1796, Messrs. Cookson and Jardine took over the Scott factory, followed by Thomas Yoole. Shortly thereafter, Thomas Rathbone, Yoole's son-in-law, was made a partner. Under Rathbone's direction (1808-1845), many flatback cottage ornaments were made. It is quite likely that almost as many of them were produced here as in Staffordshire. "T. Rathbone" over "P" seems to be the mark he used. According to Godden, "T. R. & Co." were initials used by T. Rathbone & Co. of Tunstall, 1898-1923, an altogether different firm. (*See:* Scottish Pottery; Cottage Ornaments; Inanimate Clocks.)

Illustrated is one of Rathbone's flatback chimney ornaments. Similar figures were made at Sunderland, as well as in Staffodshire.

PORTO BELLO WARE

From its name this early ware, appearing in the 1740s, suggests some type of Spanish faience made at Porto Bello. Not so. Nor has it anything to do with the later wares produced at Portobello, Scotland. Porto Bello ware was a Staffordshire product, a red or white stoneware, molded and salt glazed, named in honor of a resounding English victory.

During the 1730s, England and Spain were at odds, and

popular feeling against Spaniards ran high. When Admiral Edward Vernon, in 1739, with a fleet of only six ships, successfully assaulted Porto Bello, an important Spanish port in the West Indies, he was hailed a hero. This ware, named for his feat, appeared shortly thereafter. Henry Morgan, the privateer, was knighted for his part in the activities.

Admiral Vernon was honored in the colonies, too, for the name of Little Hunting Creek Plantation in Virginia, devised to John Washington in 1676, was changed to Mount Vernon in 1743 by Lawrence Washington who then owned it, and who had once served under Vernon's command.

Look for Porto Bello ware in museums—not antiques shops! You'll find examples at Mount Vernon.

POT LIDS

The people who saved Carrie Nation vinegar bottles in the 1930s or Lestoil bottles of recent date, had they lived a century ago, would have filled their cupboards with colorful lids from jars of hair pomade and shrimp paste and pates. And time would have proved them wise. These small round lids, printed with colored pictures have been popularly collected for a long time. The English, not usually given to Victoriana, have doted on them.

Most of these lids—and jars—were made at the F. & R. Pratt potteries in Fenton, Staffordshire, from 1845 when Jesse Austin, the senior partner, invented the process of printing pottery with oil color, to 1879 when he died, and a bit later. The process was based on the one Baxter used for his color prints, and was far from simple. Copies of paintings, landscapes, sports, scenes, city buildings, famous people, and most colorful etcetera graced these containers. Most favored by collectors today are the early "bear grease" lids—a series of sixteen, showing different bears on each one. The pots held, of course, hair pomade of bear's grease.

The Pottery Gazette and Glass Trade Review, for April 1, 1925, quoted the "Londoner's Diary" in the *Evening Standard:* "The curious craze for collecting the lids of old Fenton shrimp paste and pomade pots seems to continue unabated. At the sale of M. W. Nicholas's collection, a number of such lids, which could formerly be bought for coppers, were disposed of from £5 to £10 a piece. One, with a portrait of the Duke of Wellington, was knocked down for £15. Another, called 'Pet Rabbit,' made £11; and a third, with a portrait of Mrs. Harriet Beecher Stowe— presumably in honour of *Uncle Tom's Cabin*—fetched £21. Several were sold attached to the original pots, which were quite agreeable in shape, but for reason not apparent to the uninitiated, the presence of the pot does not appear to increase the value of the lid."

The "curious craze" is still unabated—to the point that

collectors must now be wary of reproductions. Writes John Bedford in *Looking in Junk Shops* (1964), "False ones usually stand accused by their unconvincing colors, a lack of 'crazing,' and a different sort of 'ring.' When struck gently with another plate, the genuine one in most cases will sound dead, while the false one will ring." (That's a switch for you!)

The pot lid illustrated carries a reproduction in transfer on pottery of Sully's famous painting of Washington Crossing the Delaware. It probably contained Shaving soap. (*See* Shaving Soap Boxes.)

POTPOURRI JARS

The word potpourri derives from the French and indicates a mixture of spiced flower petals in a jar, used to scent a room—a practice introduced to Europeans in the mid-eighteenth century and continued well into the late Victorian period. The special jars made for this purpose had double covers, the inner one perforated, the outer one solid. In use, the outer lid was removed for an hour or so to let the fragrance rise through the perforations of the inner lid.

The pair pictured, 11½ inches high, marked Wedgwood, are of black basalt, enamelled in bright colors to imitate cloisonne. The single jar, unmarked is similarly enamelled on terra cotta. Both date about 1810.

Later examples—and earlier ones—followed the shapes and decorations in vogue at the time they were made. Designed to be used in pairs on a parlor mantel, they were usually quality pieces, particularly the earlier ones. They became less important as the years passed and the use of potpourri became more common. You'll find some jars tall and stately, others petite and chubby, some elaborate, some quite simple, depending upon their period and the purse for which they were designed.

Potpourri itself is simple to make, and if you feel so inclined, here's an old recipe you can follow. All you need are 4 cups of dried rose petals; 1 teaspoon each of powdered orris root, ground cinnamon, ground nutmeg, ground cloves, grated dried orange rind, and grated dried lemon rind. Mix the spices and rinds thoroughly. In a pan, put a layer of rose petals, shake salt over it, add a layer of the mixture, and so continue till the pan is full. Put it away covered, for six weeks. It's ready then for your jar—and these days it may take you six weeks to find one!

BEATRIX POTTER'S PETER RABBIT

Familiar storybook characters on children's dishes seem hopefully intended to make children hungrier and milk and mush more palatable. Kewpies and Brownies and Sunbonnet Babies, who all started out on paper, have turned up on nursery feeding sets and as dolls or figurines as well. So, too, have most of the characters from Beatrix Potter's Peter Rabbit Series.

Beatrix Potter's *Tale of Peter Rabbit,* was published in 1901, followed at intervals by twenty other equally breath-taking tales, all illustrated by the author. Frederick Warne & Co., of London and New York, still publishes the whole series, with the original drawings. Many of the tales are available in translation for the delectation of young readers in Germany, France, Holland, Wales, Italy, Spain, and Sweden.

The children's plates and bowls and mugs, decorated with Beatrix Potter's characters, which Wedgwood brings out under the Frederick Warne copyright, have a wide market—the language of pictures is universal. The set we have shows central scenes from the Peter Rabbit story, with Jemina Puddleduck, Squirrel Nutkin, Jeremy Fisher and Tom Kitten in the border decoration. You'll find these sets in almost any store which carries fine china.

Another ceramic offshoot of the Peter Rabbit series is the line of character figurines in bone china made by Beswick & Co., Longston, also under Frederick Warne & Co.'s copyright. These little figures are about three to four inches tall, delightfully molded and colored, and as appealing to grownups as they are to children. Though they are in current production, finding them is like hunting antiques—you may come across them with no trouble at all or keep looking for ages. Bookshops where the Beatrix Potter books are stocked is a good starting place.

Litte Pig Robinson, pictured, came from Canada; Samuel Whiskers, from a gift shop in the Washington National Airport. These are not the best known of Miss Potter's characters, but finding just the ones you want is not always easy. The Tailor of Gloucester, a wee mouse stitching away atop a spool of thread is one of the most charming.

PRATTWARE

Prattware, with its raised figural or other decoration, is vividly colored in tones of orange, blue, purple, green, and black. Felix Pratt operated at Little Fenton, England, from the 1770s into the early 1800s.

The pottery teapot illustrated is decorated in blue, black, green, and ochre, with zigzag borders relief molded and painted.

PRESIDENTIAL CHINA
See *White House China*

PRESIDENT'S WIVES PLATES

This handsome set of plates, of which some are pictured, was produced in limited edition, of Royal Berlin porcelain (KPM), honoring the wives of American Presidents. They are ten and a half inches in diameter, with rims in gold and colors, an Ameri-

can eagle at the top, flags at each side, and a name panel, suitably inscribed, at the bottom. The central portraits are of the Presidential wives, from Mrs. George Washington through Mrs. Woodrow Wilson (Edith Galt). The one exception is Miss Harriet Lane, who served as White House hostess for her bachelor uncle, President James Buchanan. S. Wagner, a celebrated ceramic portraitist of Berlin and Vienna, was the artist.

It is evident that plates from this series will be few and far between though a whole set was sold at a Parke Bernet auction in 1953. However, they created enough interest at the time they appeared that at least one series of President's wives plates has since appeared, cheaply made in transfer-printed semi-porcelain. There is no mistaking these two sets; one is porcelain, very fine indeed, with the handsomest of decoration; the other, while interesting, is a very, very distant cousin, and a poor one at that.

PRESTOPANS

Prestopans is near Edinburgh in Scotland. In the eighteenth century, two potteries were located there—Gordon's and Watson's. In their early days, both made roofing tile, domestic wares, and some porcelain, but it is their later under-glazed figures that are most prized today.

Until about 1830, Gordon's made a series of jugs and other articles in the colorful, lively style of Staffordshire's Felix Pratt.

Watson was more inventive and produced many original figures, also with Pratt-type coloring. He also made a large number of curious and obviously nonfunctional tobacco pipes, with

twists and turns and spiralings. Watson's closed in 1840.

In their later years, both potters made blue-printed useful wares, among them the salt and pepper tobies with a pseudo Blue Willow trim (illustrated).The Prestopan "Nelson" jug pictured copies a Pratt subject and is painted underglaze in the Pratt colors of blue, ochre, brown and green.

Prestopans pots are mainly unmarked except for the blue ware. Since much of that was made for export to America, you may quite possibly come across their backstamps: "Watson & Co." enclosed in a triangle; "Willow Pattern" in a diamond; "Semi/China" in a diamond; or "Bird & Fly."

PROSCH WARE

About 1916, some most attractive service plates came on the American market. Of fine quality white china, they were superbly decorated with wide colored rims, line gold bands, and central decal motifs of rose, blue, and purple flowers, touched with hand work.

Their backstamp was completely revealing. It consisted of a crown over H & Co./Selb/Bavaria/Heinrich & Co./China Plates/ The Honesdale Pa. Decorating Co./Prosch-ware. Thus the maker of the china and the decorating company were clearly identified. The lesser known "Prosch" was the name of the owner of the Honesdale Decorating Company.

In the 1890s, Carl F. Prosch, an expert designer, was the New York representative for Bawo & Dotter's glass factories in Bohemia. As such he was well known to Christian Dorflinger whose firm was busily engaged in the manufacture of fancy glasswares in White Mills, Pennsylvania. When Dorflinger, who had been shipping his glass to New York for gilding and decorating, decided he needed a decorating shop closer to his operation, he sought out Prosch and offered to build a factory and set him up in the gold decorating business if he would decorate Dorflinger's glass exclusively. Prosch agreed. The factory, built in Seeleysville, Pennsylvania, a suburb of Honesdale, was named the Honesdale Decorating Co.; it opened in 1900.

In 1916, the year after Christian Dorflinger died, Prosch purchased the Dorflinger interest and continued to operate, under the same name, until 1932. Immediately he began to decorate china as well as glass, concentrating on service plates, some of which were marked as shown above, some with a simple "Prosch" with a blue "P" in a gold keystone. In addition to service plates, he seems also to have decorated a few demitasses, and perhaps other pieces. His chief outlets were Tiffany, Ovington, and Gilman, Collamore & Company in New York; and Wright, Tyndal and Van Roden, J. E. Caldwell & Co., and Bailey, Banks and Biddle in Philadelphia, all quality establishments.

PUZZLE JUGS

The same Old English pub crowd which thought frog mugs so funny took even more delight in the greater intricacies of puzzle jugs. These were mugs or tankards (sometimes pitchers) constructed with various spouts and apertures. The puzzle was to find the spout that could be drunk from without getting drenched. One of them worked, but it was like playing a dribbling ocarina to find it. The secret lay in a hollow handle which led to one spout only. Puzzle mugs were a source of much merriment among the bibulous and the boisterous of that olden time. The ingenious potters who fashioned them must have enjoyed their work, too.

Truly old puzzle jugs are almost impossible to find, but later examples are not. You'll meet them in many shapes and bodies from "Delft" decorated porcelains with blue twig handles and rims (made in Germany) to crude pottery jugs like the one pictured. This is Italian, hand built, buff at the bottom, green at the top. The handle and rim are hollow. Only when a hole on the underside of the handle is stoppered with a finger, will contents of the jug pour from the tiny spout.

QUAIL PIE DISHES

Bird pie, of squabs, larks, pigeons, or quail, was an early item on English menus, and in the eighteenth century, quail pie was enough of a delicacy to warrant a baking dish of its own. Such dishes, it is said, were used extensively by the wealthy during the hard times following serious wheat failures from 1764 to the end of the century. They disguised in some measure, as the pie came to table, the lack of the usual top crust and also popularized estate-supplied provisions.

The unglazed cane ware dish pictured represents a pastry shell for any bird pie. The lid is of elaborate "piecrust" strips topped by an artichoke. Josiah Wedgwood made it and signed it, ca. 1790. The dishes specifically designed for quail pie featured a quail and chicks on the cover instead of piecrust strips.

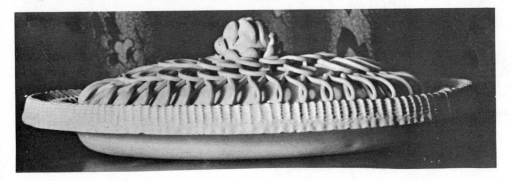

QUEEN'S WARE (or CREAMWARE)

Creamware was not invented by Wedgwood, but the radical changes he made in its body and glaze perfected the ware and made it so practical and popular that by 1759 earthenware was appearing, for the first time, on the daily tables of ordinary homes. When Queen Charlotte ordered a complete dinner set, Wedgwood changed the name to Queen's ware in her honor.

Many potteries made Queen's ware, including Leeds, Castleford, and Cambria at Swansea. Some copied Wedgwood designs, others introduced variations, but Wedgwood was the only maker who regularly marked his pieces.

The Queen's ware teapot pictured was part of a service made by Wedgwood, and printed by Sadler and Green, who used on it two of the several versions of the Liverpool Birds design.

QUIMPER

Quimper, like Limoges, is a French place name, not a factory. Located in Brittany, not far from the port of Brest, Quimper is a town of potteries, world-known for its enchanting earthenwares decorated with Breton peasants in traditional garb. Familiar farm animals and folklore notifs of the locale are other recurring decorative themes.

For almost 300 years the leading manufacturers of this charming peasant pottery have been Jules Henriot et Fils and Faienceries Bretonne de la Grande Maison H-B, the "H-B" being the initials of two families, Hubaudiere and Bousquet, long identified with the company. Henriot et Fils date the existence of its factory in the Henriot family or its forebears to 1690; Faienceries Bretonne, from 1685. (Records show there were potteries in Quimper as early as 1420.)

Both these companies are in production today, making a variety of tablewares and decorative pieces, from full dinner services to tiny souvenir sabots. Both have always marked their pieces well, using an underglaze blue "Henriot" or "H-B," as the case may be, along with the name "Quimper," and after 1891, with "France" added.

Since this ware is decorated by hand, standardization is impossible; the varying shades and irregularities of pattern are one of its charms. Collectors like to search for early pieces for their show-off shelves and to use modern ones on their tables. For information on late wares, we refer you to Alberta C. Trimble's *Modern Porcelain* (Bonanza Books, 1967). Study of present-day productions will give you insight into the past.

The quintal, or five-fingered vase, shown is in yellow, decorated in blues and orange and reds. It is marked Henriot/Quimper/France.

Quintal

To a mathematician a quintal will mean 100 kilograms in the metric system. To the antiquer, it means any five-fingered flower vase. The most usual are the rather flat, spread-fingered vases of polychrome Delft like those found in the authentically restored eighteenth century rooms at Colonial Williamsburg. Present-day reproductions, also from Holland, may be seen there, too—and purchased—in Colonial Williamsburg's gift shops. (For illustration of a late type, *see* Quimper.)

R S CHINA

In the past few years, collectors have been seeking out hand-painted china with the R S mark and paying spectacular prices for it. They have argued vehemently over the merits of the red mark, the green mark, the place names—Prussia, Germany, Suhl. Reinhold Schlegelmilch of Tillowitz has generally been considered the maker, and Erdman Schlegelmilch of Suhl whose name keeps cropping up in the discussions was perhaps a brother, a cousin, or maybe no relation.

Lack of information did nothing to hold back collecting interest, for R S hand-painted china is exceptionally attractive and well done. Importers and wholesalers offering it to the trade in the early 1890s called it a "strictly high grade line of character distinction," and listed "plates and bowls, chocolate sets, hatpin holders, and hair receivers . . . in floral designs or art decorations, blended in harmonious pastel tints with refined treatment, enhanced with gold." The shapes were fancy, often embossed, and the hand-painting was all—and more—the wholesalers claimed. The chocolate pot pictured is an excellent example of R S style.

In December 1970, Clifford Schlegelmilch of Flint, Michigan, brought out a paperback, *R. S. Prussia,* in which he shed new light, startling to collectors, about his china-producing ancestors.

In the mid-1800s, he says, Erdman Schlegelmilch, his great-great-uncle, set up a china manufactory in Suhl. Erdman's brother Reinhold (another great-great uncle) worked there for several years, then in 1869 founded a factory of his own in Tillowitz in lower Silesia. Both brothers made utility ware and luxury porcelain. Both used satin, matt, and high gloss finishes: their standards for hand work were equally high. Both made ornate portrait and scenic pieces. And, the startling part, both used the same R S mark in the same colors, the initials being in memory of their father, Rudolph Schlegelmilch. Except a piece was marked with Erdman's or Reinhold's name or with Suhl or Tillowitz, there

seems to be no way to distinguish between the work of the two factories. Reinhold specialized in floral designs and dinner sets for export, yet such pieces, bearing no more than the R S mark, cannot be definitely attributed to him.

When production at these two factories ceased is undetermined, perhaps during World War I. Little business research information comes out of Germany these days, especially about such minor, privately-owned firms. (Tillowitz is no longer on maps of the area.) Reinhold had an importing office in New York City on Irving Place as late as 1929 when the mother of author Clifford Schlegelmilch ordered a dinner set from that address. Possibly this was stock on hand and the factory itself had closed; search for definite data still goes on.

RADFORD JASPER

Alfred Radford was nineteen years old when he came to this country from England. He had been employed at the Wedgwood factory there, and easily found employment in potteries in Baltimore and Trenton. In 1891, after he had been here almost 30 years, he built a pottery of his own in Broadway, Virginia. Two years later he moved it to Tiffin, Ohio.

At Tiffin he began to make his Radford Jasper. It was quite similar to Wedgwood's jasper with sprigged-on decorations in white on background colors of royal blue, light blue, olive green, and dove gray. Since he created each piece himself, the output was necessarily limited and today examples are rare indeed.

Shortly he decided to build a plant in Clarksburg, Virginia, and while it was being erected, he went to Zanesville, Ohio, where he helped construct the pottery that became Arc-en-Ceil. There, he made a "fine vitrified ware with classic cameo relief figures in white, further ornamented with an overlay of contrasting clay resembling orange peel or the bark of a tree; either in matt or semi-matt finish." Usually the decoration was done in color— brown, tan, green, or gray—with contrasting backgrounds in light shades of pink, blue, green, dove gray, or brown. The bark was omitted on small pieces and also on some of the large ones like tankard pitchers. This ware which he made in Zanesville was not marked Radford, but bore only the model number. Color photographs of several pieces are shown in *Zanesville Art Pottery in Color*, by Louise and Evan Purviance and Norris F. Schneider (1968).

In 1903, Radford moved into his Clarksburg factory. Everything progressed nicely and he was getting ready to make his jasper ware there when, in 1904, he died of a heart attack.

His grandson, Fred W. Radford, an eighth generation potter, is now making reproductions of the jasper ware he made in Zanesville, using the original formula and the original molds.

All pieces are marked, "An A. Radford Reproduction by F. Radford," with the number of the piece in sequence of manufacture. Since he can produce only five or six a week, there are not many available—but, for the art pottery collector, an example of this unusual ware is very nice to have, particularly since there is scant chance of ever finding an original. (*See* Arc-en-Ceil.)

RATHBONE, THOMAS

See *Portobello Potteries*

RAVENWOOD

The trademark "Ravenwood," in black letters beneath the representation of a raven, on chinaware has nothing to do with Rookwood for all the plaguey similarity of rooks and ravens. When H. P. Sinclaire & Company, manufacturers of rich cut glass, moved their plant from Corning, New York, to a big new factory in Bath, New York, in 1921, they added a china decorating shop as a sideline. They used imported blanks for their hand-painted china and "Ravenwood" for their trademark. The factory closed in 1929.

REBEKAH AT THE WELL

To the hundreds of people who think of their brown-glazed Rebekah at the Well teapots as "Bennington," hear ye! This pattern was never used at Bennington factories on teapots or anything else.

Many Rebekah teapots were made by Edwin and William Bennett in Baltimore, Maryland, whose chief modeler, Charles Coxon, is credited with introducing the design to America about 1850. He copied it from one previously made in England by Samuel Alcock & Co.

The Syracuse Stoneware Company of Syracuse, New York, "manufacturers of Rockingham and yellow ware, stoneware, sewer pipe, fire brick, etc.," were offering Rebekah teapots as late as 1896, in capacities from 1½ pints to 6 pints, ranging in price from $2.40 to $6.50 a dozen.

There are many varieties of Rebekah teapots, differing slightly in design. Many different potteries, in England and in this country, made them—but none were made at Bennington. (If you still can't quite believe it, check Richard Carter Barret's *How to Identify Bennington Pottery.*)

REDWARE

The earliest potters in our country made redware for the kitchen and dairy—or even for the table—out of the same common red-burning clays they used for their bricks and roof tiles. Its making called for the simplest kind of kilns and equipment. To dress it up, they glazed it with browns and yellows, copper-greens, or a brownish black made from manganese. As late as the 1920s, potters in rural communities were still making redware for local use.

Though glazes differed according to available clays, shapes and decorations were everywhere much alike, excepting the "Dutch" counties of Pennsylvania where the Swiss Mennonites and Germans from the Palatinate settled in the eighteenth century. There, decoration was more lively, even inclined to the humorous. Pennsylvania fruit pie dishes, apple butter crocks, fluted turk's head cake molds, and standing pottery grease lamps were not items seen in New England, nor were the quaint "Dutch" banks, bird whistles, and double-walled tobacco jars. (*See:* Bell Pottery; Moravian Pottery; Zoar Pottery.)

The handsome brown-glazed redware pitcher illustrated shows decoration applied. It is New England provenance, though it was found in the Cooperstown, New York, area.

RED WING POTTERY

See *Union Stoneware Co.*

REEMS CREEK POTTERY

See *Southern Highland Potteries*

REKSTON WARE

See *Stockton Art Pottery*

RICE GRAIN PORCELAIN

Rice, in Chinese symbolism, stands for abundance, and rice grain porcelain with its delicate decoration of "see-through" rice kernels has long attracted foreigners as well as Chinese. Fifteen, twenty, or even forty years ago, rice ware in dainty bowls and other teaware pieces was commonly seen in our gift shops and china stores. These pieces were at that time being manufactured in quantity in China; genuinely old pieces are extremely rare. The ware is still available in our markets, coming to us now from Hong Kong. It is plentiful—and inexpensive—in stores which stock Oriental goods.

In the old method of production from which rice grain porcelain takes its name, actual rice kernels were pressed into the greenware while it was still wet. In the firing, the heat of the kiln burned up the rice, ash and all, leaving tiny apertures where the rice had been. With the application of the glaze, the holes filled up, and the glaze firing turned them into translucent little windows.

The Chinese writing often found on the bottom of rice grain pieces should not be construed either as an indication of profound age or as words of Chinese wisdom; it is merely the name of the manufacturer.

RING TREES

See *Dresser Sets*

RITTENHOUSE, EVANS & CO.

See *American Belleek*

ROCKINGHAM

There's confusion about this term for it applies to two very different types of ceramics. To the collector of elegant and early English porcelain, it means just that. To most of us, it means glazed brown and yellow mottled earthenware that potters everywhere used for teapots and pitchers and other homely household articles. Both designations are correct.

About 1745, at Swinton in Yorkshire on land owned by the Marquis of Rockingham, a pottery began making various kinds of earthenwares and stonewares. Here, some time later, the familiar brown mottled glaze was developed. This new brown ware was called Rockingham, honoring the Marquis, and it was so called by the multitude of potters who copied it then and continued it extensively through years to come.

The Swinton works passed through several hands, emerging in 1806 as Brameld & Co. In 1826, the Bramelds, ambitious and talented, began to produce an excellent porcelain, expensively decorated, in addition to their earthenwares. This porcelain is

also known as Rockingham. It ranked favorably with the finest manufactories of its day, and royal personages were among its purchasers.

When competition forced the factory to close in 1842, the notice of close-out sale listed on hand both useful earthenware wares (we presume some of these were brown glazed) and fine porcelains—breakfast, tea, and coffee equipages, dinnerwares, and cabinet pieces.

Recently a considerable amount of contemporary data about the Rockingham operation has come to light which corrects several misconceptions about Rockingham porcelain. For a late research account, look for *The Rockingham Pottery,* by A. A. Eaglestone and T. A. Lockett (1964), and *Ornamental Rockingham Porcelain,* by Dr. D. C. Rice, also recently published.

The example pictured is of Rockingham pottery made at the Bennett Pottery in Baltimore, Maryland. For other illustrations *see:* Bennington, Rebekah at the Well.

ROGERS GROUPS

THE FAVORED SCHOLAR

John Rogers was one of those fortunate men whose hobbies unexpectedly bring them financial gains as well as recognition. Rogers had wanted to be an artist, but "art" was frowned upon in the 1840s by his conservative New England family. It was too "unsubstantial"; he'd better be a machinist. So machinist he became, putting a six-day week (5 a.m. to 7 p.m.) at the Amoskeag Mills in Manchester, New Hampshire. But "art" was his pleasure, and for spare time fun, he shaped lumps of raw red clay from the Hooksit brickyard into lifelike little figures of the men and women around him. Later in Chicago, as a draughtsman to the City Surveyor, he continued his hobby. Not until a group he had made in clay and presented to the Cosmopolitan Bazaar, a charity affair, brought $75 at a raffle, did he realize the financial possibilities of his fun.

He hied himself to New York with two or three clay groups, learned to evolve them in plaster, and started in business for himself. Almost overnight he became, if not the most famous, certainly the most popular artist of his time. No proper parlor was complete without a putty-colored Rogers Group.

He was a salesman, too, for when stores which dealt largely with Southern trade refused to handle "The Slave Auction" in 1859, he hired a Negro to hawk them in the streets. Later his Civil War groups were much prized, and the larger-than-life plaster of Lincoln which he presented to the City of Manchester has since been cast in bronze. It stands today before one of the High Schools there.

By far the most popular of his subjects were the ordinary

scenes of everyday life, such as "Coming to the Parson," "Weighing the Baby," "Playing Doctor." Of "Checkers up at the Farm," adapted from the group raffled at the Cosmopolitan Bazaar, he sold over 5,000 copies. In all he produced more than eighty groups of plaster statuary, sold more than 100,000 copies.

Rogers Groups are always signed, and though imitators appeared, none attempted so detailed or such large size groups. Since Rogers used contemporary themes, he left today's collectors and students a wonderful insight into the costumes and customs of his age.

ROLLING PINS

The utilitarian rolling pin has been around since man started baking breads. Ancient cooks flattened their dough with stone rollers until wooden rollers evolved. Centuries of later cooks found wood rolling pins good enough for anybody. Then, in the nineteenth century, glass rolling pins came along to tempt the extravagant. Some were made of all glass, some with wooden handles, some with removable handles to allow the inclusion of ice water for chilling the dough. By the end of the century, premium hunters could buy their baking powder in glass rolling pins.

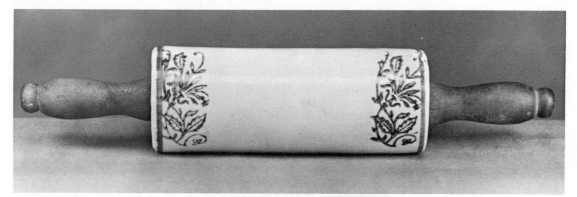

There were china rolling pins, too, making their popular appearance late in the nineteenth century. The first of this fad seems to have been those in Delft or Meissen Onion pattern which were included with complete sets of porcelain kitchen utensils —meat tenderizers, slotted spoons, ladles, funnels, and the like. Other designs followed, but by far the most popular were those with Dutch or German "blue Delft" designs of ships and windmills. These often matched a pantry set of flour, sugar, and spice jars.

Old china rolling pins are decorative in kitchens; more cooks might actually use them if they cost a bit less. The pottery roller pictured, decorated in blue, shows use, but it is not a very early one.

ROOKWOOD

Rookwood, the first art pottery in the United States—and the most distinctive—began as an amateur effort. Mrs. Maria Longworth Nichols (later Mrs. Bellamy Storer, Jr.) was one of a group of talented society women in Cincinnati, Ohio, who took up china painting under Benn Pitman of the Cincinnati School of Design. Their work was so good that some of it was exhibited at the Philadelphia Centennial in 1876. Mrs. Nichols, who went along to the Exposition, was enthralled by a display of Japanese pottery and resolved to make pottery herself, using Ohio clays.

Her father bought an abandoned schoolhouse and fitted it up for her as a pottery. She named it Rookwood for his country place and in November 1880, began operation. At first it was an expensive luxury. Mrs. Nichols was experimenting with clays and glazes and colors, and in the first year, except for her own work, the pottery turned out for sale only pitchers, teapots, and teaware of simple red or yellow clays.

In 1883, she induced William Watts Taylor to become manager of the pottery, and by 1889, it had become self-sustaining. The firm was incorporated in that year with Mr. Taylor as president, a post he held until his death in 1913. Production centered on the elegant decorative forms which made Rookwood famous.

Barber, in his *Pottery and Porcelain of the United States,* classified Rookwood finishes under three headings: Cameo, shell-tinted ware, generally of a beautiful pink color shading into white, and highly glazed; Dull Finished, similar in color, but having the appearance of being unglazed; and Rookwood Faience, highly glazed, and the most characteristic of all Rookwood wares. All varieties are distinguished by the tinting and harmonious blending of the grounds beneath the heavy, transparent colored glazes which gave brilliancy and depth to the rich tones of black, yellow, red, olive green, brown, and amber—the colors most often associated with Rookwood.

The artists who decorated Rookwood wares were exceptionally gifted. Most of them signed their work. Among these were Ketaro Shirayamandi, a Japanese artist brought over by Mrs. Nichols, and Artus Van Briggle, who later had his own art pottery in Colorado Springs. (*See* Van Briggle Pottery.)

Before 1886 various marks were used on Rookwood wares, but in that year, the reverse "R" and "P" with downstrokes overprinted, was adopted. Each year thereafter, until 1900, a small flame was added at the top of the initial. After 1900, a Roman numeral was put at the bottom. The Rookwood Pottery was purchased about 1960 by the Herschede Hall Clock Co., and moved to Starkville, Mississippi. It ceased operations in June 1967.

The eight main types of Rookwood were illustrated in *The Rookwood Book,* published by the Rookwood Pottery in 1905. We also suggest *The Book of Rookwood Pottery,* by Herbert Peck (1968), which will be easier to locate. Then, too, there is Nancy Fitzpatrick's detailed and intelligent account of the Rookwood Pottery and the endeavors which led up to it in *Spinning Wheel* magazine for April, October and November 1960. The Rookwood pieces illustrated, from Mrs. Fitzpatrick's collection are: candleholder, by Josephine E. Zettel, 1894, brown and tan with pink cherry blossoms; vellum-type vase by Shirayamandi, 1911, winter landscape against a bluish-gray background; Irish-type bud vase, by Hirschfeld, 1881, tan with gold flecks merging to blue at the base, decorated with bluebirds in flight.

RORSTRAND

There are really three distinct types of Rorstrand—the early, which is mostly in Swedish museums; the Victorian, which copied English porcelain dinnerwares, but was not heavily exported; and the late, which is available today.

Rorstrand, the oldest pottery in Sweden was established about 1726, near Stockholm, under State patronage. Its earliest wares were similar to old Delft, though experiments in hard paste porcelain were being continuously attempted. By 1760-1780, they were turning out wares with a stanniferous glaze, an enamel composed of oxide of tin, and decorated in peasant style. But for all their labor and experiments, their copying from Meissen and Sevres and Wedgwood, and the absorption of their closest competitor, Mariesberg, they were not out of the financial woods until 1867. A period of prosperity followed, and by the 1900s, Rorstrand had established several branch factories.

During and following World War II, the whole operation was moved to Lidkoping (pronounced Leedshipping), a "safe" spot in the interior. There it operates today, one of Europe's best equipped and busiest potteries.

Rorstrand's present artistic success—and it stands high—began about 1914, when their artists, with great originality, began to work along the lines of Swedish Modern. Handsomer pieces, it seems, are turned out each year. Designers to keep in mind are Carl-Harry Stalhane (dinnerware); Marianne Westman (kitchenware); Hertha Bengtsson (one of a kind stoneware pieces), and Sylvia Leuchovius (wall plaques)—all names promise to be even more significant in years to come. (*See:* Christmas Plates; Kachelofen.)

From 1904 to 1926, Rorstrand produced a limited number of Christmas plates, then no more until 1968. The 1970 plate is illustrated here, showing Nils Holgersson, the legendary boy who flew with his wild geese all over Sweden.

ROSE MEDALLION (ROSE CANTON)

Almost as popular as the blue Canton ware eighteenth century sea captains brought home from China was the Rose Medallion that second and third generation sailing ships carried in westbound cargo.

This colorful ware seems to have been made entirely for export. The shapes were western—flat plates and cups with handles, unknown to Chinese usage. The decorations, unlike other Chinese wares, seemed devoid of symbolism, rather to have been copied from a standard pattern, quite good enough for "foreigners." Thoroughly Occidental mantel vases, punchbowls, and toilet sets were made as well as dinner and teawares.

In decoration green was the basic color, used to separate large medallions of people, pink flowers, birds and butterflies. Five or six figures might be used in the panels of larger pieces, only two or three in smaller pieces. When medallions of pink flowers alternated with medallions of people, the ware was called Rose Medallion; when all the medallions were filled with flowers, it was differentiated as Rose Canton.

The whiteware itself was mostly made at Ching-teh-chen, the porcelain center of China, though some may have come from other sources. It was taken to Canton to be decorated with enamels, and shipped from that port. Thelma Shull in her *Victorian Antiques* tells of pieces marked Haviland & Co., and says this refers to the porcelain only, that the decoration, like all Rose Medallion decoration, was done in China.

The pattern remained popular long after sailing ship days.

It was being imported in quantity as late as 1912, and is still coming to us in limited amount through the port of Hong Kong.

The Rose Medallion "traveling" teapot and cup, pictured, came in a lined and padded wicker basket with elaborate brass lock and handles for carrying.

ROSE TAPESTRY

See *Royal Bayreuth*

ROSENTHAL

In 1895, in a hired room in an eighteenth century manor house, Schloss Erkersreuth, in Kronach, Bavaria, young Philip Rosenthal set up a workshop for his first porcelain factory. Much of the hard paste porcelain he produced, daintily and colorfully hand-painted in the styles of the day, came to America to brighten turn-of-the-century tea tables and china closets.

The Rosenthal marks, a crown over crossed roses with "Rosenthal" beneath or a crown with "R C" arranged in crossed diagonals, became familiar wherever quality china was sold. Marshall Field's in Chicago was an important distributor. Dr. Mickenhagen in his *European Porcelain* tells us that this was the first porcelain firm to sign its products with a full name.

Rosenthal china is still being made, still being imported;

most of it is tableware. There are factories now in Selb, Selb-Plossberg, and Munchen as well as at Kronach, and a Rosenthal glassworks at Bad Soden. Recently the present Philip Rosenthal purchased the manor house in which it all began. He and his family are living in it now, but he plans, when his children are grown, to make it into a Rosenthal Museum.

The fiftieth anniversary plate pictured shows the Rosenthal marks, as well as the founder's portrait. This was a special edition and each plate came fitted into its own velvet lined box. (*See* Christmas Plates.)

ROSEVILLE POTTERY

Roseville pottery is very "late," considering the plant opened in 1890 and did not close until 1954 and some art pottery, at least, was made to the end of its days. Pieces made between 1900 and 1930 are being quietly collected today as "antiques of tomorrow."

Zanesville potters seem all to have started with painted flower pots and cuspidors. George F. Young was no exception, beginning his career with just such items in Roseville, Ohio. He moved to nearby Zanesville in 1898, and by 1900 was ready to compete with Weller and Owens in art pottery lines. His Rozane duplicated Lonhuda and Louwelsa; he marked it with a circle enclosing a rose and the name "Rozane Ware." He continued to use the Rozane designation—a combination of Roseville and Zanesville—on various lines until World War I.

His Rozane Fugi, with incised decoration countered Weller's incised Dickens ware; his Woodland and Della Robbia were also incised. When Weller introduced Sicardo, Roseville came out with Rozane Mongol—John J. Herold, an Austrian, who had worked for both Weller and Owens before going to Roseville in 1900, designed it. (In 1908, Herold went to Golden, Colorado, and organized the Herold China Company.) When Rozane Mongol didn't take with the public, Young tried again with Rozane Mara, a metallic glaze. This met with more success, but it was never made in quantity.

Like Weller and Owens, Roseville kept busily on with its lucrative commercial lines, particularly cooking wares, but the competition with Weller in art pottery, after Owens dropped out, continued unceasing. Roseville's Donatello, decorated with cherubs and fluted borders which came out during World War I, gave Roseville the lead for the first time. This popular line was designed by Harry Rhead, an Englishman, whose brother Frederick was the designer for Weller.

The matt glazes for which Roseville won reputation in the 1920s can be credited to Frank Ferrell, the designer who replaced Rhead in 1918. Mostique, Carnelian, Imperial—what a time they must have had finding names—used conventional flowers in pastel colors, yellow, blue, rose, etc., with green foliage on pebbled grounds of gray, white, or tan, with matt finish. This is the type, so popular in the 1920s that most people associate with Roseville and recognize on sight.

About 1918, the mark "Roseville U.S.A." in raised letters on the bottom of pieces was adopted. Later pieces are still to be found with paper stickers.

The pine cone design pictured, which Roseville produced in 1913 and kept on making for fifteen years, was one Weller had rejected when Ferrell, who designed it, worked for him. It was revived in 1952 in cheapened form but was not successful. After the depression of the 1930s, Roseville concentrated on its commercial wares and its art pottery diminished to a minimum, cheaply made. The factory closed in 1954. For more details on Roseville wares, which were made in an enormous number of shapes and designs, see Norris Schneider's *Zanesville Art Pottery*, and Lucile Henzke's *American Art Pottery*.

ROWLAND & MARCELLUS

See *Historical Blue Plates, Late*

ROWANTREES POTTERY

Blue Hill on the coast of Maine was once humming with ship building and shipmasters. Those days are gone, but the village with its lovely old streets and handsome houses is still busy, embarked upon another activity as old as seafaring. It is potting.

When Adelaide Pearson, in 1934, started the Rowantrees Kiln as part of a handicraft program in the village, designed to help people who lived there, she thought of it as a hobby pottery. Miss Laura Paddock, who had trained under Edmund DeForrest Curtis in Philadelphia, came to assist her. Summer people from Blue Hill and nearby Bar Harbor, approving the pottery, the potters, and the products, started the ball rolling. Without even planning, the two hobbyists found themselves in business. Today Rowantrees, now owned and operated by Miss Paddock, is known round the world.

The tableware and accessories produced there are all handcrafted, either wheel-thrown or hand-built; no molds at all are used. The blue and gray clays used are native to Maine and dug by hand. The original glazes are made from seashore granite, rich with feldspar, quartz, black biotite mica and from copper found in an abandoned mine; there is even a manganese deposit in the neighborhood. Appropriately the colored glazes reflect the Maine coast—grays and blues, greens and blacks—and they are named in kind: Driftwood; Duckshead; Seagull; Evergreen, Jonquil, Mist Blue. Each piece is marked "R K Blue Hill, Maine."

This is not an old pottery, nor is it a large one—there are but eight fulltime potters at work—but it is one to salute. The charm, simplicity, and workmanship in Rowantrees pieces truly express the art of rural America. As such, the Kiln is represented in the Traveling Exhibits of American Handicrafts which the U.S. Department of State has sent to Europe, Latin America, and the Middle East. (More about Rowantrees in *Down East Magazine,* published in Camden, Maine, for June 1963.)

ROYAL BAYREUTH

Though Royal Bayreuth novelty items and fine quality tableware have delighted collectors for years, only recently has accurate information come to light concerning the factory; even its location has been veiled in mystery. We must all be grateful to Virginia Sutton Salley and her husband, George H. Salley, for their *Royal Bayreuth China,* published in 1970, who have at last given us something definitive about this ware. The factory is not in Bayreuth, where other researchers have hunted in vain for it, but in the mountain village of Tettau, fifty kilometers from that city. The Salleys visited the plant in 1968 and in their little book they report firsthand on what they found there.

The manufactory began in Tettau in 1794 as the Koniglich Priv. Porzellanfabrik Tettau, the first porcelain factory in Bavaria. Its early wares were on a par with Meissen. The pieces collected so assiduously today—Rose Tapestry, Sunbonnet Baby novelties, hand-painted bowls and vases, slippers, pitchers and demitasses intriguingly shaped like flowers, fruit, animals, birds, devils, and the like—were made between 1897, when the pottery was rebuilt by a new management after a Great Fire, and World War I. Little of it is found in Germany because the ware was made entirely for export.

From 1946 to 1949, the company essayed to reproduce a few novelty items such as Devil and Cards and some Tapestry pieces, mainly for export to England. This late ware was marked with the regular Royal Bayreuth crest but in a bright green color. (Earlier markings were blue or a light green.) Since almost all of the original molds were destroyed in a fire in 1917, new ones had to be made; production proved too costly to be profitable. None of the novelty pieces nor any Tapestry has been reproduced since 1949, and none is planned in the future.

The distinctive and delicately shaded Tapestry line, either in rose or scenic patterns, with its slightly pebbled surface, is the most expansive of Royal Bayreuth wares today, though none of them, even the humble tomato mayonnaise sets so commonly seen a short time ago, are inexpensive anymore.

ROYAL COPENHAGEN PORCELAIN MANUFACTORY

Because so much publicity has been given Royal Copenhagen's Christmas plates, it is easy to think that famous Denmark manufactory spends all its time making them. Actually the Christmas plates are only a minor part of its production.

The firm's specialty is dinnerware, and some of their patterns, like *Tranquebar* and *Blue Fluted* have been in use for almost two centuries. Their most famous dinner service, ordered by Catherine the Great of Russia, was begun in 1790. It was decorated by Bayer of Nurnberg with illustrations from *Flora Danica,* with the Latin names of each flower recorded on the reverse of the plate. The set was not completed until 1802, and in the meantime, the Empress Catherine had died. So it went to the Danish royal family. It's on view now in Rosenberg Castle if you'd care to see it.

Royal Copenhagen also excels in figures as everyone who visits in Denmark or in duty-free ports in the Caribbean will be quick to tell you. They're available, too, in quality chinaware shops around the world. Twentieth century figurines like their "Little Mermaid" in pure glazed white, "Boy with Umbrella," "Nodding Doll," their nursery rhyme series, and many others are now collector's items. In the late 1890s, some exceptionally fine Art Nouveau pieces were made here.

The present Royal Copenhagen Porcelain Manufactory was established in 1772 by a chemist, Frantz Henrich Muller. The artists he engaged were outstanding and the porcelain on which they painted their landscapes and flowers was of high quality. When bankruptcy threatened in 1799, the Crown took over the plant. The mark adopted then is still used—three wavy lines in blue, denoting the three belts of sea that divide the islands of Zealand and Fumen from Jutland. The manufactory passed into private hands in 1867. From 1880, when Arnold Krog was appointed art director and started underglaze decoration, the

fortunes of the company have prospered mightily.

The Royal Copenhagen Scottie figure pictured, from the collection of Mrs. H. J. Langsenkamp, Jr., is typical of the excellence found even in their smallest figurines.

ROYAL BARNUM

See *Buttons*

ROYAL BERLIN PORCELAIN

See *K.P.M.*

ROYAL CROWN DERBY

See *Derby*

ROYAL PORCELAIN COMPANY

See *K.P.M.*

ROYAL RUDOLSTADT

See *Kewpies*

ROYAL WORCESTER

See *Worcester*

ROZANNE

See: *Roseville; Zanesville Pottery*

RUBELLES FAIENCE

See *Lithophanes*

RUCKELS POTTERY

See *Illinois Potters*

RUSKIN'S POTTERY

See *Buttons*

SADLER & GREEN

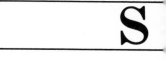

These are the men who invented transfer printing—or maybe not, authorities disagree—but at least they did more than any of the others to pioneer this new technique, and they did apply for a patent in 1756. The story goes that John Sadler, a printer in Liverpool, threw out some spoiled prints, still wet. Children found them in the trash and had a fine time sticking them on bits of broken pottery. Sadler noticed that the wet prints left a faint impression on the earthenware, and from that figured how to print designs on tissue and transfer the tissue impression to pottery. With Guy Green, another Liverpool printer, he set up a "Printed Ware Manufactory." In their patent application, they claimed that, between them, they could print 1200 tiles in six hours, and included affidavits from witnesses to that remarkable feat.

Sadler & Green did not make pottery themselves. Some ware we know they bought from Josiah Wedgwood, decorated it, and sold it back to Wedgwood for distribution; it's all recorded in Wedgwood correspondence. One of the Wedgwood designs they made and printed, in red, black, or purple, on complete dinner, tea, and dessert sets, was "Liverpool Birds." Wedgwood still uses it. (*See* Queen's Ware for illustrations.)

In 1763, Wedgwood purchased the right to decorate his own ware by their process but still continued to sell undecorated wares to Sadler & Green. Sadler retired in 1770; Green carried on till 1799. Only occasionally did they mark their work; then it was either "J. Sadler (or Sadler) Liverpool," or "Green, Liverpool," worked into the printed design at the very bottom.

The white tin-glazed tile panel, 19½ inches square, illustrated, was decorated by Sadler & Green, ca. 1789, in black transfer printing with a painted overglaze in green.

ST. CLOUD

This is early, and museum ware, but important for being, as Litchfield says in his *Pottery and Porcelain,* "the parent to the famous Sevres factory." Soft paste porcelain was being made at St. Cloud, France, as early as 1696. Before that faience had been made, and early records show that faience "vases to hold oranges," made at St. Cloud, had been purchased by the purveyor of faience to the Court of Louis XIV's *Trianon de Porcelaine.*

St. Cloud porcelain was decorated simply; the coloring being mostly blue, though sometimes red, on cream-white ground. Sprigs of painted flowers or prunus blossoms in relief were characteristic ornamentations. St. Cloud used a variety of marks and you'll find them in marks books. The factory burned in 1776, and was not rebuilt.

SAKE CUPS

Next to tea, sake, a rice wine, has long been the most important beverage in Japan. For centuries it has played an important part in every Japanese festival. It is used in the Shinto marriage ceremony and at various rites at Shinto shrines. It is also a common social drink, like beer.

Sake is served in tiny shallow cups made of pottery or porcelain, though the three cups used in the Shinto wedding are traditionally of lacquer. In olden days, it was poured from a large jar; now it is usually poured from a small porcelain bottle with a narrow neck.

The sake cups we find most easily in antiques shops today are porcelain, decorated in the early Imari style, though there are many other types of decoration and many different grades of ceramic body. The one pictured is unusual for, resembling the old frog mugs from a ribald English countryside, it is enhanced with a tiny stand-up turtle in the bottom to surprise the sipper. It is of white porcelain, with no outside decoration beyond a blue band at the base. The interior, in addition to the turtle, is decorated with a delicate hand-painted flower spray of a type which suggests an 1880 date. It is 2½ inches in diameter; 1 inch tall.

SALOPIAN (or CAUGHLEY)

This is one of the early wares, called interchangeably Salopian (for its location in Salop, Shropshire, where it was made), or Caughley (for the works), and you'll not be finding much of it in the average antiques shop. Look for examples in the larger antiques shows and in shops which specialize in eighteenth century English wares.

The Caughley Works really got underway about 1775 when Thomas Turner commenced to manufacture porcelain there. And a fine job he did of it. He had previously worked at Worcester as a designer, and the useful wares he turned out at Caughley, mostly tea and dinner wares, followed closely Worcester shapes and styles of decoration and in some respects, the body. He sold a great deal of his plain ware to Chamberlain's decorating shop at Worcester.

Particularly well known are his blue printed wares. Thomas Minton designed the famous Blue Willow pattern while he was working for Turner, and Turner himself is credited with the much-copied Blue Dragon and Nankin patterns. His blue printed porcelains were usually marked with a "C" or "S" or with Chinese style numerals, printed underglaze in blue. The mark on his later works was "Salopian" impressed.

In 1799, Thomas Turner sold the Caughley Works lock, stock and barrel to Coalport who continued it for a short while. About 1821, the factory was demolished. Recently excavations on the site have turned up much new information. F. A. Barrett's *Caughley and Coalport Porcelain* (1951) is the book for those who want to study Salopian in depth, and Geoffrey Godden in his *Encyclopaedia of British Pottery and Porcelain* tells us that a book on the recent excavations is now in the writing.

Pictured is a Caughley inscribed mug, 4½ inches high, decorated with underglaze blue print, painted name and 1776 date, and bearing the printed "C" mark. You can see it at the Victoria and Albert Museum in London.

SALT BISQUE

See *Stone Bisque*

SALT GLAZE

Salt glaze was introduced in England late in the seventeenth century from Cologne where it had long been used on heavy stoneware jugs, bottles, and tankards. This exceedingly hard glaze on white stoneware was effected by throwing salt into the heated kiln. The salt vaporized and settled on the ware in minute drops, thin and transparent. The finished product had a slightly pitted surface, somewhat like an orange peel, and was characteristically grayish in color. To English potters it was a tremendous advance over their earlier dull lead glazes, and it was used and improved until Wedgwood's creamware came along about 1760 to displace it.

Early salt glaze pieces were rather crude, with tiny flowers, leaves, birds, and other decorations individually molded and applied to the turned surface. Later, allover designs became possible; scratch blue technique was used for decoration; and between 1720 and 1760, when the finest pieces were made, an over-the-glaze decoration in brilliant enamels was in vogue.

In Victorian times there was a salt glaze revival, inspired by Parian and other molded wares. Pitchers were particularly

popular, usually in allover molded patterns in dingy shades of white, blue, or drab. Late examples are not difficult to find; early ones are. Salt glaze has never entirely disappeared. It was long used for stoneware jugs and crocks, and factories can still be found that use it so. (*See* Washington-Wakefield Pattern.)

Pictured is a salt glaze rosewater ewer and basin with basketry, scrolls and trellis design, ca. 1770, now in the Victoria and Albert Museum, London.

SAMSON

In the early 1840s, in Paris, the firm of Samson and Vivinis was busily engaged in faking whatever porcelain bibelots were attracting the attention of connoissuers. M. Edmé Samson, who started the business, was a decorator of porcelain; his son Emile, a potter. The factory was in Montreuil; the showroom, in Paris. At one time more than 200 workers were employed.

What they didn't copy is not worth writing of. They copied States Arms teapots, Oriental Export porcelain, Dresden, Chelsea, Crown Derby, Worcester, St. Cloud, and whatever else came to hand, complete with backstamps. Occasionally they used a fictitious mark, and once in a while, mainly to stay out of trouble, they added the mark of their own factory but in such small dimension it can scarcely be seen.

To add to collecting confusion, they were such excellent

potters and masters of modeling and decoration that Samson imitations were often better than the originals! One tiny help for the distressed—Samson worked only in hard paste porcelain. When a piece which was originally made in soft paste turns up in hard paste, think Samson. (*See* Martha Washington States Pattern.)

The Samson figure, illustrated, shows a lady of fashion seated on a donkey, and holding a child; two attendants and a husband stand by. The group is 13¼ inches high, and dated, but without document, about 1845.

SANTONS

Santons, or "little saints," are the finger-length clay figurines made for Christmas creches in Provence in Southern France. Signed molds in the "Old Marseilles" Museum indicate the early 1790s as the beginning of Provencal interest in this art, the earliest mold being identified as the work of Jean-Louis Lagnel (1764-1822), a professional modelist, who signed his work "Agnel."

Though figurines for decorating creches and other religious scenes had been made much earlier in Italy, southern Germany, and Spain, utilizing all sorts of materials from glass and marble to porcelain, wax, and wood, the Provencal santon-makers claim to be the first to make their figures in clay, and the first to have given them definite personalities.

Inspired by the thought that everyone had a right to come to the manger of the Infant Jesus, Provencal santon-makers added to the traditional Holy Family, shepherds, and wise men, a townful of tiny people familiar to their own locale—farmers, millers, knife-grinders, gatherers of faggots, fishermen, spinners, and such.

Santons are still being made in the same old way of natural or baked clay, meticulously hand-painted in bright colors. Most of them are sold in France, particularly in the Marseilles area, but some are now being exported for foreign collectors. Most santons are marked with the maker's name, and some collectors like to concentrate on the work of a particular artist. Carbonel is presently well known in this country, perhaps because his skillfully executed santons are most plentifully imported.

For older examples, Provence is the hunting ground, and for study of earliest types and finest workmanship, there are santons on display in most Provencal museums and in Paris at the Musée National des Arts et Traditions Populaire de France.

SARREGUEMINES

Utzschneider & Co., established in 1770, is the factory at Sarreguemines, France, where over the years soft paste porcelain, biscuit figures, and artistic stonewares have been produced. Home consumption came first, but enough of these wares, impressed "Sarreguemines," were exported to keep us aware of their Gallic gaiety and charm. Plates, in sets or singly, seem to come most often our way.

The Sarreguemines majolica, lighter in weight than English majolica, is well represented in their solid green leaf plates, which at first glance you may take for early Wedgwood. This firm is still active, very much so.

The design in center of the 6-inch Sarreguemines plate illustrated is transfer-printed in black; the border is in lavender. It's an old one.

SATSUMA

At different times, widely different types of Japanese wares have been admired by Europeans and Americans. In the late seventeenth and first half of the eighteenth centuries, fine Japanese porcelain of Kakiemon and Imari were at the head of the list. In the last half of the nineteenth century, gaudy Satsuma took over. Today, it's the simple folk ware and prehistoric sculpture that is sought.

Satsuma is an exquisite faience, among the finest made. It is cream or ivory colored, decorated with enamel colors, gold, and raised ornament. Made in Kagoshima, it was called "Satsuma" after the old name of the prefecture. The original production of Satsuma kilns, late in the sixteenth century, was tea ceremony ware in the Korean style of the Yi dynasty. Early pieces were small, restrained, and elegant. They are rare today and much desired. The Satsuma of the nineteenth century, which is still plentiful, is a different story.

After 1854, when Japan was opened again to trade by Commodore Perry, Japanese art reached high peaks of popularity in the West. The Satsuma of this period, pandering to Victorian taste, carried decoration to excess, becoming gaudier and gaudier, until it seemed every square inch of its beautiful body was covered with rich gold decoration and bright enameled depictions of Japanese legends. Europeans adored it; so did Americans.

All through the Victorian age, the rage for Satsuma continued. Vases, large and small, boxes, big and little, and all sorts of other decorative pieces, including buttons, were eagerly snapped up by Western buyers. Yet these same wares, which brought high prices fifty years ago, go begging today. So do tastes change! For further reading, Hugo Munsterberg's *The Ceramic Art of Japan* is recommended.

The Satsuma teapot pictured is one of the finer examples of late nineteenth century work. It is polychrome decorated and gilded, exquisitely painted, and goes to show that not all restraint was lost in Victoriana.

SAUT BUCKET

This you won't see often, but should you happen on one of these pottery affairs, looking like a bird's nesting house, it's a saut bucket, traditionally used in Scotland for salt-preserving or pickling fish and meats. The hen has nothing to do with it but to look pretty on its straw nest composed of fine curlings of clay. The one pictured dates about 1850; most are earlier than that. One quite similar is in the Glasgow Art Gallery and Museums. There are variations in decoration, but this one is indicative of the type.

SCAMMEL CHINA

See *Lamberton China*

SCOTT BROS.

See *Portobello Potteries*

SCOTTISH POTTERY

Little attention has been paid to Scottish potteries. Their unmarked earthenwares have been classed for years as "Staffordshire" and let go at that. What marks were used seldom appear in marks books, though Godden's *Encyclopaedia of British Pottery and Porcelain Marks* has done quite well by them. The fact is that little Scottish pottery was original; most of it was copied from the Staffordshire potteries; perhaps it deserved to be placed in that category.

Still it is interesting for us to know that Scottish potters furnished us with a great deal of tableware in early days—it did not all come from England. For instance, in 1791, Glasgow shipments to Virginia and Carolina included 21,400 lbs. of coarse pottery and 45,330 lbs. of creamware. In 1796, the figures had increased for both types to 94,100 lbs. and 168,942 lbs.

The leading potteries were in Glasgow, Portobello, Bo'ness, and Prestopans. C. Bernard Hughes, in *English and Scottish Earthenware,* in his chapter "Scottish Pottery" lists several others. (*See:* Bo'ness Potteries; Glasgow Potteries; Portobello Potteries; Prestopans; Wemyss.)

SEVRES

Sevres is the luxury name in French porcelain; everyone knows it, respects it, bows to it. This aristocrat of porcelains was first made about 1745 at Vincennes under the auspices of Louis XV, King of France. The early product was a soft paste porcelain, translucent and flawless, in plain white with gilding its only decoration. In 1756, the Vincennes factory was merged with the new *Manufacture Royale de Porcelaine de France* which had been established at Sevres. Here, too, soft paste porcelain was the order of the day, but after 1765, when the first hard paste porcelain was made at Sevres, soft paste production gradually decreased. By the early 1800s, only hard paste porcelain was being made.

The colorings of Sevres porcelains were rich and wonderful—*bleu de roi, bleu turquoise, rose Pompadour* were the most famous ground colors. Designs and decorative paintings were beautiful to behold—and typically French. The finest artists and modelers of the time lent their talents to tableware and utilitarian items as well as to elaborate decorative pieces; a handsome jonquil yellow ewer and basin is illustrated in Litchfield's *Pottery and Porcelain.* The classic bisquit groups, in pure white with gold or colored bases, first made in soft paste days, were equally popular in Napoleon's time in hard paste. The group illustrated is in hard paste.

The mark of Sevres is the royal cypher of interlaced L's, sanctioned by the King in 1753 for Vincennes use. Actually it had been used there previous to permission.

Needless to say, a ware so remarkable, so desired, and so cherished was bound to be copied. Collectors today must be very wary for Sevres imitation is nothing new. It has gone on for centuries. The best of England's nineteenth century porcelain factories copied it well, and like some present-day copyists, were not above reproducing the Sevres mark.

SGRAFFITO

In fifteenth and sixteenth century Italy, potters decorated their earthenware by cutting or incising the surface with a sharp pointed instrument before glazing. They called it sgraffito, meaning "scratched." Germany copied it, so did Holland and other European countries. Finally it got to England, and that was a long time ago, too. By then Sgraffito ware had become a traditional brown earthenware, covered with light-covered slip, the incisions being cut through the slip.

In this country, Germans in eastern Pennsylvania produced quantities of it for homely utilitarian wares from 1700 right through to 1800 and later. Today Pennsylvania Dutch souvenirs —ashtrays, plates, and the like—are made commercially by this process. It is also an effective favorite with today's amateur potters.

The puzzle jug pictured is Pennsylvania made. It is sgraffito decorated with tulips and distelfinks, and inscribed, "When this you see Remember mee that meney mules abjetent bee—1805—for Hugh and Sally Hutlin." (*See* Puzzle Jugs, though it won't help much in "unpuzzling" the inscription!)

SHAVING BASINS

A shaving basin looks for all the world like a soup plate with a giant bite taken out of the rim. It was a standard accoutrement of the barber-surgeon in the seventeenth and eighteenth centuries. The cut-out fitted under the chin of the gentleman being shaved and protected his clothes from lather drippings. These basins were made and used everywhere gentlemen were shaven, from England, Holland, and Italy to the Orient.

Earliest shaving basins were made of pewter, and an old English record, preserved from 1488, shows an entry, "Pro sowdying de le schavying Bassynnys 6d."

Shaving basins of any material can be considered rare finds today, yet if you wander the back countries of Portugal and Spain, you will see many a gay faience basin hung outside by a back

door. They are still used there and some are quite old, having been handed down from father to son.

At the Sleepy Hollow Restoration at Croton-on-Hudson, New York, there is the Japanese shaving basin pictured, in Imari style, from the early eighteenth century.

SHAVING SOAP BOXES
SHAVING MUGS

The lidded round china box to hold shaving soap, as well as pomade for the hair, seems to have entered the scene of men's foibles and frills about 1800. By the 1820s and through the 1830s, many of these earthenware containers were issued with fancy transfer printed lids. By the 1840s, shaving soap makers were packing their products in the same type boxes, but bearing their advertising as part of the design. Less expensive boxes were made of wood; these too had fancy tops and labels.

For men of the 1850s who patronized barber shops, there were personalized shaving soap boxes, generally of porcelain, with the name of the owner encircling the box in gold letters. (Two are illustrated.) These were designed for stacking on the barber's shelves, ready for use when the owner came in for his daily shave.

Then came H. P. and W. C. Taylor, soapmakers of Philadelphia, with shaving soap packed in a mug. This was purely promotional packaging; Messrs. Taylor could not have foreseen the vogue it would create—not so much for their soap as for their package. Shaving mugs became the rage. By the 1870s every shaving man, rich or poor, had a shaving mug in use, either at home or at the barber's. Mugs became fancier and fancier until the occupational shaving mug proved the *ne plus ultra*. (See: Occupational Shaving Mugs: Pot Lids.)

SHAW, ANTHONY

See *Texian Campaigne*

SHELLEY POTTERIES, LTD.

See *Foley China*

SHENANDOAH POTTERY

See *Bell Pottery*

SHENANGO POTTERY

See: *Lamberton China; Martha Washington States China*

SICARDO

This beautiful metallic lustre ware with floral or geometric designs developed within the glaze is the most outstanding—and the most expensive—of art potteries made by Weller at Zanesville, Ohio. Rich wine reds, bright greens, and peacock blue were the usual colors, highlighted with an iridescent gold or silver sheen.

To make it, Weller brought Jacques Sicard and his assistant, Henri Gelli, from France. Though the secret of their formula was never divulged—they went to enormous lengths to conceal it, like working in locked rooms and speaking always in a strange French dialect—other potteries, including Tiffany and Owens did produce quite similar wares.

Sicardo pieces are signed, usually with both "Sicard" and "Weller," though occasionally "Sicard" is used alone. Sometimes the signature is clearly visible, scratched over the design; sometimes it is included in the decoration itself and you must look hard to find it.

The vase pictured is wine red at the top, vivid green at the bottom, 5½ inches high. It's from the collection of Lucile Henzke. (*See:* Weller; Zanesville Potters.)

SILICON CHINA

See *Booth's*

SLIPWARE

Slipware was the first decorated pottery made in this country. It is a red or buff porous ware, over which slip (a white or light colored clay, thick and liquid) was poured, or trailed,

or worked with a quill to make a design. Often sgraffito and slip decoration were used together.

Though slipware was made in all the colonies, it is chiefly associated with the Germans in Pennsylvania, who brought their methods and designs from the Old Country and liked to see familiar distelfinks and tulips on their household wares.

Most of the very early slipware has long since been broken and thrown out; what remains is mostly in museums. But over the years, there was enough slipware made and enough saved so that finding good examples, not necessarily of earliest vintage, is not at all impossible.

The slip decorated vinegar jug pictured shows dot and line decoration, tulips, sunflowers, and distelfinks. This is an oldie; so is Joseph's plate.

SNOW BABIES

In the early 1900s, it was children who were making collections of these antic little one- to two-inch figurines in their white sugary snowsuits. Now, it's big people who hunt for the tiny skaters and skiers and dancers, babies on sleds, bears on sleds, babies and bears in igloos, in hundreds of happy poses.

The Snow Babies originated in Germany in the early 19th century as *Zucker Puppen* (sugar candy dolls) which along with Polar bears and igloos, were used to decorate Christmas trees and creches. Eventually confectioners changed from sugar candy to almond paste marzipan. Then Johann Moll, a confectioner in Lubeck, casting about for a window novelty, commissioned Hertwig and Company, a porcelain manufactory founded in 1864, at Katzhutte, Thuringia, to make a bisque version. The Babies that Hertwig originated—spattered with glittersand to simulate snow, and looking like marzipan—became popular knickknacks. Other German companies began to make them, and so later did the Japanese, though less skillfully.

Snow Babies sold extremely well in the United States, particularly in German communities. Though the highest peak of importation was from 1906 to 1910, their popularity lasted into the late 1930s. World War II ended their importation, and production was not resumed after the War. A few reproductions, alas, are now coming on the market. Watch mail order Christmas catalogs, particularly Miles Kimball's, for new pieces being offered.

The illustration, showing examples from the extensive collection of Mrs. Richard H. Mosher, was used by Harry Wilson Shuart in an article on Snow Babies in *Spinning Wheel* for January-February 1970.

SOLON, MARC LOUIS

In addition to his work with Pâte-sur-pâte for which he was justly famous, Marc Louis Solon was an author of at least nine books on ceramic art, from *Salt Glaze* (1890), *Old French Faience* (1903), to *Italian Majolica* (1907). His *Art of the Old English Potter,* published in 1883, is perhaps his best-known work. It may sometimes be found in second-hand bookshops nowadays, and it is well worth looking for.

Besides being a gifted artist and an author, Solon was also a collector of early English pottery and of everything in the way of literature on the subject of pottery. When his collections were sold at auction in London in 1912, over 4000 books, pamphlets, brochures, and catalogues were included.

SOUTHERN HIGHLAND POTTERIES

In the 1930s, Allen H. Eaton made a survey of the arts and crafts of the Southern Mountain region, extending from West Virginia into Georgia. His findings are recorded in his *Handicrafts of the Southern Highlands,* published in 1937 by the Russell Sage Foundation. The potteries he mentioned were in operation at that time and were ones he himself had visited. By now some of the pieces he saw being made should be turning up in antiques shops here and there, and for purposes of recognition of such pieces as are marked, we give you here some of the lesser names from his listing with his comments; the more important ones are treated separately. (*See:* Jugtown Pottery; Omar Khayyam Art Pottery; Pisgah Forest Pottery.)

In Georgia—*Meaders' Pottery,* in Cleveland, White County, was run by a family of workers—father, mother, and nine children, ranging from six to eighteen years of age. Mr. Meaders' brother, *L. Q. Meaders,* also ran a pottery in nearby Leo. Both brothers, who had learned their craft from their father in North Carolina, "made strong household pieces used in mountain homes—hard smooth vessels practical in milk houses or as mountain spring refrigerators."

In North Carolina—in Buncombe County were the *Brown Pottery* at Arden; the *Reems Creek Pottery* at Weaverville, and the *Omar Khayyam Art Pottery* at Candler. D. F. Brown, manager of the Brown Pottery had just made "what was said to be the largest single vase ever produced in any Southern pottery; it measured 9 feet, 9½ inches around, and was 5 feet, 9½ inches tall." In Wilkes County, the *Kennedy Pottery* was operating in Wilkesboro.

In North Carolina's Piedmont section, near Jugtown, "potteries which deserve special mention for form, color, and texture are *Cole's Pottery* near Seagrove, Randolph County, and the *Hilton Pottery* at Hickory, Catawba County. Some of the most attractive glazes to be found in the South are at Cole's Pottery where all the pieces are shaped by hand, most of them on the kick-wheel, and where they are fired in long, arched kilns of the old type. Hilton potters also produce some special glazes including attractive combinations of gray and blue, and they make a good many small containers to hold foods put up by the farm women of the Highlands."

In Kentucky—"*The Bybee* and the *Waco* potteries both made smooth and semi-mat glazes, in many colors, and had a rather wide distribution."

In West Virginia—at Buckhammon, Upshur County, "*Mrs. Annie Latham Bartlett,* who took up ceramics when she was well along in years, has developed a process of hardening the native clay without firing by mixing with it certain ingredients of her own discovery. She uses oil paints, then varnish, and her pieces look quite like majolica. Her figures are original and include scenes in color and arrangements of local historical or symbolical subjects."

SOUVENIR CHINA

Some local history buffs collect picture postcards of their town or state; some look for souvenir spoons. Others hunt souvenir china—cups and saucers, pitchers, plates, mustard pots, and relish dishes, all decked out with long-ago scenes. Ladies of the turn-of-the-century doted on such souvenir pieces, and merchants kept them well supplied, either from stock on their shelves or with advertising give-aways.

Though the Hampshire Pottery of Keene, New Hampshire, and the Harker Pottery of East Liverpool, Ohio, made and decorated some souvenir china, the bulk of it was imported, and the plethora of backstamps in sometimes overwhelming. There will be, usually, the backstamp of the company which made the china, with the country of origin—England, Bavaria, Austria, Germany, or whatever. Then may come the name of the concern for which it was made like "Bell Jewelers," or "Vermont Marble Co." Added to that, the name of the importer may also appear. Most likely this will be Wheelock, though sometimes it's Jones, McDuffie & Stratton or some other importer.

George Wheelock, it seems, was the largest jobber of souvenir china in this country, getting wholeheartedly into the act about 1900. He selected his whiteware in Germany and Austria, then decorated it with black and white transfer scenes at South Bend, Indiana. George Wheelock & Company was active till about 1960.

Wherever it was decorated, in this country or at some foreign factory, in black and white transfer or gaily hand-painted, all the buyer had to do was send along a sketch or photograph of the desired scene with his order to the jobber.

Souvenir china is still inexpensive, fairly plentiful, and of special interest since many of the scenes it records are now nonexistent.

The small unmarked cup and saucer illustrated is in color, orange for the background, showing "No. 1 Mill, Somersworth, N. H." This was one of New Hampshire's early cotton mills, built in 1802, the first of the Great Falls Manufacturing Company's complex. (The town was at that time called Great Falls.) No. 1 Mill was used up to the first World War, and still stands, but empty of machinery. (*See:* Centennial Souvenirs; Spode.)

SPATTERWARE

One of the tablewares Staffordshire potters sent over to tempt American buyers in the early nineteenth century was Spatter. This was a crude, soft paste ware, highly colored, with lively freehand decoration. It was uncommonly cheap. Though it was offered all along the Eastern seaboard, it found ready sale only at the Port of Philadelphia.

It was exactly what the thrifty, color-loving Germanic settlers in the Pennsylvania hinterland wanted. They took it to their hearts and made it their own. Today this humble tableware, associated entirely now with "Pennsylvania Dutch," is a choice collectible—still crude, colorful, charming, and available, but no longer cheap.

Spatterware was made in a great variety of designs and

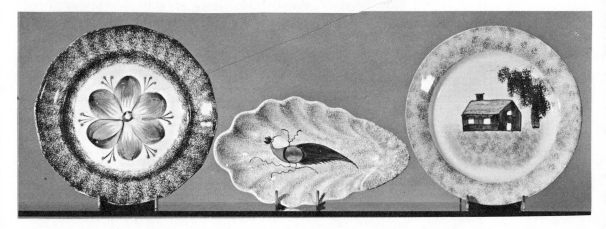

colors and color combinations. The spatter might be applied just to the border of a piece, to the center, or completely cover it. The most popular by far, and the most crudely done, of freehand center designs on spatter-bordered pieces were the Peafowl and Schoolhouse patterns. Tulips and roses were other much-used freehand centers. Spatter work is usually found on soft paste or creamwares, rarely on Ironstone, even though its popularity persisted into the Ironstone age.

On earliest pieces, the spatter decoration was accomplished by tapping a brush full of paint against the piece being decorated, the design *not* to be spattered having been covered with a paper beforehand. In 1845, a cut-sponge process was developed; thereafter, spatter was effected with a color-filled sponge, large size or small size, or cut into shapes—stars, flowers, even angels and eagles. Reds, greens, blues, yellows, in endless variation of shades were used, sometimes blacks and browns.

Who made Spatter? Practically every export potter in Staffordshire, Scotland, and Wales, even some in France, yet only about one piece in a hundred is marked. Sam Laidacker in his *Anglo-American China, Book I* lists twenty-eight makers who deigned to sign their Spatterware, beginning with Adams who made both soft paste and Ironstone. Most of them began operations between 1835 and 1840, exceptions being Vodrey, East Liverpool, Ohio (1857-1885); Meakin (1880), and Cybis, Trenton, New Jersey, who made reproductions in 1949-1950.

In their *Homespun Ceramics, a Study of Spatterware,* Arlene and Paul Greaser show pictures of 169 different designs from their collection. Perish the thought of attempting a "matched set," if ever there was such!

SPODE

W. T. COPELAND & SONS

Spode is a magic name, so magic that its present-day successors, W. T. Copeland & Sons, Ltd., still retain their trademarks. Quality was the secret of this magic for whatever Spode produced, be it blue-printed creamware, stone china, basalte, jasper, Parian, or bone china, it ranked with the best of its time. Its high standards have been upheld over the years, and today's brides are as eager for present-day Spode dinnerware as antiquers are for early examples of any description. The bride has the better of it when it comes to easy finding.

Josiah Spode established his pottery at Stoke-on-Trent in 1770, turning out the same type earthenware as other potters of his day, but just a bit better than most. When he died in 1797, his son, Josiah II, took over the business. Josiah Spode II was the innovator and inventor. By 1800 he was producing some excellent porcelain, beautifully white in body, copying in shape and decoration the styles of Dresden, Chelsea, Nantgarw, and Swansea but honestly using its own Spode marks.

In 1805, he introduced a stone china, apparently using the body patented by Turner in 1800. It is thinner and crisper than the later Mason's Patent Ironstone, though often these two used quite similar Oriental design motifs. Josiah II also pioneered in bone china, and he is usually credited with being its inventor. At any rate, his recipe is still in use today by manufacturers of the best bone chinas.

Josiah II died in 1827; his son, Josiah III, who succeeded him, in 1829. The business was continued by the executors of the estate and William Copeland, the London agent of the firm and partner since 1813. In 1833 Copeland's son purchased it, taking Thomas Garrett into partnership. This partnership as Copeland and Garrett continued until 1847 when Copeland took his four sons into partnership; since then, Copelands have owned the firm outright.

The plate pictured is a twentieth century collectible made by W. T. Copeland & Sons to mark the 1957 Centennial of Emporia, Kansas. Spode's designers, under Mr. Harold Holdway made the preliminary drawing from sketches and photographs sent from Kansas. The center memorial honors William Allen White.

SPORTSMAN MUGS

See *Occupational Shaving Mugs*

STAFFORDSHIRE DOGS

Of all chimney ornaments that found their way into every nook and cranny of Old England, the most popular were the spaniels, of a breed that exists now only in its Staffordshire replicas. Yet this breed was once one of England's great favorites. An engraved likeness of the type, found in an issue of *The Edinburgh Journal of Natural Sciences,* published the year Victoria became Queen, is identified as "The Comforter."

The Staffordshire Comforters came in pairs, designed to face each other. They were made in five standard sizes, the largest about eighteen inches tall, the smallest, six. Their coats were white with colored ears and spots. Red seemed the most favored coloring, though you will find them with ears and spots in black, brown, green, gray, or even of gold or copper lustre. Their noses were pink, and their elegant lockets and chains were gold. Some may have set-in glass eyes. Their backs were not decorated. The bases were solid, but in the old examples—these are still being made, alas—there will be a small round vent hole in the base.

Next in popularity came the whippets, then the poodles.

While the Comforters, no matter which potter created them, always seemed content to sit and stare, whippets were allowed more action. They may be found standing, lying with their paws crossed, or sitting upright, often with a hare in their mouths. Whippet racing was a popular mid-Victorian sport, and some of these statuettes are thought to have been modeled from actual "big money" racers.

Poodles were usually all white, with rough manes which were made by dropping shavings of paste on the glaze before firing. They frequently held little baskets in their mouths as poodles were then trained to do.

There were also Staffordshire Dalmations, pointers and setters, pugs and foxhounds to be found. If you'd wander father afield in the animal kingdom, look for sheep and cows, zebras, lions, gazelles—Staffordshire potters made them all.

STANGL AUDUBON BIRDS

When John James Audubon's *Birds of America,* with its 435 plates showing 480 species of American birds, was published in England in 1838 (no American publisher had been interested), his bird prints became the rage of Europe as well as America. Immediately ceramic artists began to fashion birds in his style. Rather surprisingly American potteries seemed content to leave the making of them to England, the Continent, and Japan.

However, when World War II curtailed imports, the Stangl Pottery in Trenton, New Jersey, embarked on a series of pottery birds adapted from Audubon prints. They were finely detailed, colorful, of excellent quality, complete with foliage, and usually bearing the artist's initials underglaze in blue. Besides the many pottery birds, twelve different ones were made in porcelain, but in such limited quantity—less than 50 of each—that only a most fortunate collector will find one. None of their birds, porcelain or pottery, is in production now.

Each bird wore a paper tag on a string which noted its name, such as "Audubon Warbler/ Fulper Pottery/ Trenton" on one side and "Stangl Pottery" on the other. Most such tags have been lost over the years, but fortunately for collectors, all birds were stamped with the Stangl mark on the base. Some say, "Stangl Pottery Birds"; others, just "Stangl" or "Stangl Pottery," depending on the size of the piece.

The bird pictured, from the collection of Mrs. Lucile Henzke, whose *American Art Pottery* (1970) we recommend, is marked "Stangl" though the paper label is lost. Pink, yellow, green, black, and brown are the colors used; it is 4½ inches high. Collectors seem recently to have "discovered" these birds, and the scramble will soon be on to acquire a few pieces before prices soar. (*See Fulper Pottery*.)

STATES PATTERN

See *Martha Washington States Pattern*

STEINS

We think of steins as heavy stoneware, elaborate with relief decoration and topped with towering pewter lids, like those made at Mettlach by Villeroy & Boch. But steins served too popular a purpose to be confined to one medium. You'll find them in any substance lending itself to shape and form—wood, glass, majolica, the finest of porcelain, pewter, even gold and silver.

The Tyrolean figure steins shown are bisque, with a soft matt finish. There are lithophanes of Alpine scenes in each bottom; the top rim and handrests are pewter. M. Pauson made them in Munich in 1895, and signed and dated them. The flowers he put in the lady's lap are eidelweiss.

STERLING CHINA CO.

See: *Calendar Plates; Lamberton China*

STIRRUP CUPS

When a-hunting you would go in Jolly Old England a couple of centuries ago, or a-riding to the hounds, it was customary to take a warming dram just before the hunt set out. Since this comfort was passed around to riders already mounted and ready to go, there was no need to set down the container which held it; it was simply handed back empty to the servant. So, with a conventional base unnecessary, stirrup cups were made in the round, as it were, in all sorts of shapes and forms. Most popular were animal-head shapes—foxes, hare, deer, all kinds of dogs from foxhounds and setters to bulldogs and pugs, even fish occasionally. Stirrup cups were made in finest porcelains as well as earthenwares; some, from Georgian days, were of silver.

They are rare now and expensive, and a buyer should know from their age and their long attraction to collectors that imitations are more readily found on the market than genuine examples.

STOCKTON ART POTTERY

This was a short-lived pottery, established in 1891 in Stockton, California, as the Stockton Terra Cotta Company. It closed in discouragement in 1902 after its third disastrous fire. Though little known, their Rekston ware, which they began to make in 1897, was a fine art pottery. If it had had time to really reach the market, it would no doubt have equaled any of the artware of its time.

The Rekston ware shapes are graceful; the heavy opaque glazes, mottled or blended, were effective, often striking. A rich blue streaked with dark green was one of their most successful glazes; golden brown with yellow was another. Vases, pitchers, jardinieres, umbrella stands, and teapots were among some of the Rekston items. All were marked with the Rekston name or cypher.

Of the Stockton pottery illustrated, courtesy of Paul Evans, the three largest pieces, the tallest of which is 14 inches high, are Rekston ware. The squat green glazed pitcher in the foreground is not.

STONE BISQUE
SALT BISQUE

Stone bisque is the very poor relation of Parian, aping in whiteness its distant cousin. Coarser, heavier, and a dull dead white, it served well enough for cheap little ornaments, miniature figures and vases, for penny dolls, and for doll heads, which were tinted as to hair and face. Many of the "bonnet dolls," with chapeaux molded on, were of stone bisque; these, too, were painted.

Salt bisque is a notch below. It looks like stone bisque, feels like stone bisque, and often the little figures are very well modeled. To see it on a shelf, you might not guess. When in doubt, taste it. The salt bisque is definitely salty. Pieces are inexpensive in antiques shops; some have a bit of age—you'll have to judge it by the style. We know one collector who has a penchant for salt bisque. Wise or foolish, time will tell. In the meanwhile, she has a lot of fun at little expense.

It is unusual to find a piece of salt bisque signed, but the puzzled little Italian engineer pictured, contemplating his toppling birdhouses, is marked "G. Ruggeri." The book-shaped base is 3¼ by 1½ inches.

STONE CHINA
See *Wedgwood's Stone China*

STONEWARE IN EARLY AMERICA

The salt-glazed stonewares used in early America were either brought in by colonists from England, Holland, or Germany, or imported by way of England. Though a few potters had begun to make stoneware here by the early eighteenth century, they were far between. Fragments of jugs and bottles found in sites of Revolutionary encampments and the debris of English military camps all show foreign origin, indicating that even by the late

217

1770s, American supply had not begun to catch up with the demand.

One of the earliest stoneware makers was John Remmey, a German, whose pottery was established in New York City about 1735. As Remmey & Crolius, it continued in operation until about 1820. The rich brown stoneware they made, with stamped and cobalt blue decorations, was, happily for us, marked with the Remmey and Crolius impress.

There were potters making stonewares at Norwalk, Connecticut, in 1780; in Morgantown, West Virginia, and Huntington, New York, in 1800, and the latter two producing gray ware with blue decorations. Paul Cushman, near Albany, New York, began making stonewares late in the eighteenth century and continued into the next. Dated examples of his work show him still busy in 1809. The first known marked stonewares made by John Norton in Bennington, Vermont, came out in 1823. The Bells in Strasburg, Virginia, and Waynesboro, Pennsylvania, were producing stonewares by 1834. By mid-century, many other potters had turned to stonewares, though many of them, like the Bells, continued to make redware, too.

The body of salt-glazed stonewares made in this country was brown or gray; the glazes, in brown and bluish gray were heavy, uniform, and distinctly granulated. Decorations were etched or cobalt blue designs, crudely executed; occasionally, applied reliefs were used. Jugs, jars, tankards, mugs, crocks, flagons, and water coolers were among familiar early pieces. Many of them showed a Germanic influence. (*See* Jugs and Crocks.)

SUNBONNET BABIES

Sentimentalists who first met the Sunbonnet Babies in primer book pages and their children and grandchildren who have thumbed the same book are prime collectors for the hand-painted china which Royal Bayreuth made and decorated so daintily with Mollie and May, the Sunbonnet Babies, whose faces, if any, remain forever hidden by their bonnets.

The Sunbonnet Babies Primer, written by Eulalie Osgood Grover, and illustrated by Bertha L. Corbett, a Minneapolis artist, was published in 1902. Black and white drawings of the Sunbonnet Babies had already appeared on Christmas cards and Valentines. The primer was in color. Sequels followed, and so did the *Overall Boys,* equally faceless under deep straw hats.

Color reproductions of Miss Corbett's drawings of the Sunbonnet Babies' busy week—Washing Day, Ironing Day, Mending Day, Scrubbing Day, Sweeping Day, and Baking Day—were published in 1904.

This popular series was among the first of Sunbonnet Babies designs which Royal Bayreuth used to decorate their line of children's china—teasets, mugs, bowls, plates, and pitchers. They also put Sunbonnet Babies on candlesticks, pin trays, dresser boxes, bells, and a host of small items to please little girls.

Royal Bayreuth seems to be the only chinaware authorized by Miss Corbett. The pieces you find with other backstamps and in other styles are usually products of amateur china painters who selected their own whiteware and copied or adapted the "delicious" Sunbonnet Babies to suit themselves. Occasionally you'll find a piece marked "Japan."

The rimmed baby's plate pictured is Royal Bayreuth's lively version of "Monday is Wash Day." (*See* Royal Bayreuth.)

SUTHERLAND ART WARE

Every now and then someone is set to puzzling over art pottery marked Sutherland Art Ware, Frank Beardmore & Co., Fenton. It may be a vase, decorated with chickens and roosters, with the pattern name "Poultry" on the bottom, or one called "A Wayside Inn of Old England," and decorated accordingly, or it may be a souvenir plate with local scenes. One, reported from St. John, New Brunswick, shows that city's monuments.

This ware was made, the Town Council of Fenton tells us, by Frank Beardmore at the Sutherland Pottery between 1903, when he acquired the pottery from Christie & Beardmore, and 1914, and that Frank Beardmore's wife was a sister of Arnold Bennett who wrote several excellent books about the potteries. (*See* Bennett, Arnold.)

SWANSEA

Several establishments made pottery in Swansea, in Glamorganshire, Wales. Earliest (ca. 1764) and most important was the Cambrian Pottery where willow pattern, salt glaze with enamel decoration, and black basalt, all of high artistry, were made. Illustrations and information on Swansea factories are found in E. M. Nance's *The Pottery and Porcelain of Swansea and Nantgarw.*

Names important to Swansea porcelain, which they called "opaque china," are Dillwyn, William Billingsley, and Samuel Walker, the last two having been recruited from Nantgarw. Much of Swansea's white porcelain was sold to London decorators who painted it to suit city tastes. Their styles differed greatly from Swansea's own decorations which were mainly floral patterns. (*See:* Nantgarw; Coalport.)

S. Y. P. TEAPOT

Simple Yet Perfect—such was the teapot, designed by Lord Dundonald, made and marketed by Josiah Wedgwood & Sons in the late 1890s. It had a perforated shelf inside where you put the tea. Then you poured boiling water in the pot, replaced the front-facing lid, tipped the teapot backward to rest on two small feet, and let it set. In that position the tea was immersed. In a few minutes, you had your cuppa, and no mess of soggy tea leaves in the bottom of the pot.

Wedgwood made them in Peony, Ceylon, and Oaklands patterns (the one pictured is Oaklands), and maybe others. All carried the Wedgwood marks and the SYP patent information. They were terribly expensive to produce. Wedgwood claimed each pot required the assembly of ten molded parts before firing, and gave up making them in 1921.

Arthur Wood of Longport made some after 1904, in plain color "leadless glaze"—brown, blue, yellow, and black, some with gold line trim. All of his are well marked, too, with a prominent "Patent SYP Teapot Trade Mark. Reg. No. 536554."

SYRACUSE STONEWARE CO.

See *Rebekah at the Well*

T

TAY BIRDS

Recent porcelain bird sculptures like the English Doughty Birds and the American Boehms have met with phenomenal success. Now to bear watching come the Tay birds from Italy.

Tay is the trade name for Giuseppi Tagliariol whose talent creates them and whose factory at Monza produces them. Before he opened his studio at Monza in 1952, Tay had been associate professor at the Academy of Fine Arts in Venice and an associate of the sculptor Leo Paronetto in Treviso. His birds are meticulously hand-sculptured and faithfully hand-painted in true-to-life colors. The bobolink, brown thrasher and blue jay pictured belong in the 9-to 10-inch group, which now retails in the $40-60 price range; smaller birds are slightly less; larger, more intricate pieces, like American eagles, owls, pheasants, and roosters are considerably more.

In addition to his birds, Tay has produced some small—under 6-inch—animal figures; his rabbits, foxes, and squirrels are particularly endearing.

TEA LEAF IRONSTONE

Plain white Ironstone had put in its appearance in the 1850s. It was a great success with the American farm and country set, but after thirty years, the market was ready for something new—new, but not too different. The potteries pondered and flashed up with Tea Leaf Lustre, the same good old durable inexpensive Ironstone, dressed up with a band of copper lustre and a neat little design of copper lustre leaves. They called it "Lustre Band and Sprig." By the time collectors got interested, it had picked up the catchier name of Tea Leaf Lustre.

Anthony Shaw of Longport seems to have developed this design back in the 1850s, but it took till the 1880s for the pattern to really catch fire. At least eighteen potters in Staffordshire kept busy making it—all apparently for export to the United States. Our own potteries made it, too. Though each pottery is said to have varied its designs a wee bit, most patterns look so much alike it is not difficult to match up a set with pieces by several different makers.

The design was printed on the piece before the glaze was applied and fired. The lustre went on, by hand, over the glaze, exactly covering the pattern laid on under the glaze. An abundance of dinner ware was made, with a great assortment of pieces. Comports, cup plates, butter pats, and bone dishes were often included with dinner sets. Toilet sets—bowls, pitchers, soap dishes, and the like—were popular.

Prominent among English makers were Henry Burgess, Thomas Furnival, Powell & Bishop, A. J. Wilkinson, W. & E. Corn, and Wedgwood & Co., as well as Josiah Wedgwood & Sons. The Sears, Roebuck catalogue for 1897 offered "Meakin's Gold Tea Leaf Lustre Band" in open stock. Company trademarks changed frequently though firm names were constant. Possibly as many as 100 different trademarks were used over the years by the eighteen or twenty English makers.

In the United States, Mayer Pottery Co., Beaver Falls, Pennsylvania, Wick China Co., Kittanning, Pa., and Cartright Bros., East Liverpool, Ohio, were leading producers.

By 1910, the ladies who had once been willing to move heaven and earth to acquire a set of Tea Leaf Ironstone were feeding cats and dogs from the once treasured plates and saucers. (*See* Ironstone.)

The gravy boat pictured was made by Alfred Meakin, England. It is from the collection of Mr. and Mrs. Albert Benedict of New Windsor, Maryland. At least ten makers are represented in their collection, which now numbers several hundred pieces. It began twelve years ago with a shallow soup plate, handed down in the Benedict family where it had served as a christening bowl.

TEAPOTS

Anyone who decides to collect teaware, whether teapots, teasets, or teacups, however discriminating he may be, will have a cupboard full in no time. Before the tea bag, a convenience invented about 1890 by Thomas Sullivan, a wholesale tea merchant in New York, tea was brewed in a teapot and served from a teapot. Since Europeans have been drinking tea for three hundred years or more and Eastern countries longer than that, there is no dearth of collectible teaware.

According to the Chinese, the first tea was brewed, quite accidentally, in 2737 B. C. by the Emperor Chin-nung when some dried tea leaves blew into his pot of boiling water. In India, the discovery is credited to Darma, a Buddhist priest who, some nineteen hundred years ago, vowed to spend seven years in sleepless meditation. Becoming drowsy at the end of five years, he chewed a handful of tea leaves from a convenient bush, found himself refreshed, and completed his vow.

Though Europeans had heard of tea as early as 1517, it was a hundred years later before Dutch adventurers brought it back from the East. At first it was considered a medicinal drink, but when the Chinese began sending teapots along with tea shipments to Holland, the idea of social tea drinking took hold. The fashionable Samuel Pepys wrote on September 23, 1660, in his now famous diary: "I did send for a cup of tea, a China drink, of which I had never drunk before."

The first tea brought to this country was probably to the Dutch settlements in New Amsterdam about 1650. The Dutch, who were acquainted with tea in Holland, knew how to prepare it. Not so the English in Massachusetts to whom tea was occasionally brought by sailing ships. There is record of one colonial housewife boiling the leaves and serving them with butter! By Revolutionary times, tea was a common beverage and the poor as well as the rich enjoyed it.

Perhaps in teapots, more than any other single collectible, the changing styles in tableware and the advances in ceramic techniques over the past 300 years can be most coherently and consistently illustrated.

The teapot pictured is unmarked Staffordshire, transfer printed in blue, ca. 1800-1810. (*See:* Cup Plates; for illustrations, *see* Queen's Ware; Satsuma; Tucker China.)

TECCO WARE

Made by Gates Pottery of Terra Cotta, Illinois, from 1903 to 1951, Tecco Ware finds itself in the category of art pottery by virtue of the rich green shades of its glazes and the simplicity of its form. About 1906, a matt glaze, quite similar to those used by Grueby and Van Briggle, was developed, "characterized by a smooth surface in luscious shades of green on a red or cream-colored body." The rich clay used came entirely from Brazil, Indiana. The forms, frequently derived from nature, were either molded or hand thrown; they were never hand painted or decorated with colors. There were, on the factory grounds, beautiful gardens, some aquatic, to which designers turned for inspiration. Happily, pieces are always marked on the base.

TERRA COTTA

This basic clayware takes it's name from the Italian *terra,* meaning earth, and *cotta,* meaning cooked. The ancients used it for urns and tomb figures, and succeeding civilizations were all well acquainted with it. By the early 1800s, it was in general manufacture in England—a hard, unglazed stoneware in the reddish-yellow hues of baked earth, buff pink to deep red. It was produced in special kilns, built so that the wares, to remain unglazed, were not exposed to the direct touch of the fire.

Through the Victorian years, terra cotta became increasingly popular. At the Crystal Palace in 1851, Doulton & Co.'s exhibit, which took a First Class Medal, showed a life-sized statue called "Time," made in one piece, along with vases, figures, bottles, pitchers, and other household vessels. Decorative terra cotta tiles and utilitarian terra cotta drain pipe were important in architectural work. There were all kinds of terra cotta novelties, too, from garden seats to inkstands. Sometimes embellishment was added by way of enamel painting, mosaic inlay, or application of rich colored glazes.

To be sought and found today are small well-done figure groups—French potters excelled with these—and architectural tiles, some extremely handsome, which come on the market as old Victorian buildings are demolished. There are interesting "drain pipe" vases, too.

The terra cotta "Cherub Riding Dog" illustrated was the work of the French sculptor "Clodion," or Claude Michel (1738-1814). It dates about 1800.

TERRALINE VASES

Along about 1885 to 1900, when china painting was at its height, Terraline vases and plaques appeared, tempting amateur decorators with their elaborate standout floral and fruit designs. These pieces were either of fired clay or of plastic earth and cement, molded and dried, but not fired. The entire surface was designed to be coated with enamel and colored in the same medium. The pieces were sold uncolored, along with materials to decorate them. Anyone who could hold a brush, read directions, and afford the materials could become expert in no time. Hirshberg, Hollander & Co., of Baltimore, Maryland, were extensive dealers.

The pieces were usually stamped "Terraline." Sometimes plaques show up marked "West's Terraline," presumably made by the same Mr. West of Chicago whose name is frequently found on plaster figures of the Rogers type. As pottery, coarse and overly ornate, Terraline enjoyed scant popularity with serious china painters who preferred to work with delicate porcelain pieces and demanded a wider scope for individual artistry.

TERRHEA

See *Cambridge Art Pottery*

TEXIAN CAMPAIGNE

The Mexican War (1846-1848), which expanded our boundaries to the Pacific, was fought mainly in Texas though bloody battles occurred in New Mexico and California. The firing had hardly died down when an enterprising Staffordshire potter bought out "Texian Campaigne" dinnerware, following the lines of the blue American Views which had been so popular a generation back.

The design depicted lively war action scenes enclosed in a border of military symbols and devices that look like cattle brands. It proved wildly popular, and was made in sepia, blue, purple, pink, green, and black. There were plates, platters, handleless cups, cup plates, tureens—the whole works.

The backstamp is shown here. The "J.B." which appears on many pieces is apparently the designer's initials, for enough pieces have shown up marked "A. Shaw" to credit him with the potting. Anthony Shaw established his works in Tunstall in 1851 for the production of decorated ware for export. His "Texian Campaigne" gave him a good send-off.

"Texian Campaigne" pieces are considered choice, especially favored by Texans, though stangely enough, little of this ware, even that now held in Texas collections, was found in that state. Much of it turned up in far away places like Maine or Ohio, treasured by families who had contributed a soldier to the campaign. Texans of the time had no need of souvenir dishes to remember the war.

THOUSAND FACES CHINA

This delicately translucent Japanese tea ware, with its "thousand" little Japanese faces atop bright Buddhist robes, arranged in concentric rows, was produced at Kutani as export ware, probably after 1850.

While it is neither in the age bracket nor in the monetary class with Canton, Oriental Export, or such imitation Oriental wares as were made at early Worcester, it is lively and colorful, and fraught with Oriental symbolism.

The little figures, drawn flat without perspective, represent Buddhist saints on the way to becoming Buddhas. In one variation, some carry parasols, others are studying scrolls. The faces are usually represented by two lines for eyes and a broken line for a nose, though occasionally the faces are painted in the round.

The tawny orange of the Buddhist robes is the predominating color, though pale greens and blues and gold are present, too. The feet of the lower tier of figures rest on a light blue border, representing the dome of heaven.

On flat pieces the center decoration may feature haloed figures of those who have attained Nirvana, a Japanese landscape, or a golden dragon. Sometimes cups and rice bowls have figures both inside and out. In some such cases, the outside decoration may be the Eight Buddhist Emblems of Happy Augury.

This pattern, we are told, is being presently manufactured, but modern productions are greatly inferior in all respects. Once you have seen and handled an old piece, you'll never be mistaken in a new.

While there is little on Thousand Faces ware in either *The Ceramic Art of Japan* (1965) by Hugo Munsterberg or in *Far Eastern Ceramics* (1963) by Maria Penkala, both books are excellent references on Japanese wares and Oriental symbolism.

The tea plate pictured, showing a myriad of tiny hand-painted figures with parasols and scrolls, is from the collection of Mrs. C. Albert Kuper, Jr., of Baltimore, Maryland, who over the past twenty years has assembled several hundred pieces of this colorful ware.

TIFFANY POTTERY

We hear much of Tiffany windows, Tiffany lamps, Tiffany glass, but little of Tiffany pottery. Yet for a short while around 1907, Louis Comfort Tiffany did make pottery at his factory in Corona, Long Island. Though it was distinctively designed and executed, with the same expensive elegance that characterized all of Tiffany's works, it seems never to have been very popular. It is well worth looking for today—and all the more pleasant to find because it was somewhat neglected in its own time.

The Tiffany pottery designs were developed from natural flowers and leaves, from ancient bronzes, and from marine life—octopi, seaweed, coral and the like. The initials "L. C. T." are incised on the base of each piece. The colors employed were most frequently muted green and buff-colored glaze or putty color unglazed. Less often used were dark blue, green, and reddish-brown. The 3-inch tall vase pictured is white.

TILES

The Dutch were making tiles to use about their fireplaces or to line their walls as early as 1550. These first efforts were lead-glazed over a reddish-gray body, decorated with a simple stencil filled in by hand painters. By 1600, they had improved their wares by using a fine white tin-enameled glaze and decorating them with elaborate genre scenes, landscapes, florals, and geometric arrangements in both polychrome and monochrome colors. They seldom marked their wares.

About 1675, English potters around Liverpool, not to be outdone, began making tiles, too, similar to those the Dutch had been sending over. The English used them chiefly for fireplace facings. After Sadler and Green came out with transfer printing in 1756, there was much less importation of Dutch tiles to England and increased exportation of English tiles to the colonies in America. English and Dutch tiles were used together in one of the fireplaces in the Craigie Mansion, later Henry Wadsworth Longfellow's home, in Cambridge, Massachusetts. Sadler and Green often put a signature on their tiles which makes it nice for us today.

As long as fireplaces served as the main source of household heat, architectural tiles were made in great abundance—by hundreds of potters and in thousands of designs. In collecting tiles, it seems sensible to select a potter whose work you enjoy and concentrate on his work lest you splatter yourself like an egg against the welter of available material. You'll have a wide choice from among early Dutch and Liverpool tiles through years of Wedgwoods and Doultons up to the twentieth century when several American firms were thriving on art tiles.

The U. S. Encaustic Tile Co., Indianapolis, 1877-1886; Edmund Lycett, Atlanta, Georgia; and the Trent Tile Company, Trenton, New Jersey, ca. 1886, are among those whose art tiles are represented in Smithsonian Institution collections. *(See:* Low Tiles; Beaver Falls Art Tile Pottery; Kachelofen; Sadler & Green; American Encaustic Tiling Company; Mosaic Tile Company.)

Illustrated is a blue and white Delft tile panel, ca. 1700, showing view of the River Vecht, near the city of Utrecht.

TILE STOVES

See *Kachelofen*

TOBACCO JARS

Someone has been objecting to tobacco since the day Rodrigo de Jerez, a sailor back from Columbus's first voyage to the New World, showed off what he'd learned from the Indians and got imprisioned for his "devilish habit." Though *something* was smoked in ancient days, coltsfoot for sure and maybe other herbs, it was *not* tobacco. The use of tobacco for smoking, chewing, and snuffing originated on this continent and quickly spread to others.

In 1603, King James of England declared smoking "a filthie noveltie," begged his subjects not to indulge in a habit "so hateful to the nose and harmful to the brains," and raised the duty on tobacco. A Chinese decree of 1638 threatened tobacco smokers with decapitation, and Russian offenders were deported to Siberia.

Queen Victoria, two centuries later, was still deploring it and ordered her Commanders to restrict smoking in the Army. In Berlin smoking was not allowed in public. The Victorian Church, State, and Ladies were all against it.

In spite of dire consequences and disapproval on all sides, men kept on using tobacco, and left behind all kinds of oddments to prove their independence, from ivory snuff boxes to silver cigar cutters. Lead tobacco boxes have survived from the eighteenth century, and many of wood, as well as lead, from the early nineteenth.

By the less restrictive 1880s, when a good cigar was a mark of prosperity and a pipe was permitted in the smoking room, there was no nicer present to give Dear Papa at Christmas than a tobacco jar, preferably of majolica, in the shape of a monkey's head, perhaps, or a frog, or a fish like this one pictured, or an Eastern Potentate, the uglier the better. It made Papa laugh and Mama shudder—just one more *thing* to dust!

TOBY JUGS

By and large, over the years, the Toby jug has been the most popular of Staffordshire's many collectibles. Whether these figural pieces were named for Tristam Shandy's jovial Uncle Toby or for Toby Philpot of drinking song fame is immaterial; these convivial topers have been around since 1750 and are still being made. Toby Philpot, by the way, was an actual person, reputedly one Harry Elwes of Yorkshire who downed 2,000 gallons of ale before he died.

Tobies of the 1750-1800 period, the nicest to have and the hardest to find, will be seated figures, quite large, maybe eight or ten inches tall, with fierce, ugly faces, broken teeth—and warts! Their three-cornered hats come off to be used as cups; their legs are hollow. All their fingers and buttons, garters and shoe laces are clearly defined, and the accessories they may hold—beer mugs or churchwarden pipes—are little works of art. Their body material is pale in color, light in weight, decorated underglaze or with color glaze applied. If the latter, there may be bare spots the painter missed.

These character jugs were also made to represent real people, famous and infamous, from Lord Nelson and Napoleon to Martha Gunn. Some were full figures, some three-quarters, some just heads. They came in all sizes and, through the years, were made of all kinds of material—salt glaze stoneware (Lambeth produced these in the early 1800s); Rockingham (some were made and marked at Bennington, Vt.); Belleek (Lenox made a fine Ben Franklin); Majolica (the Luneville potteries in France specialized in Majolica heads); and other earthenwares. Royal Doulton still makes a full line of inexpensive miniatures.

The removable hats, usually lost by now, belong to the early period. Just be careful if you must have an early one, that the one you find is that—they've been copied for years.

The jug pictured is a good example of an early Toby, warts and all.

TOILET SETS

Personal cleanliness was of little concern to our medieval forebears. Few of them bathed more than once or twice a lifetime, and nobody expected them to. The Kings and Queens of the seventeenth century and members of their Courts smothered themselves in perfumes and powder, and held spicy vinaigrettes to their noses. They were not much for washing, either.

But by the mid-eighteenth century, cleanliness began to raise its head. Elegant basins and ewers of beautifully painted Sevres, or silver, or silver-gilt appeared in the bedrooms of royalty and important personages.

Washbowls and pitchers for lesser folk came in with pottery for the people in the early 1800s. Mason and Minton and other early potters produced some handsome sets before 1820. These early bowls were small in circumference, and the pitchers were correspondingly squat. Since the long-sleeved ladies and gentlemen who used them were content to wash to the wrist only, they were sufficient. Washstands, with a circular cut-out to receive the basin, soon became part of fine bedroom furnishings.

By mid-century, washbowls and pitchers had become a household necessity. Pottery was abundant and cheap enough for almost everyone. Both bowls and pitchers became somewhat larger, though still chary with the water. In the next decades, the bowls grew bigger and bigger, the pitchers fatter and taller. Adjuncts were added—sponge dishes, soap dishes, toothbrush mugs, small pitchers for hot water, slop pails, and chamber pots —until by the 1870s and 1880s, the toilet set had become a veritable riot of matched crockery. Washstands grew larger to accommodate the array, with drawers and cupboards for concealing at least part of it.

By the end of the century there was a toilet set in every bedroom, public or private. Boarding houses and hotels might stop at plain white Ironstone; private families could be as gay or restrained as they pleased. In the J. Sterling Morton mansion in Nebraska City, Nebraska, in the room President Cleveland and his wife occupied on a visit there, the complete toilet sets —there were two—including chamber pots, were decorated to order to match the wallpaper.

In 1892, the Hart Brewer Pottery Co. (the Old Trenton Works, est. 1852) in New Jersey was specializing in toilet sets decorated with violets. The Havilands brought out sets in their dainty flowered gold-trimmed china. D. F. Haynes of the Chesapeake Pottery in Baltimore made such outstanding designs they were copied in England.

Since bowl and pitcher sets were produced up to the first World War and in lesser quantity into the 1920s when bathroom plumbing put an end to them in this country, there should be plenty of styles, colors, shapes, and decorations for anyone who wants one. They are, however, surprisingly hard to find, and no longer inexpensive. In 1897, Sears, Roebuck offered 12-piece English sets with floral designs and gold at $7.15 and $8.25; white granite (Ironstone) from $2.25.

Pieces are now put to uses which would have shocked their original owners. Flowers appear in pitchers, fruit in bowls, plants in chamber pots, cigarettes in soap dishes, strawberries in sponge dishes; bowls and pitchers as lamps. Even collectors who arrange their period bedrooms with appropriate washstand appurtenances hardly expect their guests to use them. (For illustration, *see* Minton.)

TOOTHBRUSH HOLDERS

So many of the large bowl and pitcher wash sets, to which the toothbrush holder once belonged, have been broken up that nowadays the toothbrush holder is usually sold as an item by itself. Thousands of toilet sets were made in dozens of different chinas, from plain white Ironstone to the most elegant Meissen. Since the toothbrush holders matched the sets, you can collect a hundred or more of them (if you should want to) without duplicating a pattern.

Toothbrush holders came in vase form or were of a covered box type. The vases were made either with a solid base or with drainage holes. The latter seem to be older and harder to find.

Those with one large hole on the side near the base have a false bottom to catch the moisture from the wet brush; those with the holes in the bottom, like an upside-down sugar shaker, drained right onto the marble top washstand. The covered box is about 8 inches long, 2 inches wide, with two raised ridges, notched to hold the brush, on the inside bottom. These boxes turn up quite often, and if you hear them called "soap dishes," as you undoubtedly will, don't believe it! Illustration from the collection of Kenneth E. Neiman, D.D.S.

TREMBLEUSE

Once in a while you'll come across a two-handled cup which fits snugly into a sort of reticulated fence in the saucer. This is a trembleuse, presumably designed—and named—for shaky-handed sippers. Most of those you'll find will date from the late eighteenth century and will bear the mark of Sevres, Augustus Rex, Derby, or some other early fine porcelain manufactory which specialized in elaborately painted decoration. They were rare and choice in their own time, more so today. Less elaborate examples appeared every now and then into the late nineteenth century.

The trembleuse pictured—you can see the stand-up collar on the saucer if you look real hard—is of early Russian porcelain, a most unusual piece.

TRENCHER SALTS

Before the seventeenth century, the entire English household sat to eat at one long table. The section at the head, reserved for the master and his intimates, was marked by a tall standing salt, an elaborate affair, sometimes sixteen inches high, of silver or gold, and not infrequently studded with precious gems. Salt was a prized commodity and containers for it were appropriately respectful. For lesser folk who "sat below the salt," smaller open salt dishes of pewter or wood were scattered about within easy reach of the wooden trenchers from which they ate. Hence the name "trencher salts."

The designation continued in use long after household tables and standing salts were outdated and the trencher salts, by the time of Queen Elizabeth I, had come into general use in important houses. With the advent of porcelain in the eighteenth century, trencher salts in that new and stylish medium became popular. Some were made in England and on the Continent, but the most desired were those imported from China. They were fashioned in various shapes, usually with a fairly deep base, and were pleasingly decorated with conventional motifs, birds, flowers, or scenes. The trencher salts pictured here are all early, all Chinese.

In Colonial New England, silversmiths made trencher salts of silver and of pewter; wealthy colonists also imported porcelain ones from England and China. After the Revolution, as more niceties became available to ordinary people, the rather robust trencher salt gave way to smaller less expensive glass salt dishes, like the lacy glass patterns made at Sandwich. These in turn passed to the even smaller individual glass or china salt dips we know today. By the time the modern salt shakers came into use in the early 1860s, porcelain trencher salts had been long out of the picture.

TRENT TILE COMPANY

See *Tiles*

TRENTON CHINA CO.

See *Lamberton China*

TUCKER CHINA

When, in 1826, William Ellis Tucker established a factory in Philadelphia to manufacture porcelain, he had to contend not only with foreign competition, but with the conviction on the part of American buyers that nothing made in America could possibly be as good as the same thing made abroad—and certainly not porcelain! Though his china won international recognition, and all kinds of prizes and citations at exhibitions, it was still American-made, and still rejected, even though it was almost impossible to tell his wares from fine French and English pieces. Now it's in museums!

Tucker's first products (1826-1828) were either undecorated or decorated with sepia landscapes in brown or charcoal. On special order, gold bands were added. In his second period (1828-1832), as Tucker and Hulme, more color and gold was used; polychrome landscapes and floral designs appeared. In his final period (1832-1838), as Tucker and Hemphill, Tucker china rivaled the most elegant French imports, with florals in large scale, lavish with color and gold. The factory closed in 1838, beset with labor troubles and sabotage—it was said workmen were sent from envious England just to break the handles off his cups and pitchers before they were fired.

The kaolin used in Tucker china was mined in Chester County, Pennsylvania, and today the Chester County Historical Society, in West Chester, has what is probably the largest museum display of Tucker china in America. In Houston, Texas, at the Bayou Bend Museum there is also an exceptional collection. One unusual pitcher there is decorated with "Rough and Ready" Zachary Taylor's portrait.

It is good to see and study Tucker china in museums for there must be pieces still around today, unrecognized or wrongly attributed. Tucker purposely did not mark all his wares. The imports he competed with were often unmarked, and for obvious reasons he followed their lead. It's a pity!

The pitchers illustrated show the three Tucker types of designs; the earliest is in the center; the latest to its left.

TURNER, THOMAS

See *Salopian*

U

UMBRELLA STANDS

For years and years, an umbrella stand, tall, tubular and vase-like, stood in every proper hall, a repository for umbrellas, wet or dry, parasols, sunshades, walking sticks, and incidentally for tennis balls, odd rubbers, forbidden Cubebs—and, in mystery stories, the murder weapon.

These useful objects were made of heavy porcelain or pottery, often of handsome Imari, Mettlach, Satsuma, or majolica; in repousse brass with lion-head rings; in cast iron, tin, and of drain pipe, lushly painted with wild roses by Aunt Louise. Where, oh where, are umbrella stands now? Where, for that matter, are front halls?

UNION PORCELAIN WORKS

This manufactory in Greenpoint, Long Island, was acquired by Thomas Smith, an architect, early in the 1860s. From a mix composed of kaolin, quartz, and feldspar, and the application of glaze by the same process as used at Sevres, Meissen, and other foreign factories, some most excellent porcelain was produced here. Karl Muller, a sculptor, was for years the principal modeler.

In keeping with the eclectic taste of the times, some of his earlier pieces were unusually elaborate. One example, now at the Brooklyn Museum, is a teaset which was exhibited at the Philadelphia Exposition in 1876. A head of a Negro serves as finial for the sugar bowl lid, a Chinese head as finial for the teapot; the handle of the creamer is a goat, and the feet of all pieces are long-eared rabbits; a design of fruit, flowers, and butterflies about cartouches of wild birds covers the surface. Later show pieces, made in the 1880s, evinced more restraint in design, but no less elegance in production. Fine quality Parian was also produced here, many of the pieces modeled by Muller.

The factory mark was usually Union/ Porcelain/ Works/ Greenpoint/ N.Y. though sometimes an eagle's head with an S in its beak was used, with or without U.P.W. above it.

UNION POTTERIES CO.

See *Great Western Pottery*

UNION STONEWARE CO.

Every now and then some happy fruit jar collector finds a stoneware screw-top jar which proclaims itself, in type taking up nearly half the jug, as a Mason's Fruit Jar, made by the Union Stoneware Co., Red Wing, Minnesota. No doubt this company made other types of stoneware jugs and crocks and perhaps marked them as conveniently for today's collectors. Though the present Red Wing Potteries, an outgrowth of the Union Stoneware Company, has no record whatsoever that such fruit jars were ever made there, a patent date, Jan. 24, 1899 is incised on the base of at least some of the jars.

At the Smithsonian Institution in Washington, D.C., there

are some amusing animal figures made by the Union Stoneware Company about 1895. Among them are a pig, two cats, a bulldog, and a frog; some are in gray stoneware, others have a brown glaze.

Decorative objects, such as vases, marked "Red Wing U. S. A." are not unusual to find in antiques shops, tucked away in some dark corner waiting the years to age them. Pottery collectors may like them as examples of late commercial Minnesota ware.

The Union Stoneware's Mason jars pictured are from the collection of Cecil Munsey, San Diego, California. The largest is gallon-size.

U. S. ART POTTERY

During the late 1880s and early 1900s, a few talented artists, in this country and abroad, began to make a conscious effort to rediscover basic art values. They had had enough of Victorian restrictions which, they felt, stifled artistic inspiration. Mass production had suffocated the vigorous handcraft of the folk potter.

Through their individual efforts, artistic potters in this country set about to revitalize American ceramics. They turned to nature for inspiration, working for free form and for mottled and streaked glazes which best expressed nature's casualness. Leaf forms prevailed, along with green matt glazes, and heavy earthen bodies in keeping with the earthenware medium. In creating fresh artistic forms, unhampered by past ideas, these turn-of-the-century potters opened the door to the modern artistic revolution.

Among these dedicated innovators whose work is represented at the Smithsonian Institution in Washington, D.C., are: Buffalo Pottery; Craven Art Pottery, East Liverpool, Ohio; Dedham Pottery; Hampshire Pottery; Newcomb Pottery; Pisgah Forest Pottery; Van Briggle Art Pottery; Weller Pottery; Wheatly Pottery; Wheeling Potteries; and, of course, Rookwood. There are many others.

U. S. ENCAUSTIC TILE CO.

See *Tiles*

VAN BRIGGLE ART POTTERY

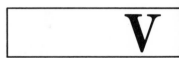

The Van Briggle Art Pottery in Colorado Springs, Colorado, was established in 1899, and with the exception of a period in World War II, has operated continuously ever since.

Artus Van Briggle, of Flemish descent, was born in Felicity, Ohio, in 1869. At the age of seventeen, he went to Cincinnati to study under Karl Langenbeck at the Avon Pottery. Later he worked at the Rookwood Pottery. In 1893, he went to Paris to study and there, at the Beaux Arts, he met Annie Lawrence Gregory, a young girl from Plattsburg, New York, who was also an art student. They became engaged in 1895.

His pottery in Colorado Springs, where he had gone for his health, was well established when they were married in 1902. He had developed a marble glaze, smooth as cut stone, for the artwares he fashioned from Colorado clays. His colors were inspired by the turquoise of Colorado skies, the sunset hues, and the many shades of Colorado's vari-colored mountains. Awards and medals came his way, many more than he lived to enjoy for he died in 1904. His pottery is found in permanent collections at the Louvre in Paris and in the South Kensington Museum in London as well as the Smithsonian Institution in this country.

His young widow, who had worked closely with him and was a talented artist in her own right, continued the pottery, using many of his designs and his original glaze. In later years, a new glaze, based upon the properties of volcanic ash, as shiny smooth as glittering glass, was developed. Both glazes are used today.

The Van Briggle Pottery has changed hands several times, but the high standards of its founder have always been upheld. There are two buildings now, one erected in 1907 by Mrs. Van Briggle in memory of her husband. Both are open to the public, the only place in the world where Van Briggle pottery is made and sold.

Van Briggle pieces are clearly marked. A cypher composed

237

of two "A's" for Artus and Anne, has long been used. Beginning in 1901 and continuing for a number of years, artists were assigned Roman numerals to use in lieu of initials. According to Mr. K. W. Stevenson of the present pottery, the Roman numeral III was Mr. Van Briggle's personal mark; from 1900 to 1920, the pieces were dated on the bottom; and from 1922 to 1929, "U. S. A." followed "Colorado Springs, Colo," on the bottom of each piece. Articles from these earlier days interest collectors most. Dorothy McGraw Bogue's paper-bound *The Van Briggle Story* (1968) is an excellently detailed account of the pottery and the Van Briggles.

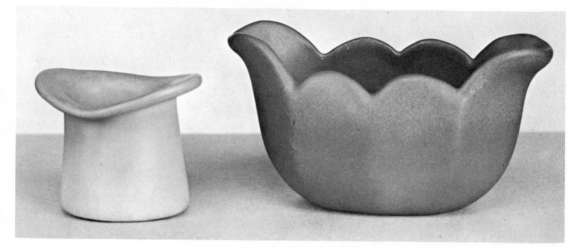

The hat toothpick holder pictured is in turquoise, dated 1938; the small flower dish, a soft raspberry-plum shading at the top to slate-blue gray, was made in 1928; both have the original marble glaze. The jug with the snake decoration is a 1902 piece, bearing Artus Van Briggle's own mark; it is from the collection of Lucile Henzke.

VAN HEUSEN CHARLES CO.

See *Historical Blue Plates, Late*

VANCE FAIENCE COMPANY

This small pottery in Tiltonville, Ohio, began in the 1880s and continued for at least thirty years. If you find the mark "Vance/F Co.," followed by a factory number, on a piece of glazed ware—tan shading into a darker brown with underglaze flower decoration—or on a matt finished piece in soft blue, green, or tan—this is the company that made it—probably about 1910.

VEILLEUSE

Getting up in the night to heat a cup of milk for the insomniac or a draught of medicine for a croupy child was no way easy in days when the heating element was the damped-down fire on the kitchen hearth. Then, in 1770, some blessed body thought up a most convenient contrivance, called *veilleuse* in France (*veiller* meaning "to keep vigil"), food warmer in England, *suppenwarmer* in Germany.

Made in three parts—a handled cup or bowl, a lid, and a matching stand with an opening for a candle or sperm oil lamp and vents to emit the smoke—these handy warmers were manufactured in considerable quantities. And broken likewise.

Many were handsomely decorated. The earliest ones were of Delftware or porcelain; later came plainer versions in creamware. Apparently there was much copying of styles between countries and some bitterness between potters, for these handy warmers were in demand everywhere. They have stayed in use, in one form or another, to the present day.

The teapot and warmer pictured is of the night light variety, with a candle in the warming compartment. It is French, ca. 1850.

VICTORIA, AUSTRIA

The "Victoria" mark found on china, usually dainty hand-painted pieces, fancy-edged tea plates and the like, often decorated in Haviland style, was used by the Porzellanfabrik Viktoria, a hard paste porcelain factory in Alt-Rohlau, Bohemia, established by Schmidt & Company in 1882. When "Austria" appears on the backstamp, the piece was made after 1891. Much of it, perhaps all, was made for export to compete with the then extremely popular—and higher-priced—Haviland and other Limoges wares.

The three-piece bread and milk set pictured is delicately flowered with rose sprays; the border color is green, the handle gold, ca. 1895.

VICTORIAN TRINKET BOXES

From the 1860s to 1890s, little china trinket boxes with elaborate lids were plentifully exported from Germany and Austria where they apparently originated. All kinds of figures appeared on the lids from babies and dogs to full blown roses and busts of Franz Josef. Most popular were the bureau-shaped boxes with a standing mirror at the back of the lid and playful children and kittens crawling on the dresser top. Common dressing table accessories were also found on lids, like washbowls and pitchers, Bibles, watches, and King's crowns. The variety was endless and seldom are two alike.

Similar boxes were made in France and England, and for years they were all—German, French, and English—quite correctly classed by collectors as "Victorian trinket boxes." Came the 1920s; Victorian was out of style, German wares were frowned on, and English wares were "in." Some super-salesman started to call them "Staffordshire boxes," and the name stuck. Few are marked; those which are usually carry the "mailed arm" trademark of Canta and Boehme, of Poessneck, which is definitely *not* in Staffordshire! (*See* Naughties and Potties.)

VILLEROY & BOCH

Never be surprised wherever the Villeroy & Boch mark turns up. This was a farflung ceramic empire. It began in 1836 when Eugene Francis Boch in Mettlach and Nicholas Villeroy in Wallerfangen, both established potters, joined forces. By 1840 they had taken over the potteries at Sept Fontaines and Schramberg. By 1856, they had built a new factory at Dresden. By 1876, they'd added a crystal glassworks at Wadgassen, a terra cotta factory at Merzig. A tile factory at Danischburg was added in 1906, earthenware factories at Bonn (1919) and Torgau on Elbe (1926), and a mosaic tile factory at Deutsch Lissu, also in 1926.

Best known to us are the stonewares, including all those beautiful steins made at Mettlach, and certain earthenwares, very similar to Staffordshire in both body and pattern, made at Wallerfangen. Much of their utilitarian terra cotta and tile was made for home consumption; but whatever you find with the V & B mark was made somewhere in the chain. (*See* Mettlach for illustration.)

VINCENNES

See *Sevres*

WALLEY, EDWARD

See *Gaudy Ironstone*

WASHBOARDS

Years back when a washboard was a lovely present for Mother at Christmas, some especially choice ones appeared with a pottery rubbing surface, set in a wooden frame. Some of these were made in Bennington, but not all. Richard Carter Barret, in *Bennington Pottery and Porcelain,* pictures one in Rockingham ware which bears Fenton's 1849 mark. Its pottery section is 10½ inches high, 10¼ inches wide. It is well mottled with yellow, and the back is plain yellow.

The washboard pictured here is smaller, the pottery section only 5¾ by 5½ inches. Printing on the wooden frame reads: The Common Sense Wash Board/Rub Lightly/It Will do the Work with Less Rubbing than any other Board/Manufactured by/The Western Reserve Pottery Co./Warren, Ohio. This is not Rockingham, but stoneware, in a solid color front and back, a light, rather reddish brown; the plain back looks quite like a pan of molasses candy set out to cool. The machine-made frame dates it considerably later than 1849. Despite its obvious differences from a Rockingham washboard, we have, to our dismay, recently seen one like it, in larger size, displayed as "Bennington," and by one who should have known better. Refinishing had erased any printing which may once have been on it.

You will not find many pottery washboards of any type; those made at Bennington are rarest of all. (*See* Bennington.)

WASHINGTON-WAKEFIELD PATTERN

Desirable collectibles aren't always old. As an example, we include this dinnerware pattern made by Lenox, Inc. in the late 1920s and 1930s. The story is this.

The birthplace of George Washington in Wakefield, Virginia, burned to the ground on December 25, 1780. (Unhappy

Christmas!) The Wakefield Historical Association, in 1925, with the assistance of the U.S. Army Engineering Corps, excavated the site to determine the original foundations of the house. Found in the dig were fragments of the Timothy Dwight salt glaze ware so greatly favored by colonists who could afford it. The Association prevailed upon Lenox, Inc. to reproduce the ware found in the Wakefield excavation and issue it as a standard tableware.

The difficulties in making this unique reproduction were many and various, with the result that the ware, when made available, carried a price that limited its sale. After a short time, Lenox discontinued its manufacture, immediately raising it to the "collectible" class. All of it is marked Lenox, and there can be no question as to its attribution.

WATSON & CO.

See *Prestopans*

WEDDING PRESENT CHINA, 1890-1910

The bride of the Gay Nineties could expect enough cut glass, silver, and china to deck her dining room and see her through any exigency of entertaining. In addition to the usual china tea plates, teasets, chocolate sets, and dessert bowls with matching saucers, she was blessed with a plethora of special-use dishes. The style of the time was gay and light, with roses and gold predominating in hand-painted designs on delicate imported china.

Likely her dinner set included butter pats and bone dishes, just as her mother's had, but someone was sure to send her extras of each. Crescent-shaped bone dishes (illustrated), meant to curve about the dinner plate, were used for just what the name implies—to put bones in. They might be elaborately scalloped and extravagantly decorated from Germany; dainty flowered Haviland-types from Limoges; or gold-rimmed, transfer-printed earthenware for family use. Butter pats also ran the gamut from plain to extra fancy.

There were pickle dishes and celery dishes; dishes for bon-bons and dishes for hot cakes—shallow soup-like plates with domed perforated covers. There were marmalade jars in fruit shapes, and straight-sided marmalade jars, with a hole in the base and a plate underneath, into which a jelly jar was set, taller ones of the same order to hold cans of condensed milk. There were sardine dishes, asparagus dishes, and strawberry bowls, with drainer holes and a base plate. (Her mother's sardine dishes had been of majolica.) There were mustard pots and salt dips, powder-ed sugar shakers and covered cheese dishes, toast racks and individual nut dishes, even toothpick holders.

Most of these dainty novelties, some gorgeous and some unbelievably garish, were made in Germany, though France and England supplied their share. China-painting friends provided the personal touch.

As the bride grew older and times and conditions changed, she carelessly pushed her out-moded pretties to the back of the shelf or discarded them altogether. All or any of them are collecti-ble today.

WEDGWOOD, JOSIAH

We hear much of Wedgwood pottery but little enough of the man behind it unless we turn to specialized study. It is all there in books to read and fascinating, indeed, are the accounts of this capable, thoroughly human, warm-hearted man.

Briefly, Josiah Wedgwood was born in August 1730, the youngest of thirteen children. He was nine years old when his father, a potter, died. At the proper age, he was apprenticed for a five-year term to his brother Thomas who had inherited his father's business. As a youth, Josiah suffered smallpox which left him with "a humour which settled in his leg." This gave him trouble until the leg was amputated some fifteen or twenty years later.

In 1752, he went into partnership with John Harrison, a banker's son who supplied the capital and from whom he absorbed considerable business training. In 1754, he entered into partner-ship with Thomas Whieldon, then the most important potter in Staffordshire, who encouraged his interest in experimentation. In May 1759, he opened his own pottery, The Ivy House Works in Burslem.

In his thirty-fourth year he married a distant cousin, Sarah Wedgwood, by whom he had four sons and four daughters. His wife was ever a help and inspiration to him, and his family life was of the happiest. He died in 1795 at the age of sixty-three, and was buried in the Church of St. Peter, Stoke-on-Trent. His practicality, united with artistic taste, brought "china" dishes to the everyday tables of everyday people, and opened the door

to expansion in the pottery industry. We should all be grateful to him.

The Staffordshire Toby jug, 5½ inches high, characterizing Josiah Wedgwood was made by Coopers at the Anchor Pottery, Hanley, founded in 1892. It is based on a contemporary bust of Wedgwood.

WEDGWOOD POTTERY

The five questions most often put to any lecturer on Wedgwood are: Is Wedgwood always marked? How do you know it's old? Is it always blue and white? Was it ever made in America? Are there any direct Wedgwood descendants still in the firm?

Wedgwood wares have been marked, almost invariably, since the beginning. The "almost" takes care of the once-in-a-blue-moon piece carelessly left bare. If a piece is properly marked, there is little doubt as to its authenticity. Unmarked pieces should be left for the experts to worry over.

The system of marks that Wedgwood used clearly indicates when each piece was made. Marks books, like Godden's *Encyclopaedia of British Pottery and Porcelain Marks,* list them in full; several books and pamphlets deal solely with Wedgwood marks.

Jasper ware is so generally well known that a surprising number of people have an idea it was Wedgwood's only product; that Wedgwood alone made it; and that it was made only in blue. *(See* Jasper ware.) Actually Wedgwood has made almost everything in pottery there ever was to make, from calendar tiles and drug mortars to dinner sets for Royalty. *(See* Empress Catherine Service.) The great service Josiah Wedgwood I did for the world, and on which his reputation was based, was his work with cream-wares whereby he brought "china" dishes into common use, expanding the industry, delighting women, and putting pewterers out of business.

All of Wedgwood's wares have been made in Staffordshire, first at the Ivy House Works in Burslem where Josiah I started in 1759, then at the "new" factory in Etruria, and since 1940, at Barleston in the "most up-to-date pottery in the world."

Until quite recently there have been direct descent Wedgwoods active in the firm of Josiah Wedgwood & Sons, but time has taken its toll. Arthur Bryan, director of the United States branch, has for some time been the Chairman of the Board, the first "outsider" to serve as chief executive. Of the surviving members of the Wedgwood family, one is a nuclear scientist, one a specialist in geriatrics, and the third, a professor of pediatrics.

Dozens upon dozens of books and articles have been written about Wedgwood. Because Wedgwood output was so diversified, writers have a wide range for specialization. And because Josiah

244

himself, then those who followed him, kept meticulous records of everything that went on at the plant and saved them all, including correspondence, researchers have quantities of accurate material to call on. *Wedgwood* by Mankowitz, and *Wedgwood Ware,* by Honey, are good books to look for in your library.

For Wedgwood collectors, there are two national associations to join in this country, at least one in England, and an International Wedgwood Seminar.

For seeing and studying, the Buten Museum in Merion, Pennsylvania, just outside Philadelphia, has the largest, most comprehensive collection of Wedgwood in this country. (*See:* Chessmen; Clockcases; Egyptian Black; Empress Catherine Service; Flaxman, John; Historical Blue Plates, Late; Jasper ware; Jelly Molds; Lessore, Emile; Moonlight Lustre; Mortars and Pestles; Queen's Ware; Sadler & Green; SYP Teapots; Wedgwood, Josiah; Wedgwood's Stone China.)

WEDGWOOD'S STONE CHINA

Stone china was introduced by Josiah Spode II about 1805. It was a dense hard earthenware having china stone as an ingredient. Spode may have hoped his ware, decorated with Oriental motifs, would take the place of coarse Chinese export porcelain. But it was the Ironstone china, supposed to contain pulverized slag of iron, patented in 1813 by Charles James Mason, that took the public fancy and set up a popular demand for this cheap and durable ware. However, the two wares were essentially very much alike.

To compete with the popular Mason product, practically every potter in Staffordshire had soon perfected his own version of the ware, Wedgwood among them. Like everything the Wedgwood factory produced, their "Stone China" was of superior quality, and it is reasonable to surmise it was made in some quantity.

The unusual thing about Wedgwood's Stone China is its present rarity. Even collectors who for years have studied intensively all aspects of Wedgwood production may never have seen a piece. Surprising, too, is the paucity of reference to it. Jewitt, in *The Wedgwoods,* wrote in 1865 that production had ceased in 1825 and that examples were then rare. Tom Lyth, Curator of the Wedgwood Museum and archivist of the Wedgwood Society of London, corrected Jewitt's dates in 1957, from his study of Wedgwood papers, which showed that Wedgwood's experiments for Stone China were begun in 1819 and that manufacture stopped in 1861.

How examples of a ware produced for sale over a span of forty or more years could almost totally disappear seems remarkable, yet Wedgwood's Stone China is as rare today in England as it is in this country. Even the backstamp is omitted from most reference books on Wedgwood marks.

The plate shown, from the Buten Museum of Wedgwood in Merion, Pennsylvania, is a water lily pattern, printed in blue, hand-enameled on glaze in yellow and cobalt, with some gilding. The ware itself is faintly bluish-gray; the backmark appears in blue. We recently saw its mate in the historic Robertson Mansion in Salido, Texas, tucked away back on a pantry shelf with kitchen dishes! So—they're not impossible to find.

WEIR STONEWARE FRUIT JARS

Though the Weir Pottery Company of Monmouth, Illinois, made other items (*see* Old Sleepy Eye), their stoneware fruit jar, patented March 1, 1892, was their best known. These were sold "through dealers everywhere," and an advertisement in the *Ladies Home Journal* for June 1903, claimed that H. J. Heinz Company, makers of "57 Varieties," had ordered one million Weir jars for packing their preserves and apple butter.

The advantage of their jar, Weir claimed, was that being stone, the light was excluded so that the natural color was retained and the fruit stayed as fresh and flavorful as the day it was picked. The enameled interior and the fact that the fruit never touched metal made it perfectly sanitary.

In 1906, the Weir Pottery consolidated with five other potteries to form the Western Stoneware Company, which still operates in Monmouth. The crockery jars the company makes these days are mainly for the Kaukauna Cheese House in Wisconsin. The closure on present-day jars is much like that used fifty years ago on the old Weir Stoneware Fruit Jar.

WELLER WARE

Late on the collecting scene, and late, too, in period of manufacture, are the various artwares made at the Weller pottery in Zanesville, Ohio, from 1895 to 1948. During these fifty-three years a multiplicity of types and styles were produced, which makes collecting it today fun without frustration. Pieces made before 1925 are the ones to look for.

In 1895, Samuel A. Weller bought the Lonhuda Pottery at Steubenville, Ohio, moved its manufacture to Zanesville where he was already established, and became the first in the area to produce art pottery. Up to then he had been a successful manufacturer of painted flower pots, jardinieres, cuspidors, and umbrella stands. Art pottery offered a challenge, and he liked the prestige of it. His own talents were for production and promotion, so he hired the best designers he could find, and kept them busy.

By 1904, when Edwin Atlee Barber published his *Marks of American Potters,* he credited Weller with six lines, all successful: *Louwelsa* (underglaze decoration on blended brown background); *Eosian* (characterized by pale blue, gray, and green); *Aurelian* (resembling Louwelsa); *Aurora; Dickensware* (scratched designs in sgraffito technique); and *Turada* (varied colored clays, brown, orange and cream, with applied ornaments of pierced work).

Sicardo, a metallic lustre ware with floral and conventional designs on dark grounds, was produced just too late to be included in Barber's list. Jacques Sicard, whom Weller had brought over from France, designed it. This was Weller's most expensive ware to produce, and the least profitable to him. It is, understandably, the most sought and most expensive today. Even when it was first produced, some of the more elaborate pieces cost as much as $300.

LaSa, another metallic lustre, and *Chengtu,* a red glaze, both created by John Lassel in the early 1920s, are also high on the Most Wanted list.

Zanesville Art Pottery in Color gives full details on Weller ware, and shows many pictures, as does Lucile Henzke's *American Art Pottery. (See:* Dickens Ware; Lonhuda; Sicardo.)

WEMYSS WARE

Earthenware, made at the Fife or Gallatown Pottery, established at Sinclairtown, Kirkcaldy, Scotland, around 1820, was called Wemyss in honor of Wemyss Castle, an ancient and famous pile. It is pronounced *weems*. The Wemyss Ware on which cocks and hens, fruits and flowers are painted so meticulously—and so engagingly—was introduced about 1880, when the pottery was under the proprietorship of Robert Heron & Son. It was popular in Scotland, not made for export.

While Scots settlers coming to America undoubtedly brought examples with them, very little of it came to light in this country until after World War II, when American dealers, buying in London, wandered into Scotland and "discovered" Prestopans, Wemyss, and other Scottish potteries. There is still a Wemyss Castle, and in 1954, at least, Sir Michael and Lady Victoria Wemyss were living in it.

The ware is a very brilliant white, very glossy, and very colorfully decorated under glaze. A deep green and a deep rose are traditional Wemyss colors; foliage is always luxuriant. An incised "R. H. & S" with "Wemyss Ware" in a semi-circle, is the usual marking. Look for it in useful wares—jam jars, honey pots, plates, bowls, and mugs.

WEST LOTHIAN POTTERY CO.

See *Bo'ness Potteries*

WESTERN POTTERS IN AMERICA

Moving westward from Ohio across the country, potteries of consequence became fewer and farther between. Notable among them in the late 1800s and early 1900s were the Burley & Winter Pottery Co. in Crooksville, Ohio, dating from 1850, who sometimes used a heart-shaped backstamp; the Peoria Pottery, Peoria, Illinois, dating from 1873; the Crown Works at Evansville, Indiana, from 1891; the Van Briggle Pottery in Colorado Springs, from 1901; the Pauline Pottery, Edgerton, Wisconsin, from 1883—this was operated by Mrs. Pauline Jacobus, an extraordinarily gifted amateur; the Miss Mary Chase Pottery in Detroit and the Linna Irelan Pottery in San Francisco, dating from 1899, both amateur efforts and, like the Pauline Pottery, worthy of professional status.

At Golden, Colorado, was the Geijsbeek Pottery, a commercial venture, established in 1899, where three kilns turned out a whiteware product said to be "very much like modern Delft without blue decoration." Also, at Golden was the Herold China Company, founded in 1908 by John J. Herold who had worked for the three leading potters in Zanesville, Ohio. (This later became the Coor Porcelain Co.) W. A. Long also moved from Zanesville to Colorado, establishing the Denver China and Pottery Company in Denver. Later Western potteries whose work is received favorably are the Niloak Pottery, Benton, Arkansas, about 1910 to 1946, and Camark Pottery of Camden, Arkansas, active from 1930s on.

Pottery from these Western firms makes an exciting collection for any specialist, and an especially rewarding one for Westerners. (*See:* Arequipa Pottery; Lonhuda; Niloak Pottery; Van Briggle.)

The Geijsbeek Pottery marks are pictured.

WESTERN STONEWARE CO.

See *Old Sleepy Eye*

WEST'S TERRALINE

See *Terraline Vases*

WESTERN RESERVE POTTERY

See *Washboards*

WHAT-NOT JUGS

What-not jugs, sometimes called crazy jugs, were Victorian creations, the home work of exuberant young ladies and unskilled children with nothing better to do on a rainy afternoon. Maybe they got the idea from the girl next door; maybe they followed directions in some *Lady's Book;* in any event making a crazy jug kept their busy fingers out of worse mischief.

They started with a solid base, something that was no good anyway—a cracked saucer, a jug with the handle off, a broken bowl or candlestick, a bottle. This they covered completely with thick globs of clay, building it to some sort of reasonable shape. Into this mass, they stuck, as closely as they could, all sorts of pretty little odds and ends they found around the house—broken doll heads, tiny toys, buttons, safety pins, seashells, grandma's old spectacles. The bristling product was either gilded or shellacked before it took its proud stance in the parlor as a monument to Something from Nothing.

Occasionally these oddities show up at country auctions or even in antiques shops. Some people buy them to pry off penny dolls or other treasures or to dig out picture buttons or tiny teaspoons. Some like them as they are, quaint reminders of a "save-everything" past.

The one pictured is gilded, built up over a Mason jar on a 7-inch Ironstone plate marked Cookson and Chetwood.

WHEATLEY POTTERY

The pottery founded by T. J. Wheatley Co. in 1880, in Cin-

cinnati, Ohio, continued to operate until 1906. One of the interesting decorations used there resembled the pitted surface of ancient pottery. A process patented in 1880, having to do with slip-painted scenes and florals underglaze was much copied by other potteries. But Wheatley pieces are well marked. The vase pictured (yellow flowers on glossy brown and green ground) is incised "T.J.W.Co." on the base with the 1880 patent date.

WHEELING POTTERY CO.

The Wheeling Pottery Co. was established in Wheeling, West Virginia, in 1879 for the purpose of manufacturing "Ironstone and C.C. wares." ("C.C." was an abbreviation used extensively in advertisements of that time for "cream-colored" earthenwares.) Apparently this company, like others, held with the popular idea that imported wares had more sales appeal than domestic products, for they were exceedingly reticent about using their name in their various backstamps and trademarks. Occasionally they used a "W," or a "WPC," or a "WP." More often they dreamed up elaborate trademarks with flags, eagles, beehives, laurel wreaths, and other English-type motifs ostensibly to make their wares look imported. On their earthenwares they often used the name "LaBelle" or "LaBelle China" with no further identification.

One of Wheeling's most successful patterns was their Moss Rose which appeared on Ironstone dinnerware and teasets. Roses had always proved appealing in china decoration from the earliest days, and the fuzzy moss rose which was then grown extensively was a particular favorite.

The design the Wheeling Pottery used on their Ironstone showed three large buds and a single green leaf in a spray. Other potteries used and had used for years similar designs on both Ironstone and porcelain; to match up sets nowadays, it is best to go by the backstamp. The mark of Wheeling's Moss Rose was typically English, with "Royal Ironstone China" above a lion, unicorn, and coat of arms, and "Warranted" below. According to Minnie Watson Kamm in *Old China,* Wheeling made 131 items in this line. Montgomery Ward was offering it in teasets and dinner services in their 1896 catalog, but, allowing for changing preferences, as "of American manufacture."

Wheeling's flown blue wares, marked LaBelle China were also extremely popular when they came out, and as much or more so with today's collectors. You'll also find the LaBelle name on a good many odd bone dishes, some of which did not come with a dinner set but were made up to sell by themselves. (*See* U.S. Art Pottery; Flown Blue.)

WHEELOCK, GEORGE & CO.

See *Souvenir China*

WHIELDON

Thomas Whieldon appears to have been in business in Little Fenton in Staffordshire as early as 1745, making knife handles. By his own efforts, he advanced to become the leading potter of his time. His pieces are now collectors' items; his teapots and milk jugs in "Tortoise-shell ware" of mottled brown and green, and his teapots molded in shapes of cauliflowers, melons, and the like are choice today. He was a great experimenter and an excellent potter. His Toby jugs are supremely ugly as they should be. (*See* Toby jugs.)

Many of Staffordshire's leading potters were at some time his apprentices, among them Aaron Wood, Josiah Spode, William Greatbach. Josiah Wedgwood, before he started his own potting works, was Whieldon's partner for five years.

The Whieldon cruet stand pictured, complete and in perfect condition, is among Colonial Williamsburg collections. The decoration is molded; the lead glazes are colored, ca. 1765.

WHITE HOUSE CHINA

Until quite recently, incoming First Ladies were free to discard such appointments in the White House as did not please them, and a great many incomplete sets of chinaware, used by previous administrations, found their way to auction sales or second-hand shops, thence into hands of collectors.

Both Mrs. Rutherford B. Hayes and Mrs. Benjamin Harrison made some slight attempt to start a collection of White House china, but it was not until Abby Gunn Baker, a Washington writer, interested Mrs. William McKinley in the project that the Presidential china collection, now in the White House China Room, was begun. (There is also a scattered collection at the Smithsonian Institution.)

Mrs. McKinley and Mrs. Baker began with the china already in the White House; none of it dated further back than Lincoln's administration. Mrs. Theodore Roosevelt, with Mrs. Baker's help, began a search for pieces used by earlier Presidents, relying mainly on gifts from patriotic donors. Mrs. Baker wrote prolifically about the chinaware, and her writings seem to have been accepted as Gospel. Since she was more reporter than researcher and relied heavily on what donors told her, a deal of confusion has arisen over the years as to which pieces were used by which Presidents. Now Marian Klamkin's *White House China* (1972) has taken the hearsay out of identification—to the delight or dismay of the surprising number of collectors who own pieces of White House china.

In 1972, a Washington, D.C. woman took six State dinner plates to auction. Lincoln had patronized her grandfather's barber shop and had given him the plates as a token of appreciation. The family always called them, "Lincoln's dishes." The auctioneer's appraisers first said they were from the Grant administration, but before the auction (and perhaps after checking Mrs. Klamkin's book) set them correctly in the Polk administration, making them a much rarer find than either Lincoln or Grant plates. They brought $7,000.

Pictured is one of the purplish-red bordered plates from the Lincoln service. Mrs. Lincoln ordered the set, made by Haviland and Company in Limoges, from E. V. Haughwout and Company in New York. Haviland made several other sets for the White House, and has recently begun reproducing some of them, all suitably marked. The first American-made White House china was the Lenox set made for President Woodrow Wilson. (*See:* Haviland; Lenox.)

WILLOW PATTERN

Willow, the most popular tableware pattern ever made, was first put on English porcelain in 1780 at the Caughley Pottery in Shropshire, which Thomas Turner then owned and where he made his Caughley or Salopian wares. Thomas Minton, one of his apprentice decorators, adapted the design from Oriental wares.

(This same Minton later founded his own factory, which is still in operation.)

It is a pattern that has never gone out of style. At some time or other every English potter used it on something —stoneware, pottery, or porcelain. It was produced in Scotland, France, and Germany. Japan is making it today.

The colors may vary from a fine old blue to an almost purple shade; the transfer printing may be sharp and clear or badly blurred; but the pattern is basically the same—the Mandarin's pagoda, the willow tree, the bridge and the runaway lovers crossing it, the boat that took them to their island, and the doves they turned into. Variations are few, though sometimes a third figure, presumably a pursuer, appears on the bridge.

Because so many potters used the Willow pattern over such a span of years, and it's all so repetitious, collectors tend to find it of little interest *per se,* though they will pick up pieces when the potter particularly interests them. (*See:* Salopian; Minton; Glasgow Potteries.)

The porringer pictured was made at Campbellfield, Glasgow, in 1850.

THE WOODS OF BURSLEM

There were so many potters in the Wood family in Staffordshire—and so many with the same first name—that to unconfuse yourself completely, we suggest you turn to *The Wood Family of Burslem* (1912) by F. Falkner, who manages somehow to get them straight and give each one proper credit. The Ralphs and Enochs are of most concern to today's collectors.

Ralph Wood (1716-1772) and his brother Aaron were sons of a miller in Burslem; both worked as potters. Ralph made rustic figures, Toby jugs, and groups. Aaron was a modeler and made models for other potters. Ralph marked his wares "R. Wood," and his son Ralph, who also became a potter, marked *his,* "Ra Wood, Burslem."

Aaron's son Enoch (1759-1840) served his apprenticeship with Humphrey Palmer, and later in his own pottery made cream-colored wares, black basalt, and jasper, as well as the portrait busts for which he became famous. About 1790, Enoch Wood took James Caldwell as a partner, and from then until 1818, his figures and busts were marked "Wood & Caldwell." From 1818 to 1846, the style of the firm was Enoch Wood & Sons. In this period, the firm made a huge amount of dark blue printed ware for the American market; a contemporary account says it was the largest exporter of pottery earthenwares to America. *(See* American Views.)

The "Ra Wood Burslem" statuette pictured is of St. Philip,

with long beard, wearing a puce jacket, flowered trousers, and mauve flowing cape. It is 15½ inches high, and of the 1790 period.

WORCESTER
ROYAL WORCESTER

The strict and serious Worcester collector confines himself to the Dr. Wall period of production which extended from the inception of the company in 1751 to 1785, though Dr. John Wall himself, the activator of the concern, died in 1776. The ware made in this period was perhaps the most distinctive of eighteenth century porcelains, well proportioned, carefully finished, richly decorated, and with superlative gilding. Most early pieces were useful items; rarely were vases, figures, tureens, and other large pieces made. One of the early inventions was the so-called "Japan patterns," which were produced well into the nineteenth century.

Changes came in 1793, when the business, then owned by Thomas Vernon and the William Davises, senior and junior, was sold to Thomas Flight, then passed successively to Flight & Barr; Barr, Flight & Barr; Flight, Barr & Barr; Chamberlain & Co.; and Kerr & Binns, until the Royal Worcester Company emerged in 1862, a company that persists today.

Worcester china is noted for its creamy white lustreless surface. Its decorations have varied with the times, but it has always retained its extremely high standards both as to potting and decoration. (*See:* Doughty Birds; Equestrian Figures.)

Much has been written on Worcester porcelain. You'll find information on early blue and white in Dr. B. Watney's *English Blue and White Porcelain;* on transfer printing in Cyril Cook's *The Life and Work of Robert Hancock* (Hancock is the engraver who went to Worcester about 1756, and from whose plates more than 100 subjects were used there); on early decorated ware, H. Rissik Marshall's *Coloured Worcester Porcelain of the First Period,* and for general and later coverage, R. L. Hobson's *Worcester Porcelain;* R. W. Binn's *Worcester China–1852-1897;* and Geoffrey Godden's *Victorian Porcelain.*

For seeing examples, trip it to England and visit the exhibits at the Worcester Works Museum and at the Victoria & Albert Museum in London. Museums nearer home will have examples, too. For buying, look in quality antiques shops specializing in English wares.

Illustrated are a tureen in Imari pattern by Flight, Barr & Barr; and a creamy mat finish pitcher with painted and enamel decoration in Royal Worcester, a turn-of-the-century type, easier to find today.

WYLLIE, JOHN & SON

See *Great Western Pottery*

ZAFFER

Scrabble players will find "zaffer" a paying word to have on tap. Pressed, they can glibly explain it's cobalt oxide in powder form from which smalt was made, smalt being the blue coloring used by potters. Show-offs can also mention that potter John Bell of Waynesboro, Pennsylvania, in 1848, wrote his brother Samuel in Strasburg, Virginia, that "graffee (zaffer) is calcined cobalt or flystone, which is the same thing," and it is "rank poison."

ZANE POTTERY

See *Moss Aztec*

ZANESVILLE ART POTTERY

Zanesville, Ohio, became "the Clay City" in the 1890s and the scene of some lively competition. Samuel A. Weller and the J. B. Owens Pottery Company were the early giants in the trade, with Roseville Pottery Company close behind. All three panted for fame and fortune from prestige artwares. What one did, the others tried to do better. All of them snooped a bit, duplicated methods, imitated successes, hired away each other's employees and, in the end, put on the market surprisingly distinctive pieces, most of them clearly marked and identifiable.

Weller, who produced his first art pottery in 1893, stood from 1882 to 1948; Owens from 1881 to about 1930, though his artware production was limited from 1896 to 1906. He turned then to more profitable tile. Roseville, begun in 1892 in nearby Roseville and moved to Zanesville in 1898, entered the art pottery field in 1900, and continued until 1945. All three made "bread-and-butter" utilitarian lines but, as of yet, late-date pie plates and custard cups, however clearly marked, raise little interest. It is the artware these companies made which engages collector attention.

Owens' and Weller's early art pottery has already reached "antique" status. Roseville—was there ever a bride in the 1920s who didn't receive at least one Roseville vase or bowl or console set—is now being quietly sought as a "coming antique."

Norris F. Schneider's *Zanesville Art Pottery,* an excellent treatise, gives all the ins and outs of the rival three, lists and describes their various artwares, and mentions twenty-one other potteries in Zanesville between 1883 and 1961; many of them short-lived, some still at work. *(See:* Weller; Owens; Roseville.)

ZOAR POTTERY

From Worttemberg, in 1817, came the Society of Separatists, called Zoarites, to settle in Tuscarawas County, Ohio. Theirs was a communal settlement; they named it Zoar, and it prospered until it was dissolved in 1898.

Like the Shakers, the Moravians, and other communal sects, they practiced many trades—weaving, building, blacksmithing, printing and, of course, potting. Red roof tiles, dated 1834, still remain on some of their buildings; porringers, sold to farm folk in the locality in the 1830s are choice finds today, as are other pieces of common brownware and black or buff-glazed redware, known to have been made there until 1853.

At the Henry Ford Museum in Dearborn, Michigan, is a washbowl and jug, with buff-glazed interior, whose handles are stamped "Zoar" and "1840." The bowl is 17 inches in diameter; the jug is 11¾ inches tall.

ZONA

One of Weller's Zanesville productions was dinnerware with an apple motif decoration; he called it Zona. It was designed about 1920 by Rudolph Lorder. Gladding, McBean & Company of California, having acquired the rights to this design, now manufacture it under the name Franciscan Ware. Look for the Weller mark on the early pieces.

ZOUAVE PITCHER

Col. Elmer Ephraim Ellsworth of the N. Y. Zouaves, whose dramatic death occurred in Alexandria, Virginia, on May 23, 1861, is known as the "first commissioned officer to lose his life in the great fraternal struggle" of the Civil War. When the Union forces seized Alexandria, young Ellsworth rushed impulsively to cut down a Confederate flag flying atop the Marshall House. While descending the stairs, he was shot dead by James W. Jackson, proprietor of the hotel. Jackson was immediately shot down by Corporal Brownell.

To commemorate the event, Josiah Jones modeled a quart-size patriotic "Zouave" pitcher for Millington, Astbury & Paulson of Trenton, New Jersey. That firm made the Zouave pitcher in Ironstone, some with the raised design in color, using the blues and orange reds of the Zouave uniforms, others in plain white. The Zouave pitcher was also made up in Rockingham ware.